P9-AQL-712

FEMINIST READINGS ON SPANISH AND LATIN-AMERICAN LITERATURE

Edited by

L. P. Condé and S. M. Hart

The Edwin Mellen Press
Lewiston/Queenston/Lampeter

Library of Congress Cataloging-in-Publication Data

This volume has been registered with The Library of Congress.

ISBN 0-7734-9440-5

A CIP catalog record for this book
is available from the British Library.

The Edwin Mellen Press
Box 450
Lewiston, New York
USA 14092

The Edwin Mellen Press
Box 67
Queenston, Ontario
CANADA L0S 1L0

The Edwin Mellen Press, Ltd.
Lampeter, Dyfed, Wales
UNITED KINGDOM SA48 7DY

Printed in the United States of America

FEMINIST READINGS ON SPANISH AND LATIN-AMERICAN LITERATURE

Contents

THE DARK CONTINENT

INTRODUCTION

'Tremate, tremate,
le streghe sono
tornate'.[1]

Early on in *A Room of One's Own*, Virginia Woolf alludes to the Manx cat which bequeathed an informal title to this collection of essays.[2] Virginia Woolf is describing her thoughts while having lunch at an un-named Cambridge college:

> If by good luck there had been an ash-tray handy, if one had not knocked the ash out of the window in default, if things had been a little different from what they were, one would not have seen, presumably, a cat without a tail. The sight of that abrupt and truncated animal padding softly across the quadrangle changed by some fluke of the subconscious intelligence the emotional light for me. It was as if someone had let fall a shade (...) Certainly, as I watched the Manx cat pause in the middle of the lawn as if it too questioned the universe, something seemed lacking, something seemed different. But what was lacking, what was different, I asked myself, listening to the talk?[3]

Woolf seems coyly unaware of the implications of her text, or at least that is the impression she wishes to give. But given the parallels between the Manx cat shut outside while the sumptuous dinner takes place within, and the earlier scene in which Woolf herself had been debarred from entry into an un-named college library, the Manx cat stands - or better, sits - as a symbol of the female ostracized from the discourse of phallocratic society. Woolf's use of the cat as a symbol of femininity is perversely apt. She alludes to the symbolism which has linked cats in an archetypal manner to women. As Beryl Rowland has pointed out: 'Aristotle stated that the female cat was peculiarly lecherous and wheedled the man on to sexual commerce. Misogynist clerics in the Middle Ages frequently repeated this evaluation, seeing man as the mouse and woman as the sleek, enticing, and predatory cat'.[4] Pointing in a similar direction, the persistent question in Woolf's text 'what was lacking?' is clearly a reference - via the absent tail - to the phallus, the term Freud re-invented and which Lacan expanded to signify the power adhering to the male within patriarchal society. But there is a deep irony in the historical fact that Manx cats come from the Isle of Man, and that one of their species should appear surreptitiously in Woolf's text to embody an ostracized female consciousness.[5]

And yet the metaphor fits the facts, for literature written by women is also like a species on its own which is born from within literature's Isle of Man. Feminine writing occupies the empty centre within the literary canon. This is only to be expected since its author, woman, has invariably been seen in terms of lack, deficiency, incompleteness. As Aristotle once suggested with a phrase that feminists will never allow to slip into oblivion, 'woman is, as it were, an impotent male, for it is through a certain incapacity that the female is female', a view which was echoed by one of the intellectual architects of the western renaissance, Thomas Aquinas (d.1274) who viewed women as 'mutilated males'.[6] The parallels drawn between women and lack even permeate the discourse of twentieth-century ego-psychology. As Charlotte Wolff, argues, surprisingly, since she is a feminist psychiatrist: 'The effect produced by a group of women alone is different from that of a group of men. Women by themselves appear to be incomplete, as if a limb were missing. They do not come into their proper place and function without the male'.[7] Yet, this sense of Lack, 'as if a limb were missing' (to quote Charlotte Wolff), this 'truncated animal' (to quote Virginia Woolf), can also be a source of unsuspected power. Lack need not be seen solely in negative terms, for it could be argued that the discourse of womenkind has now begun to speak *through* its absence, *through* its silence, *through* its lack. Since discourse itself, as Lacan argues, can only emerge through the death of the signifier, through its own absence, women's discourse can be seen as embodying the very lack of discourse. It stands nearer the absence, silence and death of words.

The discourse of womenkind has certainly begun to emerge in the field of criticism on Spanish and Latin-American literature. In the last decade, more significant feminist studies have been published on Spanish and Latin-American literature than in the previous seven decades combined. In past years, studies on female writers seem to have aroused an interest comparable to that elicited by articles of the 'Further reflections on the evolution of Czech ship building 1747-1751' type. Important pioneering studies were published early on, such as Sidonia Carmen Rosenbalu's self-explanatory *Modern Women Poets of Spanish America: The Precursors: Delmira Agustini, Gabriela Mistral, Alfonsina Storni, Juana de Ibarbourou (1945),* and Giuseppe Bellini's *Figure della lirica femminile ispanoamericana* (1953), which traced a female poetic tradition from Alfonsina Storni to Delmira Agustini. But it was not until the 1980s that studies of women writers, studies of images of women, and feminist readings of the male (and, of course, the female) canon began to make significant inroads into the academic canon of hispanism.

In 1982 Gabriela Mora and Karen S. Van Hooft edited a pioneering collection of essays entitled *Theory and Practice of Feminist Literary Criticism,* which offered new readings of literary texts mainly drawn from the male canon. Beth Miller edited a collection of challenging essays the following year which focussed on the image of women in hispanic literature; Mary Crow edited a significant collection of contemporary Latin-American women poets in 1984, revised in 1987, provocatively entitled *Woman Who Has Sprouted Wings.* Canon-defining journals such as *Revista Iberoamericana* (1985) and *Anales de Literatura Española Contemporánea* (1987) brought out special issues on women writers. A. Flores and K. Flores were joint editors in 1986 of *The Vibrant Muse: Hispanic Feminist Poems from the Middle Ages to the Present,* and Lorenzo Saval and J. García Gallego edited and introduced, in the same year, a good anthology of modern Spanish literature written by women, *Litoral femenino: Literatura escrita por mujeres en la España contemporánea.* L. M. Jiménez Faro published a helpful *Panorama antológica de poetisas españolas* the following year (1987). Two books on Spanish women writers came out simultaneously a year later, both of which fundamentally recharted the lost territory of women's writing in Spain. Janet Pérez's study *Contemporary Women Writers of Spain* lists more than 300 works of fiction by contemporary women writers in Spain, while Biruté Ciplijauskaité's *La novela femenina contemporánea (1970-1985)*, published in 1988, covers an even wider range of material and focuses on women's narrative as autobiography. Also published in 1988, Robert Manteiga, Carolyn Galerstein and Kathleen McNerney's collection of essays on *Feminine Concerns in Contemporary Spanish Fiction by Women* deals with specific feminist issues in the work of some fourteen contemporary Spanish women writers, while Patricia O'Connor's study, *Dramaturgas españolas de hoy: una introducción*, brings Spanish female dramatists nearer centre-stage.

Two significant studies of feminine literature were published the following year: Helena Araújo's *La Scherezada criolla: Ensayos sobre escritura femenina latinoamericana*, and Jean Franco's *Plotting Women*, the latter of which draws upon historical and literary texts in order to trace images of women from the colonial period in Mexico to the present day. Still more recently Susan Bassnett has edited an important collection of essays, *Knives and Angels* (1990), which brings together a number of notable studies on writers ranging from Victoria Ocampo, María Luisa Bombal, Alejandra Pizarnik, Rosario Castellanos, Clarice Lispector and Griselda Gambaro. That such a recent book as this should still feel the need for biographical information on the authors covered (John King on Victoria Ocampo, 9-25; Marjorie Agosin on María Luisa Bombal, 26-35; and Susan Bassnett on Alejandra Pizarnik, 36-51) suggests that, even nowadays, women writers in the hispanic world still need a formal introduction. On the other hand, Noël Valis and Carol Maier stress in the Preface to their current collection, *In the Feminine Mode: Essays on Hispanic Women Writers* (1990), that 'despite our eventual decision not to focus on conventional biography ... we were both drawn to reflect on the relation between biography and elusiveness in writing by and about female authors' (15). These essays cover a range of Spanish and Latin-American women writers and include an exploration of some of the ways in which Hispanic women writers have been aware of and at times collaborated with the work of other women.[8]

The essays included in the present collection were selected from papers given at a conference held in June 1990 at Queen Mary and Westfield College (Hampstead), University of London. In this sense they might be characterised as the British contribution to the ongoing debate on the interaction between feminism and hispanism which mushroomed in the 1980s. Indeed, this conference, conceived and organised by Stephen Hart, was the first of its kind to be held in the United Kingdom, with its coverage of feminist readings of male and female writers, both Spanish and Latin-American, from the Golden-Age to the present day. While such diversity is reflective of the complexity of feminism today, some attempt to impose order upon what Jane Gallop so aptly describes as 'the unruly material of an anthology'[9] has resulted in the division of these essays into three sections: The Male Canon, The Female Canon, and The Dark Continent, and their appearance in a roughly chronological order within these sections.

The portrayal of women by classic 'masters' of the Spanish Golden-Age, nineteenth century and '98 Generation is reassessed from a range of feminist perspectives and not always found so wanting as one might expect. Melveena McKendrick argues that Calderón places feminine issues at the heart of plays which might appear to be focussing audience interest elsewhere, as in *El mágico prodigioso* where Justina refuses to accept the role that society expects women to occupy. This determination of the heroine to shape her own destiny is seen as constituting a powerful feminist statement on the part of the dramatist. Lisa Condé finds such recognition of female potential for self-determination also present in the work of Pérez Galdós, and reinforced through his repeated use of the image of wings: an image of continuing pertinence in the feminist debate. In the evolution of Galdós' *mujer nueva* on stage, the *alas cortadas* of the writer's earlier novelistic heroines are allowed finally to spread, as the new woman's full potential is realised. A more unlikely candidate for consideration as 'pro-feminist' is Valle-Inclán, seen by many as the phallocentric writer *par excellence*. Jean Andrews pursues Noël Valis' recent challenge to this view by applying Cixous' theory of bisexuality to the character of Mari-Gaila in *Divinas palabras*, thereby suggesting a transition on the part of the writer from the phallocratic realm of the proper to the feminine realm of the gift.

Ambiguity and ambivalence are more apparent in the portrayal of women by Clarín and Unamuno, as explored respectively by Jo Labanyi and Alison Sinclair. Jo Labanyi's study of mysticism and hysteria in *La Regenta* raises many vital questions concerning Clarín's depiction of Ana's behaviour; above all, whether this represents the conquest of an inner female space that resists male codification, or shows her to be the projection of a male view of woman as lack. Alison Sinclair illustrates how, in *La tía Tula*, Unamuno's ambivalence (characteristic of envy) in relation to the feminine and the maternal results in their being portrayed in such a destructive manner as to disenfranchise female characters from being placed in the ranks of the most valued of the writer's protagonists.

Turning to the female canon, the classic 'mistress' of the nineteenth-century Spanish novel, Emilia Pardo Bazán, was, as is now known, also the mistress of her male counterpart, Galdós, and one is immediately reminded of the inferior connotations so often attached to female equivalents of male nouns. Language, however, is to be dealt with more specifically later. Judith Drinkwater's essay sets out to defend Pardo Bazán's early novel, *Un viaje de novios*, against the charge of sentimental 'romanticism' through an ironic reading of the text.[10] Thus the downfall of the heroine Lucía is seen to serve as an indictment of the social myths which circumscribe her existence, and the romantic intrusions in the text seen to indicate the impossibility of female attainment of the romantic ideal of freedom.

Moving on to the twentieth century, Abigail Lee Six explores how Rosa Chacel depicts masculine and feminine aspects of the senses of sight and sound in her novel, *Desde el amanecer*, and finds not only that these frequently transcend their physiological sex, but that they are not so easily categorized as modern theorists would have us believe. The theme of difference is pursued by Stephen Hart in a study of the concept of 'écriture féminine' and its development from psychoanalytic feminism. Irigaray argued that what had been specifically excluded from the discourse of psychoanalysis was the female body, and in Cixous' subsequent pioneering work, the role of the body was to become a central metaphor and the double meaning of 'voler' an apt image. Clarice Lispector and Esther Tusquets both allude in their writing to this new language, written through the body, and to a (still unrevealed) new world of difference. Catherine Davies pursues the notion that 'the personal is political' and focuses on the contemporary writers, Montserrat Roig, Rosa Montero and Luisa Valenzuela, who have attempted to represent the political in terms of personal sexual relationships. Drawing upon their own, essentially female experience at crucial moments of political change, their 'semi-fictions' indicate the need for a redefining of gender identity and the reconstruction of female subjectivity and desire.

An equally wide range of approaches is offered in the section dealing specifically with the 'Dark Continent' of Latin America, where political change in particular is more a way of life and feminism inextricably linked to the struggle against oppression. Evelyn Fishburn traces the trajectory of one of the first and foremost Latin-American feminist poets, Alfonsina Storni, and finds her work to be more subversive than has generally been recognised. She also perceives a foreshadowing of Cixous' call for woman to 'write herself' in a poem from Storni's early collection, *El dulce daño* (1918). The critical revision of traditional fairy tale discourse found in the work of the Cuban poet, Dulce María Loynaz, and the novelist, María Luisa Bombal, is analysed by Verity Smith. Of particular interest is her study of the former's lesser known experimental novel, *Jardín*, published in 1951, some twenty years after its conception. In this novel, as in those of María Luisa Bombal, the critique of the fairy tale relates closely to the whole question of 'a woman's place' being in the green world, from which she is as yet restrained from seeking renewal.

Linda Craig's study of Luisa Valenzuela's later work, *El gato eficaz* (1972), reveals the novelist's awareness of the difficulties arising around the subject of women and language. Parallels with the carnivalesque are found in this novel, where nothing is fixed and the imagery and language are in constant flux. In this way, the barriers of tradition are transcended and the falsity of the generally accepted feminine role exposed. Giovanni Pontiero focuses on Clarice Lispector's 'swansong', *The Hour of the Star*, which he sees as both a rebellious and a questioning personal work, as the writer strives to establish truth before arriving at 'the ultimate freedom' of death. At the same time, he explores Lispector's obsession with silence and her insistence that 'emptiness, too, has its value and somehow resembles abundance'.

Finally, we return to male depiction of women characters, this time in modern-day Cuba. Nissa Torrents reports that, despite cosmetic social advances, the (women's) revolution within the revolution has not occurred, as popular fiction - largely written by men - testifies. Sadly, notwithstanding the promotion of 'el hombre nuevo', we learn that 'to this day there has been no mention of the new woman', and witness a return to the misogynistic attitudes of pre-revolutionary texts.

Redundant stereotypes persist, and the struggle continues.

S. M. H. & L. P. C.

NOTES

1.   'Tremble, tremble the witches are back' was a popular feminist slogan in Italy where feminism was one of the most vocal organizations in Europe in the 1970s; quoted by Susan Bassnett, *Feminist Experiences: The Women's Movement in Four Cultures* (London: Allen and Unwin, 1986), 95.

2.   The originally intended title of *The Manx Cat* has now been superseded by its more traditional subtitle for cataloguing purposes.

3.   *A Room of One's Own* (London: Hogarth, 1929), 18.

4.   Beryl Rowland, *Animals with Human Faces: A Guide to Animal Symbolism* (London: George Allen and Unwin, 1974), 52.

5.   Woolf was not the first to make an association of this kind between the woman and the Manx cat. In 1881 Carlyle made the connection in a roundabout way using the middle term 'Manx penny' in the expression: '[He] hadn't the heart to ... watch a woman making a Manx penny of herself' as cited in the *OED*, which furthermore defines a 'Manx penny' as 'a coin stamped with the device of three legs arranged in a form suggestive of a Catherine wheel'. Other examples of metaphorical uses of the term Manx likewise carry associations of oddness; see *The Oxford English Dictionary* (Oxford: Clarendon, 1933), vol. VI, 146.

6.   Aristotle quotation from Juliet Mitchell, *Women: The Longest Revolution* (New York: Pantheon, 1984), 115; Thomas Aquinas citation quoted by Uta Ranke-Heinemann, *Eunuchs for Heaven: The Catholic Church and Sexuality* (London: Deutsch, 1990), quoted in a review of this work by Mary Flanagan which appeared in *The Sunday Times: Books* (8 April 1990), 10.

7.   Quoted by Nina Auerbach, *Communities of Women: An Idea in Fiction* (Cambridge, Massachusetts: Harvard University Press, 1978), 7.

8.   Full references are: Sidonia Carmen Rosenbalu, *Modern Women Poets of Spanish America: the Precursors: Delmira Agustini, Gabriela Mistral, Alfonsina Storni, Juana de Ibarbourou* (New York: The Hispanic Institute, 1945), and Giuseppe Bellini's *Figure della lirica femminile ispanoamericana* (Milano: Edizioni Universitarie, 1953); Gabriela Mora and Karen S. Van Hooft (eds.), *Theory and Practice of Feminist Literary Criticism* (Ypsilanti, Michigan: Bilingual Press, 1982); Beth Miller (ed.), *Women in Hispanic Literature: Icons and Fallen Idols* (Berkeley: University of California Press, 1983); Mary Crow (ed.), *Woman Who Has Sprouted Wings: Poems by Contemporary Latin American Women Poets* (Pittsburgh: Latin American Literary Review Press, 1984); *Revista Iberoamericana*, nos. 132-33 (July-December 1985), *número especial dedicado a las escritoras de la América Hispánica; Anales de Literatura Española Contemporánea*, 12, 1-2

(1987), *Reading for Difference: Feminist Perspectives on Women Novelists of Contemporary* Spain. A. Flores and K. Flores (eds.), *The Vibrant Muse: Hispanic Feminist Poems from the Middle Ages to the Present* (New York: Feminist Press, 1986); Lorenzo Saval and J. García Gallego (eds.), *Litoral femenino. Literatura escrita por mujeres en la España contemporánea* (Granada: Litoral, 1986); L. M. Jiménez Faro, *Panorama antológica de poetisas españolas* (Madrid: Torremozas, 1987); Janet Pérez, *Contemporary Women Writers of Spain* (Boston: Twayne, 1988); Biruté Ciplijauskaité, *La novela femenina contemporánea (1970-1985)* (Barcelona: Anthropos, 1988); Roberto C. Manteiga, Carolyn Galerstein and Kathleen McNerney (eds.), *Feminine Concerns in Contemporary Spanish Fiction by Women* (Maryland: Scripta Humanistica, 1988), Patricia O'Connor, *Dramaturgas españolas de hoy: una introducción* (Madrid: Espiral, 1988); Helena Araújo, *La Scherezada criolla: Ensayos sobre escritura femenina latinoamericana* (Bogotá: Universidad Nacional de Bogotá, 1989); Jean Franco, *Plotting Women: Gender and Authority in Mexico: 1650-1970* (New York: Columbia University Press, 1989; Susan Bassnett (ed.), *Knives and Angels: Women Writers in Latin America* (London and New Jersey: Zed Books Ltd., 1990); Noël Valis and Carol Maier (eds.), *In the Feminine Mode: Essays on Hispanic Women Writers* (Lewisburg: Bucknell University Press, 1990).

9.   'Reading the Mother Tongue: Psychoanalytic Feminist Criticism', *Critical Inquiry* 13 (1987), 327.

10.   There is a further irony here, of course, in Pardo Bazán's own failure to accord Galdós' "feminist" novel, *Tristana*, an ironic reading.

THE MALE CANON

CALDERÓN'S JUSTINA:
THE ASSUMPTION OF SELFHOOD

Melveena McKendrick

Years ago, when talking about Calderón's *La devoción de la cruz*, I stated that the heroine, Julia, is presented as an individual like her brother, that for Calderón she is as much a representative of mankind as he is, as capable of evil and of salvation; and I concluded that at this level of inquiry into the human condition, gender is no longer of significance for Calderón.[1] I still think this to be the case. However, it seems to me now that the implications of Julia's role are more radical than this suggests. That Calderón should accord Julia her full place in the Christian scheme of sin and redemption is to be expected, in spite of the misogyny enshrined in the scholastic tradition, though we might want to reflect on the fact that Renaissance theologians still felt it necessary to ask themselves whether women really were human beings and whether they too were created in the image of God.[2] More significant, I think, is Julia's status in the play as a *representative of humankind*, a representative equal in spiritual terms with her twin brother; their very twinning, indeed, would seem to accord them inseparable status and link them anthropologically to the divine. At the same time, Julia's forceful insistence on her right to self-determination in Act I acknowledges that in Calderón's theatre, as in life, the fates of men and women were not interchangeable, that there were dilemmas more specific to women (sexual exploitation, self-alienation, self-determination) as there were dilemmas more specific to men (notably the uneasy adjustment of public and private selves which brings the concept of honour into play) - even if the larger questions to which an exploration of those dilemmas is directed are the same, as they are in the case of Julia and Eusebio, or in that, say, of Semíramis and Segismundo. There is in Calderón's drama an ontological engagement with women at both spiritual and human levels.

In fact the conviction has grown in me over the years that for all Lope's fascination with women on and off the stage, and for all of Tirso's apparent tolerance of female independence and his talent for creating intelligent women, it is in Calderón that we find the most significant female roles, the most memorable female speeches, the most substantial confrontation with issues now called feminist. I am thinking not only of self-assertive characters with their eyes firmly fixed on goals of their own choosing which they may or may not achieve, women like Julia, Justina or Rosaura, but of those passive figures like Isabel, Mencía and Serafina, whose enforced removal into silence at the end of their stories stands as eloquent testimony to their terrifying helplessness in a phallocratic world. Julia's defiant interchange with her father in *La devoción de la cruz*, Rosaura's ecstatic bisexual celebration of identity in Act III of *La vida es sueño*, Isabel's anguished lament of shame, anger and despair after her rape in *El alcalde de Zalamea*, these are potent moments in the fictional chronicling of female experience. Justina in *El mágico prodigioso* is given no such memorable words, but she is nonetheless an intensely memorable figure and an unusually interesting example, I think, of the way in which Calderón places feminine issues at the heart of plays which might appear to be focussing audience interest elsewhere. In this play there is no strategic renunciation of sexual identity, no temporary assumption of the manhood necessary to make headway in a man's world, such as we find elsewhere in the *comedia*, simply an outright refusal to accept the role that society expects women to occupy.

El mágico prodigioso is Calderón's dramatization of the Faust theme. Cipriano is a student in Antioch in the early days of Christianity whose deliberations have brought him so close to belief in God that the Devil decides to distract him with the beauty of the virtuous Justina, a secret Christian whom the Devil also wishes to destroy. Cipriano sells his soul to the Devil in return for Justina, but the Devil's attempt to corrupt her fails and the woman whom Cipriano eventually embraces turns out to be a horrifying skeleton. When Cipriano prises out of the Devil the admission that Justina was able to resist the assault on her free will because of her belief in the Christian God, his search is at an end. He becomes a Christian and the two meet their deaths together on the executioner's block. The play has a sub-plot involving Lelio and Floro, who as rivals for Justina's hand employ Cipriano as their intermediary, which is when he falls in love with her. Their rivalry is the tool the Devil uses in his campaign to destroy Justina's reputation.

Justina is the fulcrum of the play's action and its theme. Her virtue is absolutely central to her role. God's purpose is to test it, the Devil hates her for it, Lelio and Floro are attracted by it, even the Governor of Antioch, who arrests her for being a Christian, overreacts because of it. Her beauty acts as the catalyst. It enables the Devil to attempt her downfall via Lelio and Floro; it likewise enables him to attempt the downfall of Cipriano; these two are closely linked in that it is through Lelio and Floro that Justina is revealed to Cipriano as an object of sexual passion. Her virtue and her beauty together make her the unwitting source of the play's spiritual and physical conflict. Her human and moral perfection is the magnet which attracts desire (i.e. love) in Lelio, Floro and Cipriano, and envy (therefore hatred) in the Devil; it thus becomes the instrument of chaos. The chaos is all-enveloping. Lelio and Floro sacrifice friendship, filial duty, honour, even freedom; Cipriano sells his soul; Justina loses her reputation, her honour, and her adoptive father's love and respect; Lisandro loses his trust in his daughter and the Governor imprisons his own son, Lelio. Justina's virtue and beauty are seen by the world as complementary to each other, but in the event, through the Devil's offices, they are brought into complete opposition. What enables the Devil to use her beauty to try to destroy her virtue, of course, is the existence of her honour - the measure by which human society has chosen to judge virtue and nobility.

The Devil's combined purpose means that where Justina's honour is concerned he can do a thorough job. First he brings her virtue into disrepute with his activities in and around her house, which give Lelio and Floro's jealous fantasies corporeal form. The balcony scene where each separately sees the Devil leaving Justina's house and thinks it is the other is crucial, for as a result of Justina's apparent shamelessness first Lelio and later Floro feel free to penetrate the house and violate Justina's privacy; a sexual parallel may obviously be drawn here - compare the relevance of the victim's sexual past in the history of rape legislation. The subsequent discovery of the two suitors duelling in Justina's house then makes public her assumed dishonour. The Devil's *coup de grâce* comes with his attempt to lead Cipriano into eternal damnation. Justina's dishonour will, he hopes, then become a real disintegration of virtue when she yields to the temptings of her imagination and goes in search of Cipriano.

But the Devil underestimates Justina. The extraordinary seduction scene (extraordinary because there is no seducer other than her own imagination), in which her senses are ravaged by aural and visual representations of love, affects her only briefly. As soon as the Devil tries to push home his advantage and lead her to Cipriano, she recovers her reason and her will, and in one of the great emblematic moments of the Golden-Age stage she resists his attempt to drag her off. What he has not bargained for is her total commitment to her own view of her life. In her rejection of her suitors there is not a hint of playing hard to get. Justina is intellectually immune to the three of them. The point is hammered home immediately afterwards in a grotesque scene of inverted parody in which her maid, Livia, far from rejecting her two suitors, cannot bear to forfeit either and takes them both on alternate days. While she lives through and by her senses, her mistress has consistently lived above hers. We learn later from Justina's own lips that from the day she first met Cipriano she like him has felt confused and troubled. But their love affair must be the least tangible in the seventeenth-century Spanish theatre. It is as if Cipriano, rather than being loved for himself, becomes through his passionate advocacy of love the embodiment of Justina's other self, the focus of awakening thoughts and imaginings which she has never before experienced. And Justina senses that her commitment to a spiritual life is threatened (hence her call on her *albedrío*), that a monumental conflict of flesh and spirit is to take place within her. When physically confronted by Cipriano in the street at the beginning of Act II, however, she does not weaken and she leaves him with a rigid declaration that she cannot love him until death, a warning misconstrued by Cipriano, who chooses to interpret her words in terms of the hectic conceits of the courtly lover. The real temptation, significantly, is felt in his absence, in her imagination, and she will not meet him again until they are locked in the room in the governor's palace from which they will walk out together to their deaths. Justina is unassailable because her mind is all along fixed on a higher order of values. The woman whom the Devil assumed it would be easy to overcome precisely because she was a woman thus emerges as the invincible one, her integrity absolute, her singleness of purpose (that quality traditionally regarded as a property exclusive to the male) unimpaired. All the other characters in the play, by contrast, fail in intellectual rectitude.

Justina at first sight appears to be yet another of the Golden-Age theatre's sexual icons, those unruly beauties so intent on preserving their chastity that they have to be "humanized" by love in the course of the play. The socio-psychological basis of their position is clear. It is their only way of retaining a modicum of independence from male dominance and social subservience; they reject love and marriage because of the way in which these are used by men to subject women to the values of a patriarchal world. *Esquivez* is a bid for control, and its defeat in the *comedia* marks the reassertion of prevailing patriarchal attitudes. Calderón, however, takes a different approach here, as becomes the play's hagiographical identity. By placing the motif in the context of the persecution of the early Christians and of the theology of the Devil's temptation of the human race, he transforms it into a struggle to maintain an order of values that applies not only to woman's personal independence and dignity but to the proper structuring of human society. Justina has the moral absolutism of Shakespeare's Isabella, who sincerely believes that her spiritual integrity, inseparable for her too from chastity, is worth more than her brother's life: 'more than our brother is our chastity' (II, iv). And Justina's scene with the Devil is as outstanding as are those between Isabella and Angelo. In both *Measure for Measure* and *El mágico prodigioso* what corrupts is not sex but its elevation into the primary good and final end of human existence. Justina knows the right order of values, Clarín, Moscón and Livia blatantly defy it, Lelio and Floro forget it when their selfish behaviour sabotages the very virtue that attracts them. Cipriano learns it from experience, and from Justina's example: she has retained her independence while he has become enslaved. There is nothing evil in human love or passion, the play suggests, provided they do not usurp the values of the spirit. It is through Justina, though human love, after all, that Cipriano ultimately comes to know God. Thus the human union longed for earlier on by Cipriano is both mirrored and transcended by their martyrdom together. The executioner's block becomes their marriage bed in fulfilment of Justina's warning that she can love Cipriano only in death.

It might be argued that it is Justina's spiritual goals that empower her rejection of gender stereotypification and it is certainly true that they would have legitimated her behaviour for a seventeenth-century audience. Sanctity and chastity, as we know, go together. Justina is a Christian. But of course although Christianity has idealized chastity, it has not, for obvious reasons, insisted on it; even St. Paul did not recommend it for all.[3] In the sixteenth century it became a Reformation issue. In most Christian societies the normal human model has been that of the family, and woman's role, unlike that of men, has been located exclusively within it. The choice of chastity has been an admired choice, but a choice against the grain for both sexes. In freeing herself from the ties of tradition, custom and expectation in embracing celibacy, Justina defies her female destiny, which is reflected in her suitors' assumption that she will have one or other of them. And just as early Christian resistance to the idea that human worth was defined by social contribution has been seen by historians to contain the seeds of the later Western idea of the absolute worth of the individual, so Justina's resistance to her socially determined role can be seen, in the context of both early Christianity and seventeenth-century Spain, as a prefiguration of our belief now in the absolute value of woman. The spiritual scope of Justina's role within the scheme of the play does not for us now invalidate the paradigmatic significance of her stand against social coercion, and I doubt whether the point would have been lost on audiences at the time, a significant proportion of which, it must be remembered, were women. After all, a seventeenth-century daughter who insisted on entering a convent against the wishes and interests of her family would have been challenging the system, for all that age's acceptance of monastic life.

The real issue is the free exercise of choice. Justina's refusal of the role she is expected to occupy in itself marks her out as a rebel. In terms of *comedia* convention all her motives do is allow her to remain one: she remains unmarried because she is called to a higher destiny - unlike Isabella, whose vocation falls victim to a shameless sell-out to the constraints of a happy ending (unless one chooses to see it as the immature enthusiasm of a passionate young girl destined all along for marriage, as some Shakespearian directors have done). Yet the *nature* of Justina's choice is itself not without its significance here. In spite of the advent of Christianity, seventeenth-century Europe, like classical antiquity, still largely accepted Aristotle's definition of the human being as a political animal, that is, as being defined by membership of and contribution to society and the state. The choice of chastity, the privileging of the individual will, can therefore be seen as a political act. It is, clearly, an act of the spirit as well - Peter Brown, in his masterly study of the body and society in early Christianity, maintains that chastity was used by early Christians as a means of achieving a radical spiritual transformation which would help them regain the lost perfection of Adam.[4] But this goal in itself of course was, in the Roman Empire, socially and politically subversive. Foucault sees such conduct in early Christianity as an exercise in power and liberty, which closely echoes Justina's adherence to the principle of self-determination.[5] Elaine Pagels, another historian of early Christianity, develops this point: 'For many Christians of the first four centuries and ever since, the greatest freedom demanded the greatest renunciation - above all, celibacy. This identification of freedom with celibacy involved a paradox, then as now, for celibacy ... is an extreme form of self-restraint. Yet as Christians saw it, celibacy involved rejection of "the world", of ordinary society and its multitudinous entanglements and was thereby a way to gain control over one's own life.'[6] St. Augustine's pagan contemporaries regarded sexual renunciation not only as social suicide but as impiety and dishonour;[7] in the play, Justina's covert Christian beliefs are similarly seen as dishonouring her and her chastity is denounced as hypocrisy by the Governor. Clearly, in societies like those of early Christianity and Calderón's Spain, where marriage was a social contract arranged with little reference to the couple concerned, particularly the woman, and where childbirth took a high toll in suffering and mortality,

8

celibacy could seem an attractive option. Pagels points out that in the days of early Christianity celibacy offered women earthly benefits such as control of their own wealth, freedom to travel and engage in intellectual and spiritual pursuits and to found institutions.[8] In seventeenth-century Spain celibacy was a legitimate, even ideal, choice, but in the context of a powerful Church and a declining economy it was again a choice inspired by diverse motives (the Church was the only career structure open to women at the time) and worries were expressed about its economic and demographic effects. The argument for seeing celibacy as a possible instrument of the individual's control over her or his own identity and destiny is historically, therefore, a strong one, and in *El mágico prodigioso* the motifs of celibacy and free will, or control, are indeed inextricably intertwined.

Justina remains faithful to the truth of her life as she sees it, bound up as this is with absolute truth as she knows it to be. She rejects her suitors out of hand, not because she is prudish or through any misconceived notion of honour, but because her life is following a different course from that of love and marriage. Her honour is not something it occurs to her to worry about until she is actually accused of being without it. Like her mother before her - murdered in childbirth by her husband for being a Christian - Justina dies a violent death; but unlike her mother, Justina has rejected the possibility of husband and children in favour of the life of the spirit, and for her, therefore, martyrdom is not a tragedy but a fulfilment and a deliverance. Her posthumous birth prefigures her spiritual rebirth and apotheosis at the end of the play. Her life and her death represent the triumph of will, of control, over those things - internal and external - which militate against them. If, like Isabella, she is not a woman we instantly recognise or even sympathize with now, this is because the conflict between life's alternatives and its different realities, which takes place in and around her, is presented in a socio-historical context, that of religion and honour, which is less familiar to the modern world. Nevertheless, the integrity of her inner resolution, the pathos of her bewilderment, the humanity of the feelings that rise temporarily to the surface, above all the strength of her determination to shape her own destiny, to refuse to be what others want her to be, all make her a moving and powerful dramatic figure.

The play, after all, is a play about choice. Cipriano's story is that of the transformation, in the crucible of experience, of wrong choice into right choice. Justina's story constitutes a confirmation, a reiteration of choice in that same crucible. She has chosen the life she wants to lead, the sort of person she wishes to be. But the choice has been made from a position of innocence, of ignorance of the claims of normality. Cipriano's impassioned outpourings bring her into direct confrontation, not merely with a man who attracts her, but with something much more vast - a reality outside her experience, the call of a completely different life. The temptation scene is the resulting crisis, in which intellectual conviction and spiritual devotion grapple with the stirrings of the body and the emotions (sexual fantasies were, for obvious reasons, a familiar form of diabolic temptation for the celibate). When her will prevails, her choice of destiny becomes unassailable. Her choice, like Cipriano's, involves death. Like her mother she dies, but unlike her mother she dies *for* her faith and not merely because of it. Through the exercise of choice, the mother's tragedy becomes the daughter's triumph.

Sexual renunciation was presumably something Calderón himself came to know about when he suddenly entered the priesthood at the age of fifty-one, and was required to measure at first hand the value of celibacy as a means of acquiring freedom through self-control. *El mágico prodigioso* was written, of course, some fourteen years before this, and it is probably significant that he himself as a young man had insisted on exercising control over his own life by refusing, against the wishes of a domineering father, to enter the priesthood. The relationship between celibacy and choice was therefore a matter as central to his life as it is to this play. As to what Calderón's considered thoughts on woman's place in the scheme of things might or might not have been, of course we cannot know. But the portrayal of splendidly independent, though by no means idealized, women such as Justina must correspond to some 'psychic reality', as Stevie Davies puts it, somewhere in Calderón's mind.[9] If a fictional character represents no more than an imaginary psychology as Ortega y Gasset held, then the mere act of imagining a Justina, or a Rosaura, or a Julia, concedes the possibility of her existence for the author. Justina is given licence by Calderón to speak with a double voice, that of her kind and that of her sex, and the play endorses all that she has to say, effectively turning her role into a remarkable assertion of female selfhood.[10]

NOTES

1. *Woman and Society in the Spanish Drama of the Golden Age* (Cambridge: Cambridge University Press, 1974), 126.

2. Ian Maclean, *The Renaissance Notion of Woman* (Cambridge: Cambridge University Press, 1980), 12; Stevie Davies, *The Idea of Woman in Renaissance Literature* (Brighton, Sussex: The Harvester Press, 1986), 10.

3. I Corinthians, 7:7; and Peter Brown, *The Body and Society. Men, Women and Sexual Renunciation in Early Christianity* (London: Faber and Faber, 1989), 54.

4. *The Body and Society*, 83-102.

5. Michel Foucault, *The History of Sexuality.* Vol. II *The Use of Pleasure*, trans. Robert Hurley (Harmondsworth: Viking Press, 1986), 22.

6. Elaine Pagels, *Adam, Eve and the Serpent* (New York: Random House, 1988), 78.

7. Pagels, 79.

8. Pagels, 88.

9. *The Idea of Woman*, 2.

10. Interestingly, the centrality and power of Justina's role are reflected in the fact that in the nineteenth century D. F. McCarthy chose to call his translation of *El mágico prodigioso*, *Justina, a play* (London, 1848).

THE SPREAD WINGS OF GALDÓS'
MUJER NUEVA

Lisa Condé

*No le cortéis las alas, y veréis
hasta dónde se remonta...*
(Pérez Galdós, *Voluntad*)

Contemplating the poor, truncated Manx cat in *A Room of One's Own*, Virginia Woolf ponders: 'Was he really born so, or had he lost his tail in an accident'?[1] From an early point in his career, Galdós can be seen to pose a question similarly linked to Freud's notion of castration through his depiction of woman's clipped wings. This image of wings might be further linked to the concept promoted by Luce Irigaray of an alternative, female symbolic which is labial rather than phallocentric.[2] In this way, and in answer to Thomas Aquinas' view of women as 'mutilated males', Galdós is arguably exploring the phenomenon of the mutilated female through the metaphor of 'las alas cortadas'.

Until recently, of course, Galdós scholars had generally concluded that, while sympathetic to the problems faced by women in society, the great writer was not an advocate of feminism. Such scholars based their judgement primarily upon the *novelas contemporáneas* and often cited *Tristana* of 1892 as conclusive evidence.[3] However, the current resurgence of interest in Galdós' turn to the stage that same year[4] has led to a reassessment of this view in the light of his subsequent contemporary drama.

The phenomenon of *la mujer nueva* of Galdós' contemporary drama and last novels has now been acknowleged by several critics,[5] although it has not generally been seen as part of an evolutionary process in the writer's approach to the role of women in society. In her latest study, *Galdós* (1988), Carmen Bravo-Villasante stresses the radical nature of what she sees as a fundamental change in ideology from 1892 as 'en tres años, nada más, Galdós nos sorprende con el estreno de *Voluntad*. Su cambio es radical ... Esta Isidora es la mujer nueva de Galdós ... Estas mujeres representan el cambio en la ideología galdosiana'.[6]

It is my view that, although there was a distinct shift in Galdós' approach to the *portrayal* of women's roles which coincided with and was facilitated by his turn to the stage in 1892, his vision of *la mujer nueva* was the culmination of a lengthy and complex process of evolution rather than the result of an abrupt and inexplicable change in ideology.[7] Daria Montero-Paulson speculates on this possibility in the Conclusion to her recent work, *La jerarquía femenina en la obra de Galdós*:

> ¿Cómo es la mujer "nueva" y por qué aparece en la obra tardía de Galdós? No es fácil contestar esta pregunta, como tampoco es fácil delinear el proceso creador e ideólogico de un escritor tan complejo, enigmático y genial como lo es Benito Pérez Galdós.[8]

Although space does not permit Montero-Paulson to pursue possible answers to the second part of the question she poses, she does acknowledge in a footnote that 'se pueden percibir algunas huellas de la mujer nueva en estado embriónico en la obra más temprana de Pérez Galdós'.[9]

These early signs of *la mujer nueva* can be more clearly perceived by tracing Galdós' persistent use of such unmistakable images of imposed female passivity and confinement as *la muñeca* and *el corsé*, and of potential female awareness and ability as *la luz* and *las alas*.[10]

For the purposes of this essay, it is proposed to explore the development of Galdós' "feminist" interest in the roles of women in society through his use of the image of wings. Notwithstanding the limitations and prejudices of the writer's time, race, class and gender, the term "feminist" might reasonably be applied if one accepts such definitions as that offered by Rosalind Delmar, who concludes 'in the writing of feminist history it is the broad view which predominates: feminism is usually defined as an active desire to change women's position in society',[11] while at the same time acknowledging Toril Moi's qualification, 'men can be feminists - but they can't be women'.[12] Through Galdós' use of the image of wings, repeatedly shown as being clipped by society in the *novelas de la primera época* and the *novelas contemporáneas* but ultimately allowed to spread in his more "utopian" contemporary drama and last novels, the writer's desire to change women's position in society is manifest.

The insistent use of this image in Galdós' early novel, *Gloria* (1877), reveals his already keen awareness of society's suppression of female potential. It is clear from this point in his work that the image denotes woman's capacity for independent reasoning and action, at the same time as linking such potential with both the freedom of the bird and the perfection of the angel. Yet Galdós' particular use of the image of *las alas* in *Gloria* and in later novels and plays appears more specific than the general, arguably more "random" use of bird imagery found in *Fortunata y Jacinta* and studied by Stephen Gilman,[13] Carlos Blanco-Aguinaga,[14] Agnes Gullón[15] and Roger Utt.[16] Of course, there are strong links in so far as such imagery is almost invariably applied to female characters and, as Gilman's later work on Fortunata stresses: 'the special quality of her way of being alive, both of rebelling against captivity and of celebrating freedom, is winged'.[17] Utt also emphasises the obvious connection between 'la imagen del ave' and 'la libertad y la sensación del espacio abierto'[18] and further points to Fortunata's 'pícara idea' which emerges from her 'como sale el pájaro del cascarón'.[19]

The continuing pertinence of images of wings and flying to the feminist debate has been stressed recently by several feminist writers, notably Hélène Cixous who insists, 'To fly is woman's gesture'.[20] Rosette Lamont declares that 'women must invent their own style, both new and rebellious, and thereby emerge from the restricted spaces assigned them for their existence. Their discourse will then take flight on the wings of words that grow out of their flesh, like those of birds and angels ...'.[21] Regretting Freud's failure to acknowledge the cultural tradition which has to do with lips, Irigaray points to the Jewish tradition where the lips figure as a reversed double Yod, a double reversed tongue, and furthermore to how 'the same motif is used for the Holy

Spirit, when, in the form of a bird, it soars above the earth and its seas. At this point, it signifies the creative spirit ...'.[22]

The frequent use of images of flying by women writers is stressed by Gabriela Mora:

> El hallazgo repetido de construcciones metafóricas del concepto *volar* pareciera confirmar el juicio de Hélène Cixous de que "Flying is women's gesture". Estas construcciones que en los niveles más aparentes se asocian, casi siempre, a la prisión doméstica que sufren heroínas y narradoras, en niveles más profundos pueden ser, a veces, índices de fenómenos que contradicen directamente las características asociadas con lo "femenino" tradicional.[23]

Through his early and contemporary novels, Galdós himself can be seen to expose the limiting reality of 'lo femenino tradicional' and then to transform same through his depiction of *una sociedad nueva* on stage. Images of 'el ángel de la casa' confined to the domestic prison of which Mora speaks, with wings well clipped, abound in Galdós' novels from *Doña Perfecta* of 1876 to *Tristana* of 1892, the year of his turn to the stage.

The particular significance of the image of the clipped wings is soon made explicit in *Gloria* (1877) as the heroine begins to recognise her own intellectual potential, telling herself: 'Tú puedes volar hasta los astros, no te arrastres por la tierra' (OC,NI,569).[24] Yet she is repeatedly and, it would seem, well meaningly, restrained and rebuked over this instinct, to the point where she concludes:

> Mi padre me ha dicho varias veces que si no corto las
> alas al pensamiento, voy a ser muy desgraciada ...
> Vengan, pues, las tijeras. (OC,NI,534)

Throughout the novel, this image reflects Gloria's constant struggle between assertion and denial of her intellectual capacities and of her will. This struggle is not just concerned with her wish to marry the man she loves, but with philosophical matters both related and unrelated to this issue. As in subsequent novels, Galdós describes the limited education afforded to his heroine, aimed primarily at providing a veneer to improve her matrimonial prospects and leaving her 'en completa posesión del Catecismo ... mascullando el francés sin saber el español ... y tocando (mal) el piano' (OC,NI,521). Her father, don Juan, recognises how atrocious Gloria's piano playing is, yet when, having gained unauthorised access to certain books in his library, she dares to proffer the opinion that 'los reyes de España habían hecho mal en arrojar del país a judíos y a moriscos', he retorts angrily: '¿Qué entiendes tú de eso? Vete a tocar el piano.' (OC,NI,521). Likewise, following Gloria's independent reasoning on the merits of Golden Age literature, don Juan 'afirmó que el entendimiento de una mujer era incapaz de apreciar asunto tan grande ...' (OC,NI,524).

Clearly, women were brought up to suppress and, indeed, be ashamed of any independent thought as being naturally inferior and presumptuous. Such is Gloria's respect and admiration for her father that she temporarily experiences 'un convencimiento profundísimo de que había pensado mil tonterías y despropósitos abominables' (OC,NI,525). Many a young woman's intellectual development would, of course, have become permanently stifled at this point. In Galdós' sympathetic depiction of Gloria's suppressed initiative, he can be seen to anticipate such challenge to tradition as portrayed by Pardo Bazán in her later novel, *Memorias de un solterón* (1896), wherein Feíta's father is equally appalled by the fact that his daughter, 'como si fuese un hombre, ha leído los libros más perniciosos...'.[25] By gaining such access to the inherited knowledge on which male authority resides, Feíta has similarly crossed the barrier into the sphere of male knowledge and thus, as Bieder observes, 'violated the strictures of female experience'.[26] We are further reminded here of one of the key confrontations recounted in Virginia Woolf's *A Room of One's Own*, where she is denied access to the "Oxbridge" library.[27] Such denial of access to knowledge remains, as Chris Weedon points out, a key political issue, since knowledge brings with it the possibility of power and control.[28]

Gloria is condemned for this unwitting intrusion upon the rights of men, and temporarily subdued. Yet her struggle continues, as she subsequently recognizes her inability to accept blindly the judgements of her father and uncle who, in her opinion, 'se fijan en la superficie; pero no ven el fondo' (OC,NI,569). She resolves, 'si no puedo menos de pensar, al menos callaré' (OC,NI,525). Again there is a parallel with Woolf's response, 'Lock up your libraries if you like; but there is no gate, no lock, no bolt that you can set upon the freedom of my mind'.[29]

While Gloria's frustration persists, so does her father's refusal to discuss any subject in depth with her to the point where, in one brief and highly charged statement, we are told, 'Tenía cortadas las alas' (OC,NI,525). Subsequently, however, on overhearing a conversation which revealed the hypocrisy behind the Catholicism of Rafael, the suitor her father wishes her to marry, Gloria sees the hypocrisy in her own submission:

> Yo he sido hipócrita; yo me dejé cortar las alas, y cuando me han vuelto a crecer, he hecho como si no las tuviera ... He afectado someter mi pensamiento al pensamiento ajeno, y reducir mi alma, encerrándola dentro de una esfera mezquina. (OC,NI,569)

Such submission to the will of others, intent on subduing and moulding women to suit their own and society's purposes, is a theme Galdós was to pursue in subsequent novels from *La familia de León Roch* (1877), and most notably in *Fortunata y Jacinta* (1887).[30]

Gloria's inner voice continues to insist: 'Rebélate, rebélate. Tu inteligencia es superior' (OC, NI, 579)[31] and, again, Galdós uses the image of the fluttering wings which will not yet be stilled: 'Gloria movía con más vigor a cada instante las funestas alas de su latitudinarismo, que debían conducirla Dios sabe a qué regiones de espanto' (OC,NI,580).

Although Gloria rebels against the dogmatic form of religion extolled by her aunt Serafina, she becomes a more suitable candidate for such doctrine as a result of the guilt she experiences following her loss of innocence. With this loss of innocence, Gloria also suffers a loss of strength as those same wings which might have led to some freedom and ability to control her own destiny, are broken. The apparently forced seduction of Gloria by Daniel is less than totally convincing, although this 'fall' is crucial to the heroine's subsequent development and manipulation by doña Serafina. With 'las alas rotas' (OC,NI,592), Gloria is now crushed spiritually, intellectually and physically. Her hopes for the future all but lost, she shuts herself away in her room, where 'como el laborioso insecto, ha tejido un capullo, y, quedándose dentro, con intención, sin duda, de no salir sino con alas, o sea en espíritu' (OC,NI,606). From her room, nothing can be heard except 'quizás un rumor más tenue que el de las alas del más pequeño insecto batiendo en el aire' (OC,NI,607).

The forceful crushing of Gloria's wings in this early novel can be directly paralleled with the crushing of Tristana's hopes for the future, illustrated through this same image, in Galdós' later novel. Here Emilio Miró concludes of the heroine's destiny: 'Las alas cortadas o la pierna cortada; todo es lo mismo'.[32] The analogy is clearly a highly pertinent one to the continuing feminist debate, and a similar question is begged to that posed by Virginia Woolf when contemplating the Manx cat. Was Tristana's failure really due to Nature, as Leon Livingstone would have us believe?[33] Or should Freud's theory of the castration complex be re-defined? Is Galdós in fact illustrating the brutality of society's suppression of female potential, as one might well conclude from his insistent use of the wings image, now reinforced through the untimely loss of a limb?

Tristana's potential is acknowledged by both don Lope and Horacio through this image of wings. Don Lope admits 'No sabemos más sino que tienes alas ...' and wonders '¿hasta dónde volerás?' (OC,NIII,397). Likewise Horacio recognises his lover's 'alas de extraordinaria fuerza para subirse a los espacios sin fin' (OC,NIII,413). Yet both feel threatened by this potential and attempt to suppress it, Horacio directly appealing, 'No te me vuelvas muy filósofa, no te encarames a las estrellas' (OC,NIII,390). Just as Gloria had wanted to reach for the stars, telling herself, 'tú puedes volar hasta los astros', but ultimately 'tenía las alas cortadas', so Tristana's ambitions are similarly curtailed.

Although Tristana is ultimately forced to conform to society's demands, the amputation of her leg dramatically (if not melodramatically) reinforcing the symbolic clipping of her wings, the case is not completely closed through this unsatisfactory conclusion. For, through Horacio, one can perhaps detect the writer's own tentative suggestion that Tristana:

> quizás ve más que todos nosotros; quizás su mirada perspicua, o cierto instinto de adivinación concedido a las mujeres superiores, ve la sociedad futura que nosotros no vemos. (OC,NIII,413)

It is this new society, this 'sociedad futura', that Galdós immediately proceeds to explore on stage, and which is activated through his vision of *la mujer nueva*. In her depiction, the images one might well call "feminist" (including that of *las alas*) which were not just lurking but actively employed in the preceding novels, are redeployed and serve to reinforce her achievements.

The secondary role of Clotilde in *Realidad*, the dialogue novel adapted for Galdós' dramatic début of 1892, is notably developed for the stage rather than being condensed or even dispensed with as might be expected. Clotilde can be seen as the immediate precursor of *la mujer nueva* as she is finally allowed to assert her will without restriction. The maid Bárbara is at first blamed for encouraging Clotilde in her rebellion and accused: 'tú le has dado alas'. Nevertheless, Clotilde's wings are not clipped and, consequently, Villalonga is able to observe: 'Clotilde ha decidido de por sí de su suerte' (OC,CTC,149).

The strength and power of the will of Galdós' new heroine is further developed through Victoria in *La loca de la casa* (1893) and fully realised through Isidora in *Voluntad* (1895). The contrast between the victimised heroine of the past and the victorious *mujer nueva* of the future is vividly illustrated through the redeployment of the same "feminist" images, found throughout Galdós' work. Thus where Gloria's wings, struggling to develop in the early part of that novel, are crushed by her fall from innocence, the wings of Galdós' new Isidora in *Voluntad* are conversely allowed to expand and mature *subsequent to* her "fall", reflecting the desired change in social attitudes promoted by the new dramatist.

Like Gloria and Tristana before her, Isidora reaches for the stars, but, unlike her predecessors, she is not restrained from realising her ambition. Having taken charge of her father's business, Isidora not only saves it from ruin, but aspires to greater successes, as illustrated in the following discussion with her father, Isidro, and uncle, don Santos:

Isidro	Contentémonos con conservar lo presente ...
Santos	Alientos tiene la niña para mucho más.
Isidora	¡Ya lo creo!
Isidro	Yo, no; mis aspiraciones son más modestas.
Isidora	*Las mías pican alto.*

Here the image of *las alas* returns to encapsulate the determination, ambition and potential of the heroine, as don Santos exclaims:

Santos   ¡Viva el águila del comercio matritense!   No le
cortéis las alas, y veréis hasta donde se remonta ...
(OC,CTC,382).

At last the wings of the heroine's *voluntad*, so long restrained, are allowed to
spread fully, as Isidora fulfils her ambitions and takes control.

It is the force of the will of Galdós' *mujer nueva* which activates the
realisation of his vision of *una sociedad nueva* on stage. In terms of class
politics, this vision has been seen as romantic and unrealistic in its utopianism.
In terms of sexual politics, however, it might well be considered progressive
and potentially realisable. In seeking solutions on stage to both problems,
Galdós is in accord with Simone de Beauvoir's view of feminists as 'those
women or even men who fight to change the position of women, in liaison with
and yet outside the class struggle, without totally subordinating that change to
a change in society'.[34]

Galdós' stance, essentially liberal with increasingly "socialist"[35]
overtones, has been likened by Carla Her to the early "liberal feminism" of
John Stuart Mill.[36] Emilia Pardo Bazán was preparing an Introduction to the
Spanish translation of Mill's study of *The Subjection of Women* at the time
Galdós was writing *Tristana*, and it is highly likely that they would have
discussed his views. Ibsen's *A Doll's House* had also just been translated into
Spanish, so the question was clearly a topical one at the time Galdós explored
the concept of a more radical form of feminism in *Tristana*. The "liberal
feminism" reflected through his subsequent contemporary drama, in which the
institution of marriage is retained but renegotiated and the Krausist ideal of
conciliation pursued, might be seen as a compromise better suited to the
contemporary society than the more radical measures considered in *Tristana*,
to which arguably society rather than Galdós or Nature could not concede.[37]

It is apparent that Galdós was acutely aware of the roots of the female
dilemma, whether or not he intentionally set out to explore solutions. All the
related issues and problems which he had portrayed through his preceding
novels recur and are re-explored through the process of adapting *Realidad* for
the stage, together with their corresponding imagery. At the same time the
role of Clotilde, significantly played by Concha-Ruth Morell,[38] is expanded
and developed as the precursor to *la mujer nueva*. From this point the

evolution of Galdós' new heroine is rapid, and as her wings unfold her potential is released.

Despite the retention of the traditional institution of marriage, the release of this potential and the corresponding power afforded to Galdós' *mujer nueva* implies a transformation of its internal structure. In this way, Galdós can be seen to follow Aristotle in allowing for the retention of many traditional characteristics as well as for 'potentiality as a dynamic attribute of living organisms',[39] in contrast to Plato who makes his Republic immune to change once formed. At the same time, however, through his insistent use of the image of the clipped wings, Galdós might well be challenging the former's notion of woman as 'an impotent male' with the suggestion that her own particular potential is not only unnaturally but undesirably suppressed by society. Beyond this, the suggestion that a different form of power might arise from a different source of potential can be linked to the current ideal of the feminist Hermione Lee for power 'to take on its most promising and least hurtful meaning, that of potential'.[40]

While Galdós' vision of *la mujer nueva* may be considered utopian, we are reminded by Toril Moi how 'utopian thought has always been a source of political inspiration for feminists and socialists alike'.[41] Whether Galdós is finally accorded either of these titles and despite the many contradictions in his writing, there can be little doubt that in the depiction of the spread wings of his new heroine he is promoting his declared belief that 'el día que la mujer consiga emanciparse, el mundo será distinto'.[42]

NOTES

1. *A Room of One's Own* (London: Hogarth, 1929), 20.

2. Luce Irigaray, 'The gesture in psychoanalysis' in *Between Feminism and Psychoanalysis*, ed., Teresa Brennan (London: Routledge, 1989), 135-136.

3. The most vociferous of these critics is Leon Livingstone in 'The law of nature and women's liberation in *Tristana*', *Anales Galdosianos*, VII (1972).

4. Recent full-length studies on Galdós' theatre include Carmen Menéndez Onrubia's *Introducción al teatro de Benito Pérez Galdós* (Madrid: *Segismundo,* Anejo, 1983) and Stanley Finkenthal's *El teatro de Galdós* (Madrid: Editorial Fundamentos, 1980).

5. See, in particular, Carmen Bravo-Villasante, *Galdós* (Madrid: Mondadori, 1988) and Daria Montero-Paulson, *La jerarquía femenina en la obra de Galdós* (Madrid: Editorial Pliegos, 1988). Michèle Guerrini's enlightening Ph.D. dissertation, 'Galdós and nineteenth-century Spanish feminism: women and marriage in the *novelas contemporáneas* (1881-1915)' (University of Pennsylvania, 1978), also stresses the feminist nature of Galdós' last novels, particularly *La razón de la sinrazón* (1915).

6. *Ibid.*, 88.

7. I have traced this evolution in *Stages in the Development of a Feminist Consciousness in Pérez Galdós* (New York: Mellen Press, 1990).

8. *Op. cit.*, 195.

9. *Ibid.*, n. 1.

10. See my work *Stages ...* , *op.cit.*, for more detail on these images.

11. Rosalind Delmar, 'What is Feminism?' in *What is Feminism?*, eds. Juliet Mitchell and Ann Oakley (Oxford: Blackwell, 1986), 13.

12. Toril Moi, 'Feminist, female, feminine' in *The Feminist Reader*, eds. Catherine Belsey and Jane Moore (Basingstoke: Macmillan Education Limited, 1989).

13. Stephen Gilman,'The birth of Fortunata', *Anales Galdosianos*, Vol. 1 (1966).

14. Carlos Blanco Aguinaga, 'On the birth of Fortunata', *Anales Galdosianos*, Vol. 3 (1968).

24

15. Agnes Gullón, 'The bird motif and the introductory motif: structure in *Fortunata y Jacinta'*, *Anales Galdosianos*, Vol. 9 (1974).

16. Roger Utt, '"El pajaro voló": Observaciones sobre un leitmotif en *Fortunata y Jacinta'*, *Anales Galdosianos*, Vol. 9 (1974).

17. Stephen Gilman, *Galdós and the Art of the European Novel* (Princeton University Press, 1981), 315.

18. *Op. cit.*, 40.

19. *Ibid.*, 46.

20. Hélène Cixous, 'Sorties: out and out: attacks/ways out/forays', *The Feminist Reader*, 115.

21. Rosette C. Lamont, 'The off-centre spatiality of women's discourse', *Theory and Practice of Feminist Literary Criticism*, eds. Gabriela Mora and Karen S. Van Hooft (Michigan: Bilingual Press, 1982), 138.

22. *Op. cit.*, 135.

23. Gabriela Mora, 'Crítica feminista: apuntes sobre definiciones y problemas', *Theory and Practice* ..., 7.

24. Textual references are to the 1973 Aguilar edition of the *Obras Completas*.

25. Emilia Pardo Bazán, *Obras Completas*, II (Madrid: Aguilar, 1964), 473.

26. Maryellen Bieder, 'En-gendering strategies of authority: Emilia Pardo Bazán and the novel', *Cultural and Historical Grounding for Hispanic and Luso-Brazilian Feminist Literary Criticism* (Minnesota, Minneapolis: Institute for the Study of Ideologies and Literature, 1989), 486.

27. *Op. cit.*, 12.

28. Chris Weedon, *Feminist Practice and Poststructuralist Theory* (Oxford: Blackwell, 1987), 14.

29. *Op. cit.*, 114.

30. This theme is explored in *Stages* ... , *op. cit*.

31. The innate superior intelligence of such women was to be stressed by Pardo Bazán in an article published in *La Epoca* in 1896, wherein she declared:

    El número de mujeres verdaderamente superiores, sin que por esto sean célebres, sería incalculable; la mujer española es inteligente y la instrucción hacía aquí maravillas.

(Quoted by Bieder, *op. cit.*, 491)

32. Emilio Miró, '*Tristana* o la imposibilidad de ser', *Cuadernos Hispanoamericanos, Núms.* 250-252 (1970-1971), 520.

33. See n. 3 above.

34. Quoted by Gabriela Mora in *Theory and Practice*..., 2.

35. Galdós declared socialism to be 'la última palabra en la cuestión social'. Quoted by Olmet y Carraffa, *Los grandes españoles: Galdós* (Madrid, 1912), 111.

36. Carla Her, 'Pérez Galdós, Pardo Bazán y Stuart Mill: una aproximación literaria y filosófica de la problemática femenina en el siglo xix', *Actas del Tercer Congreso Internacional de Estudios Galdosianos*, I (Las Palmas, Excmo. Cabildo Insular de Gran Canaria, 1989).

37. Based on an ironic reading of the novel. See, for example, Edward Friedman's study '"Folly and a woman": Galdós' rhetoric of irony in *Tristana*', *Theory and Practice* ...

38. Concha-Ruth Morell had provided the inspiration (and the letters) for *Tristana*.

39. Lewis Mumford, 'Utopia, the city and the machine', *Utopias and Utopian Thought*, ed. Frank E. Manuel (London, Souvenir Press 1973), 23.

40. Hermione Lee, 'Power: women and the word' in *The State of the Language*, eds. C. Ricks and L. Michaels (Berkeley: University of California Press, 1990), 117.

41. Toril Moi, *Sexual/Textual Politics: Feminist Literary Theory* (London, Routledge 1985), 121.

42. Reported by Angel Martín, Galdós' coachman, in *Excelsior*, 11-11-1917.

SAINTS AND STRUMPETS:
FEMALE STEREOTYPES IN VALLE-INCLÁN

Jean Andrews

In 1904, José Ortega y Gasset proclaimed himself shocked to learn that the author of *Sonata de estío* was not 'a muscular male, great-limbed and meaty of forehead, massive like a Borgia and bursting with cruel instincts, someone who would spend his spare moments bending iron bars or smashing horseshoes with his fist'. To his immense consternation, he reveals to his audience, the author is 'thin, impossibly thin, he has a long beard full of dark mysterious reflections and little, round horn-rimmed glasses'.[1] The world of the *Sonata de estío* and of the *Memorias del Marqués de Bradomín* is unremittingly masculine, the noblemen are 'hombres galantes, altivos, audaces que derrumban corazones y doncelleces, que pelean y desdeñan', soldiers and seducers, in other words, who would just as cheerfully lay siege to and capture a town as a woman (25). Ortega is enamoured also of the women portrayed in these stories:

> Las mujeres suelen ser o rubias, débiles, asustadizas, supersticiosas y sin voluntad, que se entreguen absorbidas por la fortaleza y gallardía de un hombre, o damas del «Renacimiento», de magnífica hermosura, ardientes y sin escrúpulos. (26)

The women, sufferers or saints the first category and courtesans or strumpets the second, provide the soldier-seducers with contrasting military-cum-amorous objectives, the equivalent perhaps of launching an assault on a convent, and on a brothel. This is not an exaggeration. In Ortega's analysis, the women in these early stories by Valle-Inclán are defined only in terms, firstly, of how desirable they are to men, and, secondly, of how easily, or at what cost, their defences may be breached. For Ortega, the writing of Valle is uselessly beautiful, impossibly heroic, gloriously amoral. Most importantly, the decadent Renaissance world created by the apparently unmasculine Valle is perceived, without too much difficulty, by this very influential male critic as a phallocentric paradise.

Thirty-two years later, César M. Arconada published a tribute to Valle-Inclán on the day after his death in the socialist *Mundo Obrero*. He divides Valle's work, like most critics, into two cycles, before and after the *esperpentos*. Even though his political viewpoint is radically different to that of Ortega, his interpretation of Valle's first period is similar:

> En las «Sonatas» y en las «Comedias bárbaras», el ideal caballeresco, feudal, noble, está sostenido, incólume, con una virilidad y una grandeza epopéyica que asusta. En esta época, su ideal está con el señor, ... por aquello que el señor tiene de fuerte, de orgulloso, de excepcional, de insubornable e indomable.[2]

The ideal of nobility identified by Arconada in these works depends on overtly masculine qualities for its survival: virility, patriarchy, strength, pride, indomitability. According to him, Valle eventually loses faith in his decaying aristocracy and begins to portray the proletariat not as the loyal servants of feudal masters but as individuals persecuted by the ruling classes. When this happens, Valle's writing loses much of what this critic condemns as its effete *modernismo*, 'para adquirir expresión sustancial, racional y popular' (151). In Valle's early writing the masculinity of the *caballeros* compensates for the decadence of the style, in the *esperpentos* there are no spectacularly masculine characters but the new form finally reveals a writing worthy of Spain's great literary past: Valle becomes the true descendent of 'nuestros grandes clásicos, Rojas, Cervantes, Quevedo'. The tradition of these writers is one of satire, social comment and sympathy for the harshness of life among the underclass, it can be made to exemplify Marxist social realism with little effort. It is also, however, an unremittingly phallocentric canon.

In tracing the history of the proletariat within the work of Valle-Inclán, Arconada makes a passing reference to the lampooned Isabel II but does not mention any of Valle's other female characters. He could, perhaps, have cited

Adega in *Flor de santidad* as an early example of the oppressed peasantry or La Sini in *La hija del capitán* as a late manifestation of picaresque enterprise amongst the urban poor. That he does not is probably due to a pattern in Valle's portrayal of female characters which Sumner Greenfield identified thirty years later. Speaking of Mari-Gaila in *Divinas palabras* he emphasises how she differs from most of Valle's women 'quienes rara vez responden a un estímulo fuera de un contexto de amor'.[3] Greenfield does admit that Mari-Gaila has the very freedom to act, with only herself to answer to, that he claims is denied to the rest of her sisters in Valle-Inclán's work. In his summing-up, however, he betrays himself:

> Sigue invencible hasta el fin, esta insensible e incorregible Mari-Gaila, quien es una cosa curiosamente bella de contemplar dentro de su ignorancia moral. (580).

Greenfield attributes Mari-Gaila's unfettered sexual behaviour negatively to moral ignorance whereas the same attitude in Valle's male characters is uniformly explained as amorality, a knowing refusal to conform to expected standards. Secondly, she remains for this critic an object, a curiously beautiful, primitive thing for the male audience to contemplate. Effectively, the critic has stripped Mari-Gaila of whatever independence she possesses and reduced her almost to the passivity of Ortega's 'mujeres débiles y sin voluntad'.

The extent to which all of Valle's women can be fitted into the categories of angel or whore which feminism, especially Gilbert and Gubar, has developed in response to the portrayal of women in the patriarchal canon is uncanny. Amongst the saints can be counted the loyal and long-suffering wives Doña María de Montenegro and Madama Collet, the innocents Adega, Sor Maximina, the young Gaetani princesses, Claudinita, Simoniña; amongst the strumpets, la niña Chole, Mari-Gaila, Isabel II, la Lunares, Ernestina, la Sini. Some of the female characters do not fit so neatly into either pigeonhole, for example, Concha, Sabelita, and, to a lesser extent, Loreta, but, in each case, their dilemma is confined within the boundaries of these definitions, that is to say, within an amorous context. Each character struggles between the impulses towards moral behaviour and fulfilling sexual desire, between holiness and prostitution.

The other great female archetypal figure in the male canon is that of the muse. Woman as object permeates the writing of Valle-Inclán but, curiously, woman as inspiration is absent. In the third section of *La lámpara maravillosa*, his book of gnostic aesthetics, entitled *Exegesis trina*, Valle postulates that the mortal who roots all his actions in love will return to the primitive state of supernature and behold the face of God. This will come about through ecstasy, which is the contemplative enjoyment of all things in the act of being created. Art is the harbinger of that divine knowledge because it provides, on earth, an ideal of consciousness, and because the study of aesthetic doctrine leads to an apprehension of beauty, which is an attribute of the divine essence.[4] Valle mentions Christ in the introduction to this section. Later on, he invokes the image of the three persons of God, the 'padre creador', 'Cristo Señor Nuestro' and 'el Paracleto' in his description of the mystic-gnostic way. This goes through three stages, termed 'rosas estéticas', to union with God. The three roses are the 'rosa erótica', the 'rosa clásica' and the 'rosa enigmática del matiz'. The first represents physical regeneration of the human race through eroticism, the Demiurge. It therefore constantly assures the Future and is, ultimately, the function of the 'padre creador'. The second rose, the 'rosa clásica' or 'rosa andrógina', is the rose of the Present, of thesis and antithesis, of humanism. Valle implies, but does not state, that this rose, which opens 'en el cielo, todo amor, del verbo', is associated with Christ, the Word of God and the Enunciator of His great love. The third rose is the rose of quietism and ecstatic contemplation of beauty in all things. It is the rose of the Past or, rather, of forgetting the Past. It allows the contemplative to overcome Time, to conquer the enigmas of Past, Present and Future and to enter into mystical awareness of the divine consciousness.

In all of this there is no mention of the feminine. The aesthetic rose has become utterly androgynous in the writing of Valle-Inclán and has none of the feminine connotations to be found in the work of contemporaries like Yeats or Juan Ramón Jiménez, for example. Yeats's 'rose of all the world', the 'rose upon the Rood of Time' is quintessentially a female figure.[5] The rose is an even more heteroerotic symbol in the poetry of Juan Ramón, in the sequence of four 'Rosas' poems from *Piedra y cielo*, for instance.[6] Indeed, the Christian mystical tradition which Valle invokes in *La lámpara* contains, in the writing of such figures as San Juan, Santa Teresa and Sor Juana Inés, a very powerful use of heteroerotic imagery to convey the ineffable mystical experience. The images Valle employs, on the other hand, are completely patriarchal, dominated by the 'padre creador' and the male, Christian Holy Trinity. Eroticism, which should at least imply an important female presence, is categorised as a function of the Father Creator and of the equally male Demiurge. Valle does mention the Chaldean occult concept of antagonism between male and female principles but only as a preface to the hermetic belief that woman must resist man and man fascinate her in order to subdue her. Thus a myth of reciprocal opposition and complementarity becomes an assertion of male superiority. His whole discussion of eroticism is set in classical Greece, surely more reknowned for its homoerotic culture, and he even describes the icon of female eroticism, Venus Aphrodite, as sculpted in androgynous marble.

John Lyon compares Valle as a theorist of Symbolist drama with Wagner, D'Annunzio, Maeterlinck, Gordon Craig, Yeats and John Millington Synge.[7] Yet, there is certainly a great difference between Valle and these aforementioned in the importance given to the feminine in their work. Throughout male Symbolist writing there is a constant search for a female Other. She may be an erotic object or an elusive muse, but in either manifestation, or, more usually, in some combination of both, she is necessary to the poet's fulfillment. In her analysis of the use of gynaecomorphic imagery in Rubén Darío's *Prosas profanas*, Catherine Davies identifies the female image as 'the dominant sign of the poet's paradoxical endeavour to find the eternal and absolute in himself'.[8] She appears in the first guise in practically all of Wagner's music dramas, in much of Maeterlinck, in Yeats and, to a lesser extent, in Synge and D'Annunzio. The very fact that many of these writers produced plays about tragic, legendary lovers - Tristan and Isolde, Pelléas and Mélisande, Deirdre and Naoise - shows how important the figure of the female Other, or rather the ideal, subservient feminine complement, was in their work. Less accessible to the poet, the airy presence of the female muse dominates the early poetry of Antonio Machado and Juan Ramón Jiménez, Symbolist plays such as Maeterlinck's *L'Intruse*, and much of Yeats's poetry. In most of these writers, the feminine is of the utmost importance, as the means through which the male poet looks for fulfillment. Naturally, in such phallocentric writing, the female figure, be she muse, idealised lover or a combination of both, is almost always passive.

At the beginning of her manifesto of feminine aesthetics, *La jeune née*, Hélène Cixous states that woman has always been identified with passivity, that this is true in phallo-logocentric philosophy and therefore in literature, which she believes is based on patriarchal philosophy.[9] In phallocentric literature woman is either passive or she does not exist. Any other possibility is either unthinkable or unthought in male writing. Interestingly, she quotes Mallarmé's inscription for his dead son's tomb, "Pour un tombeau d'Anatole" (118). She uses the poet's dream of a new alliance with his son which would bypass the need for a mother ('donc pas mère alors?') in support of her argument that all male literature comes back to the masculine desire to be the origin of all things. Thus, the ideal woman must also be the creation of the male, like the sleeping beauty who awakens and finds her field of vision exclusively occupied by the male prince come to rescue her, he in place of everything. In the phallocentric edifice, the sleeping beauty is absent, therefore desirable, *inexistant*, dependent, therefore adorable, when she wakes she will be a creature of phallocentrism, and therefore passive. This is the ideal woman of male Symbolist writing, the *inexistant*, dependent, passive lover-muse, who, in the Mallarmé poem, is at her most desirable because she is absent.

This analysis leads inevitably to the conclusion that Valle-Inclán must be the most phallocentric of all the writers discussed so far because the feminine is least prominent in his work. His women are most easily categorised as muses or lovers, saints or strumpets, defined only in terms of their relationship to men, from the exotic women of the *Sonatas* to the almost non-existent wife of Max Estrella, Madama Collet. Even in *La lámpara maravillosa*, the feminine is not present as the traditional symbol of poetic inspiration and aesthetic beauty.

However, there is another way of looking at this, and it relates to the prominence of androgyny in Valle's aesthetics. Hélène Cixous's striking reassessment of Freud's theory of penis envy divides masculine and feminine attitudes into two categories: the masculine realm of the proper which, as a result of the male fear of castration, obsessively defines that which is possessed or desired by the (male) subject and that which belongs to another; and the feminine realm of the gift, an unfettered, fearless, continually expanding economy of giving. For Cixous, the male is negative, retentive, the female affirms and is generous. This she accepts as the status quo, but, she envisages a new future where each sex will acknowledge and encourage the elements of the opposite sex within. 'Elle est bisexuelle' she proclaims. She defines two types of bisexuality. The first is the hermaphrodite, more asexual than bisexual, composed not of two types but of two halves, a ghost of unity (155). This is a fusion of the sexes which cancels out the sexuality of both halves. In effect, it is worse than castration and still part of the realm of the proper. The second type of bisexuality rejoices in the differences between the sexes, 'each subject not enclosed in the false theatre of phallocentric representation institutes its own erotic universe'. The different elements complement each other, in this instance, in mutual generosity. She believes that this could only take place within the female realm of the gift.

If this theory is applied to Valle's aesthetic pronouncements in *La lámpara maravillosa*, then, he, with his 'rosa andrógina' of humanism, of thesis and antithesis, of love, and his equally androgynous Venus Aphrodite has, in some measure, approached Cixous's ideal of bisexuality. It could be argued that the use of the overtly patriarchal symbol of the male Trinity of Christian tradition and especially that of the father creator is undermined by the traditionally feminine image of the gnostic rose, despite the attempt to make it asexual. It seems evident, however, that the bisexuality of *La lámpara* belongs to the first of Cixous's categories, that of the hermaphrodite, where one sexuality cancels the other out. She relates the first type of bisexuality to Ovid, a tacit admission that there is nothing revolutionary in it. In *La lámpara*, Valle also sets it in the context of classical antiquity.

The hermaphrodite is the intemediate stage in Cixous's scheme. Before that, the situation defined by Simone de Beauvoir in *The Second Sex*, in which woman is perceived, feared and manipulated as the ideal and unknowable Other by the male writer, prevails. Valle's work up to the publication of *La lámpara*, especially pieces like the *Sonatas*, the *Corte de amor* and even the *Comedias bárbaras* reflect this.[10] The women here, be they saints or strumpets, are erotic objects for the male characters. After the publication of *La lámpara*, a change can be discerned in the writing of Valle. Usually this is described as the evolution of the *esperpento*, but, in terms of Cixous's theory, it is perhaps the appearance of the second type of bisexuality. Mari-Gaila in *Divinas palabras* and Max Estrella in the first *esperpento*, *Luces de Bohemia* belong to the realm of the gift. Mari-Gaila does not abide by any of the conventions of the phallocratic society in which she lives, she takes for herself the same social freedom as a man but she continues to give of herself as a woman. She certainly seems to enjoy an enhanced erotic experience as a result and, despite the persecution of the villagers, she enters the church unbowed and unviolated at the end. Max Estrella is a Tiresias-figure, a hermaphrodite, it is true, but he also spans the masculine and the feminine in a positive way. He displays a feminine generosity in his selfless, almost obstinate devotion to his poetic ideal, his discourse is free-flowing and imagistic, almost *écriture féminine*, and, as a result, he enjoys moments of enhanced visionary ecstasy, just as Mari-Gaila revels in her increased erotic pleasure, her *jouissance*. His death is the culmination of his refusal to be bound by the esperpentic or, better still, the property-oriented phallocratic society in which he finds himself.

Can one come to the heretofore unthinkable conclusion therefore that Valle's work is the least phallocentric of his era? Or at least argue that, in a long career, his writing made the transition from the phallocratic realm of the proper to reside finally in the feminine realm of the gift, through a bisexuality that even Cixous claims is much more accessible to the female? Is his work as revolutionary in the fields of gender aesthetics and sexual politics as masculine critics recognise it to be in the areas of social politics and literary aesthetics? Much more so than in the case of any contemporary writer, the work of Valle-Inclán is enigmatic, ironic, playful. The sands are constantly shifting beneath the reader's interpretive strategies, making it possible to essay any number of violently contrasting readings, but constantly undermining them. So, ultimately, it is for us to choose whether we agree with Sumner Greenfield that Mari-Gaila 'es una cosa curiosamente bella de contemplar dentro de su ignorancia moral' or prefer to read triumphantly that 'elle est bisexuelle'.

NOTES

1. 'Acabo de leer *Sonata de estío* y creyera a su autor un varón musculoso, amplio de miembros, de frente carnosa, grueso como un Borgia y rebosando instintos crueles: alguien que ha de entretener sus ocios en retorcer una barra de acero o en romper en un puñetazo una herradura, según cuentan del hijo de Alejandro IV. Por esas páginas los amores y los odios carnales andan sueltos, toman bellas posturas y fácilmente logran su empeño. Así debieron ser Benvenuto y el Aretino. Aquellos esforzados héroes del *risorgimento* sabían dar un sabor de galante malicia a sus narraciones tremebundas. Pero el autor de ese libro no se parece en nada a estos soberbios ejemplares de la humanidad: es delgado, inverosímilmente delgado, con largas barbas de misteriosos reflejos morados, sobre las que se destacan unos magníficos quevedos de concha.' 'La «Sonata de estío» de D. Ramón del Valle-Inclán', *Valle-Inclán visto por...*, José Esteban, ed. (Madrid: Espejo, 1973, 17-28) 17-18.

2. César M. Arconada, 'Valle-Inclán ha muerto', *Mundo Obrero* (6/1/36) (ibid., 149-152) 150.

3. Sumner Greenfield, '*Divinas palabras* y la nueva faz de Galicia', *Ramón del Valle-Inclán: An Appraisal of his Life and Works*, A. N. Zahareas, ed. (New York: Las Americas, 1968).

4. *Obras completas de Don Ramón del Valle-Inclán, Tomo II.* (Madrid: Editorial Plenitud, 1954 584.

5. W. B. Yeats, *The Rose* (1893) in *The Variorum Edition of the Poems of W. B. Yeats*, Peter Allt and Russell K. Alspach, eds. (New York: The Macmillan Company, 1957, 100-139) 100, 113.

6. Juan Ramón Jiménez, *Piedra y cielo* (Madrid: Taurus, 1981) 94, 105, 121, 136.

7. John Lyon, *The Theatre of Valle-Inclán.* (Cambridge: Cambridge University Press, 1983) 12.

8. Catherine Davies, 'Woman as Image in Darío's *Prosas profanas*', *Romance Quarterly* Vol.36 No.3, (Aug. 1989) 281-288, 281.

9. Hélène Cixous, *La jeune née* (with Catherine Clément). (Paris: Inédit, 1975, 115-246) 117ff.

10 Noël M. Valis, 'The Novel as Feminine Entrapment: Valle-Inclán's *Sonata de otoño*', *MLN* 104 (1989) 351-369. This article challenges the phallocentric base of Valle's *Sonata* in a very subtle and interesting way, seeing it undermined by a pre-linguistic feminine conspiracy, a previously undetected *écriture feminine*.

MYSTICISM AND HYSTERIA IN *LA REGENTA*: THE PROBLEM OF FEMALE IDENTITY

Jo Labanyi

> Some have felt that these blundering lives are due to the inconvenient indefiniteness with which the Supreme Power has fashioned the natures of women ...
>
> Here and there is born a Saint Theresa, founder of nothing...
>
> George Eliot
> "Prelude" to *Middlemarch*

As she returns to the cathedral at the end of the novel, Ana feels a sudden inner 'estallido' and 'estrangulación deliciosa' which she does not know whether to interpret as mystical rapture or hysterical attack: '¿era voz de lo alto o capricho del histerismo, de aquella maldita enfermedad que a veces era lo más íntimo de su deseo y de su pensamiento, ella misma?' (674).[1] Her contradictory experiences of exploding (release from constraint) and suffocating (subjection to constraint) have in common the sensation of self-annihilation: liberation and constriction are both experienced as loss of self. At the same time, this loss of self is felt by Ana to be herself. What is interesting here is not just that she experiences her femininity as lack - one of many ways in which the novel anticipates Freudian theory - but that this sense of lack puts her in a double-bind. Regardless of whether she breaks free or succumbs to restraint, she is still 'nothing'. Restraint means not being oneself in the sense of accepting alien definitions; release means having no boundaries and thus being formless. Ana's dilemma illustrates the fundamental problem of feminism: the impossibility, if there is no such thing as an essential feminine nature (a position most feminists would support), of defining woman as anything other than lack.

In her book *Spéculum de l'autre femme*, Luce Irigaray argues that woman is condemned to lack both because she is perceived in patriarchal discourse as an inverted mirror-image of man (as not being/having what man is/has), and because there is no representation possible outside the specularity of patriarchal discourse.[2] When the Magistral looks at himself in the privacy of his bedroom mirror, he sees his real self in the shape of huntsman. When Ana looks at herself in the privacy of her bedroom mirror, she sees herself as what she is not (the way others see her) and as what she does not have: the *Virgen de la Silla* without a child.

However Irigaray argues that, if woman cannot escape specularity, she can at least take the mirror in her own hands in the form of the speculum that reflects the inner void that is her sexual being (as opposed to the external castration, or lack of a visible sexual organ, reflected in the patriarchal mirror). In the central section of her book - punningly titled 'La Mystérique' - Irigaray considers two specifically feminine forms of experience which constitute just such an exaltation of non-being and which through their use of language affirm woman's sexuality: mysticism and hysteria.[3] Both, it is suggested, are refusals of the rationality of patriarchal discourse. The mystic resorts to paradox, metaphor, disjointed syntax and the speechless trance; the hysteric to non-sense, inarticulate cries and the speechless fit: both dissolve the boundaries of the conscious self.

In Ana's case, mysticism and hysteria are closely linked. Sometimes nervous illness induces mystical rapture, at other times mystical rapture induces nervous illness, to the extent that the two - as in the previously quoted passage from the end of the novel - become indistinguishable. In both cases, she describes her mental states as a burning that is an intensification of feeling as well as a loss of consciousness. That mysticism and hysteria are affirmations of female sexuality is shown by the fact that Ana uses identical language to describe her desire for Mesía. There is, however, a certain difference between the heightened feeling/loss of self caused by religious rapture and that caused by nervous illness. The latter produces a fragmentation of the self, represented linguistically by the suspension marks that punctuate Ana's speech: 'a veces se me figura que soy por dentro un montón de arena que se desmorona ... No sé cómo explicarlo ... siento grietas en la vida ..., me divido dentro de mí ..., me achico, me anulo ...' (387). While religious rapture dissolves the self in a formless totality: 'Y como si sus entrañas entrasen en una fundición, Ana sentía chisporroteos dentro de sí, fuego líquido, que le evaporaba ..., y llegaba a no sentir nada más que una idea pura, vaga, que aborrecía toda determinación' (452). What splitting and fusion have in common is their annihilation of the boundaries that allow self to be defined in opposition to the other. If hysteria has traditionally been attributed to a 'displacement' of the womb, mysticism involves a state of 'transport': in both cases the boundaries that keep the self in place cease to hold. The problem is whether this loss of ego boundaries is - as Irigaray argues - a specifically feminine transcendence of the dichotomies of western metaphysics; or whether it represents an annihilation of the female self.

Irigaray interrupts her discussion to ask whether the 'mysterical' experience, despite its apparent offer of an escape from male discourse, does not after all reflect back male definitions of woman as lack, incoherence, unclassifiability: 'mystery', in short. Earlier in her book she describes hysteria as a 'mimicry' of male discourse: the hysteric performs for the (male) doctor in the sense that she is behaving as women are expected to behave.[4] The implication is that the mystic is also mimicking stock expectations of women for the benefit of her (male) confessor. In the chapter on mysticism in her seminal work *The Second Sex*, Simone de Beauvoir had pointed out that, although - unlike the hysteric - the mystic is master of her body, mysticism constitutes a 'mimicry' of feminine passivity, in which the woman is 'possessed' by an object of love who remains forever absent. As Beauvoir notes, the insistence on 'the sovereign gaze fixed attentively, amorously, upon her' encourages feminine narcissism.[5] 'Egoísta' is an adjective frequently applied to Ana; mysticism fulfils her need to feel adored by a lover who - unlike Mesía - remains at a safe distance. Béatrice Didier, writing on Santa Teresa, stresses her confessor's control over her writing, and also notes that she claims not to be speaking herself but acting as medium for the (masculine) word of God.[6]

The control exerted over Ana by her confessor is a major theme of *La Regenta*, though it should be pointed out that the Magistral discourages Ana's mystical tendencies because they give him few opportunities to see her (is he perhaps jealous of Ana's intense relationship with Santa Teresa also because the latter is a woman?). Didier's scepticism about the authentic 'femininity' of the mystical experience is echoed by Jean Franco in her discussion of Mexican women mystics, where she goes on to make two further points. First, that the mystical flight of the imagination can take place only within the enclosure of the convent, which it confirms. It could be argued that mysticism and hysteria, by confining Ana to her bedroom, represent an equally illusory escape that in fact assigns her to her 'proper' women's place. Second, Franco points out that the tropes of mystical discourse are not spontaneous emanations of the female soul, but are highly conventionalised.[7] The imagery used by Ana to express her mystical raptures is directly borrowed from her reading of Santa Teresa's *Vida*; indeed the narrator stresses her imitation of her illustrious predecessor (441, 444). One is forced to ask whether Ana's mimicry of Santa Teresa is any different from the second-hand imitation of models satirised in the rest of Vetustan society.

A parallel debate over whether the hysteric should be seen as rebel or mimic has arisen in the varied responses to Freud's famous case history of Dora. Hélène Cixous and Catherine Clément propose that Dora's hysteria should be read as a refusal of male manipulation (that of the father, of Mr. K. as sexual predator, and of Freud as psychoanalyst).[8] But Juliet Mitchell justifies Freud's view that hysteria represents the woman's refusal to admit to her own sexuality, arguing that this does not project on to woman a male view of female sexuality as castration, but provides an understanding of how both men and women are conditioned into repudiating femininity. Hysteria thus illustrates male power but at the same time exposes it.[9] I would argue that Mitchell's reading of Freud is confirmed by a reading of *La Regenta* (if one can talk of a literary text 'confirming' psychoanalytic theory; Freud, however, frequently turned to works of art to support his propositions). The psychosomatic nature of Ana's hysterical condition does affirm female sexuality in the sense that it suggests in a remarkably radical way that female psychology is rooted in biological sexual drives; but at the same time it is also clearly the result of Ana's repression of those drives. Puberty triggers Ana's mystical and nervous crisis, but one can interpret this as Ana's way of refusing to acknowledge her access to womanhood, having been traumatised by accusations of precocious sexuality after the earlier episode in the boat with Germán. A further contributing factor to this first crisis is the loss of the father, which leaves Ana without any sense of self definition: the father is, it seems, necessary to set boundaries to female existence. Indeed, one of Ana's major problems is that her father, as an absent-minded freethinker, had never set clear boundaries to her existence in the first place: she has no clear sense of a male-imposed femininity to rebel against.

It is perhaps this original lack of ego boundaries that leaves Ana so vulnerable to the states of 'possession' represented by mysticism and hysteria: both mystics and hysterics were in earlier centuries persecuted as witches; that is, women possessed.[10] Just as Ana feels 'taken over' by Santa Teresa, so in her nervous attacks she feels that her body is at the mercy of an alien will: 'creía de repente que aquellos dedos no eran suyos, que el moverlos no dependía de su voluntad' (394). Ana does not feel dominated by her doctors in the same way that she does by her confessor, but she is nonetheless described as a docile patient who obeys doctors' orders. Of course, hysteria was in the nineteenth century treated by hypnosis: the 'possession' of the patient by the doctor. Víctor is being uncharacteristically perceptive when he admits that there are two things that terrify him: hypnotism ('magnetismo') and ecstasy (452), for his wife's hysteria and mysticism are both forms of hypnotic possession that parallel her eventual sexual possession by Mesía. Alas shows hysteria and mysticism to be forms of 'alienación' in every sense of the word ('alienista' in Spanish meaning 'hypnotist'): not the expression of an authentic female self, but a usurpation of self. And yet it is a female character he selects to represent this problem: Alas is exploring the difficulties of female self-affirmation, but he also seems to be suggesting, in keeping with patriarchal discourse, that women have an intrinsic disposition to neurotic forms of hypnotic possession. The question that needs to be asked here is whether this hypnotic possession represents a loss of the female self; or whether the usurpation of self is precisely what constitutes femininity.

As we have seen, Irigaray suggests that mysticism and hysteria offer a way out of patriarchal discourse because they dissolve the inner/outer opposition that allows woman to be defined as man's 'other'. With this she comes close to suggesting that women are defined by their capacity to blur oppositions, as opposed to men who think in terms of dichotomies. Such a suggestion only reintroduces the definition of woman as man's 'other' that feminist theory is supposedly trying to subvert. I would prefer to argue that the 'mysterical' dissolution of the inner/outer opposition represents an acknowledgment of the fact that inner and outer, self and other, or - to put it slightly differently - biology and history, are inevitably bound up with one another. Patriarchal discourse has, in fact, traditionally regarded woman as a complex blend of nature and culture: a natural product 'socialised' through marriage to man.   In his book *Adultery in the Novel: Contract and Transgression*, Tony Tanner has argued brilliantly that the realist novel's concern with female adultery represents an anxiety over the increasing difficulty, in an age of capitalist commodification, of distinguishing the natural from the cultural: a difficulty which becomes acute in the case of woman since she inevitably represents an ambiguous mixture of the two categories, an 'adulteration' that is rendered critical by her recourse to adultery.[11] I have argued elsewhere that *La Regenta* constitutes just such a depiction of the impossibility of separating the natural from the cultural.[12]   If this is so, the dissolution of the inner/outer boundary produced by Ana's mysticism and hysteria is merely one key example of a problem shown to affect society as a whole: a key example because woman has of necessity always known that self is a form of possession by the other, and has traditionally been represented by men in such terms; whereas men have - in western discourse at least - tended to represent themselves as discrete entities in conflict with the outside world rather than invaded by it.   Hélène Cixous and Catherine Clément have proposed that hysteria, by acknowledging the otherness of self, offers the possibility of a bisexuality that transcends the traditional dichotomies of gender stereotyping.[13]   If mysticism and hysteria are to be seen as forms of liberation, it is not because they affirm an essential femininity defined by its rejection of male dualistic thinking, but because they destabilise the whole concept of an essential self.

In his discussion of Santa Teresa, Paul Smith insists that we do not have to choose between biology and history - that is, between the view that 'Teresa is spontaneous because she is a woman' and the supposedly contrary view that 'she is ingenious because she is the product of a sophisticated, Renaissance culture' - because she is, of course both: a woman who is the product of culture.[14] The psychosomatic merging in Ana of hysteria (biology) and mysticism (derived from her reading of religious literature) shows her to be an inextricable mixture of nature and culture. It is in this sense that her loss of self is her self. Or, to paraphrase Santa Teresa, it is in this sense that she lives because she dies and dies because she lives. At the same time, it must be noted that Alas depicts Ana's hysterical and mystical tendencies as a form of indisposition or sickness: the male writer seems to be reluctant to accept as normal the fusion of inner and outer that constitutes Ana's self (and here we should remember Alas's resistance to the deterministic theories of Zola's naturalism).[15] The popularity of *La Regenta* in recent years may well owe itself to the fact that the otherness of self depicted in Ana is more readily accepted as a condition of both male and female ego formation than it was at the time of publication.

By way of a postscript, I should like to suggest that Alas as novelist himself succumbs - partially at least - to the supposedly feminine neurosis that he depicts in Ana. In his classic study of narrative strategy in Freud's case history of Dora, Steven Marcus notes that 'Freud is implying that a coherent story is in some manner connected with mental health', and that 'Inversely, illness amounts at least in part to suffering from an incoherent story or an inadequate narrative account of oneself'. Marcus observes that, despite his attempts to establish coherence, Freud's own narrative lapses into a virtually Proustian 'geological fusing of various time strata - strata that are themselves at the same time fluid and shifting'.[16] The reason is of course that Freud was forced to put himself inside the mind of his hysterical 'protagonist', for his story is her story. The use in *La Regenta* of *estilo indirecto libre* to blur the point of view of narrator and female protagonist is well known. One feature of the novel that has not been commented on sufficiently is the fluidity of its time sequence, which departs radically from the chronological presentation characteristic of classic realism. I am not including here the flashbacks in Part 1 over the childhoods of Ana and the Magistral, for flashbacks - by explaining what happened 'before the beginning' of the story - confirm the causal coherence inherent in chronological presentation. I refer rather to the temporal loops - sometimes doubling back over each other in superimposed layers - that characterise the narrative for much of Part 2: precisely at those points where Ana is confined to bed by nervous illness. These temporal loops refer to experiences beyond the confines of the bedroom; what is important is that Alas chose to narrate them out of chronological order from the viewpoint of the bedroom: that is, from the viewpoint of the hysteric. We can hardly call this narrative assumption of the hysteric's refusal of coherent, chronological, causal presentation an example of 'feminine writing', for the novel's depiction of female psychology as diseased supposes that the narrator is speaking from an external (male) position. The appropriate phrase, given the suggestion that Ana's inability to achieve a coherent sense of self is an 'enfermedad', would seem to be 'contagion by femininity'.

NOTES

1. References are to the 7th edition published by Alianza, Madrid, 1974.

2. Paris, Editions de Minuit, 1974.

3. There have, of course, been male mystics, but the equation of the self with Christ's bride in the form of the soul (a feminine noun in Romance languages) places the subject of mystic discourse in a feminine position whatever his/her biological sex. Hysteria was until relatively recently thought to be an exclusively female disorder caused by a wandering or unstable womb (Greek *hystera*): see Ilza Veith, *Hysteria: The History of a Disease*, Chicago, Chicago University Press, 1965; and Alan Krohn, *Hysteria: The Elusive Neurosis*, New York, International Universities Press, 1978. Freud regarded hysteria as a feminine neurosis that could manifest itself in both men and women: see Juliet Mitchell, *Psychoanlysis and Feminism*, Harmondsworth, Penguin, 1974, 91, 404; Charles Bernheimer and Claire Kahane (eds), *In Dora's Case: Freud, Hysteria, Feminism*, London, Virago, 31. As Kahane notes (*loc. cit.*), recent feminists have reclaimed hysteria as 'the dis-ease of women in patriarchal culture'.

4. *Spéculum*, 245-246, 86.

5. 'The Mystic', in *The Second Sex*, Harmondsworth, Penguin, 1972 (French original 1949), 679-87.

6. 'Thérèse d'Avila et le désir de Dieu', in *L'Ecriture-femme*, Paris, Presses Universitaires de France, 1982, 51-70.

7. 'Writers in Spite of Themselves: The Mystical Nuns of Seventeenth-Century Mexico', in *Plotting Women: Gender and Representation in Mexico*, London, Verso, 1989, 3-22; in particular 16 and 21.

8. Hélène Cixous and Catherine Clément, *The Newly Born Woman*, Manchester, Manchester University Press, 1987; Hélène Cixous, *Portrait de Dora*, Paris, Edition des Femmes, 1976. Clément, however, (*The Newly Born Woman*, 155) admits that Dora is a failed rebel. For a range of views on the question of whether Dora's hysteria makes her a feminist rebel or a victim of patriarchy, see the above-mentioned anthology *In Dora's Case*.

9. *Psychoanalysis and Feminism*, 404.

10. See *In Dora's Case*, 3, 13. Freud himself saw connections between the hysteric and the witch: see Cixous and Clément, *The Newly Born Woman*, 5 and 12.

11. Baltimore and London, Johns Hopkins University Press, 1979. Tanner draws on Lévi-Strauss's anthropological analysis of woman's

46

traditional function as an exchange object that mediates the nature/culture contradiction, arguing that this traditional function comes into conflict with post-Rousseau society's belief in the need for a social contract that keeps nature and culture apart.

12. 'City, Country and Adultery in *La Regenta*', *Bulletin of Hispanic Studies*, 63 (1986), 53-66.

13. See *The Newly Born Woman*, xv, 8, 86.

14. *The Body Hispanic: Gender and Sexuality in Spanish and Spanish American Literature*, Oxford, Oxford University Press, 1989, 23-24

15. For Alas's views on naturalism, see his article 'Del naturalismo', his prologue to Pardo Bazán's *La cuestión palpitante*, and his review of Galdós's *La desheredada*, included in Sergio Beser (ed.), *Leopoldo Alas: Teoría y crítica de la novela española*, Barcelona, Laia, 1972, 101-53, 225-239.

16. 'Freud and Dora: Story, History, Case History', in *In Dora's Case*, 71, 73.

THE ENVY OF MOTHERHOOD:
DESTRUCTIVE URGES IN UNAMUNO

Alison Sinclair

Gertrudis, the central character of *La tía Tula*, is a forceful woman, who achieves the objective of the status of motherhood (and the opportunity of providing mothering) by unusual means. Other women close to Tula bear children, whose upbringing she then takes over, as a consequence of which she becomes their mother in all but the concrete, physical sense. Unlike the terrifying Raquel of *Dos madres* in the *Tres novelas ejemplares y un prólogo* (1920), Tula is less than explicit about the accomplishment of her personal project of motherhood. What does make her similar to Raquel, however, is the fact that her urge towards motherhood is the product of quite complex and unexpressed emotions, and not simply the desire to have children. I have argued elsewhere[1] that Raquel's desire to be a mother stems from the intolerable feeling of emptiness and incompletion that she suffers. At the heart of Tula's unconventional path towards the maternal state, I would argue that there is an analogous feeling of emptiness, of lack of possession of a state or of an object, but that in the case of this novel, the experience of emptiness is expressed in, or gives rise to the feeling of envy, a primitive emotion which then colours Tula's whole attitude to the state of maternity.

It is in the light of the concept of envy, then, that I propose to explore the idea of maternity in *La tía Tula*. My discussion will focus on the topic in two ways: first an examination of how Tula's own attitude to and experience of maternity is arguably coloured by the feeling of envy, and secondly a consideration of how the concept of envy may help us to understand the overall treatment of motherhood in this text. The first is an internal, straightforward discussion of the psychological dynamic existing between characters in the text, and in particular, concerning Tula as a character who, I shall suggest, is motivated by her feelings of envy about motherhood in others. The second is a discussion that takes place in a space already annexed by Unamuno in Chapter 31 of *Niebla* (1914), that is, a space existing between the author and the text he has created, with its characters. This second part of the discussion explores the way in which Unamuno's destructive portrayal of Tula is a phenomenon which itself may be related to an attitude of envy towards the feminine (that is, to the feminine as a concept as defined and understood by Unamuno himself).

According to Chaucer, envy was the worst of the seven deadly sins.[2] The reason why it may be felt to be so fundamental and so pervasive is that it is of the feelings which relate to the earliest reactions of the sentient human being, preceding the feeling of jealousy, for example. It holds a particularly prominent place in the work of Melanie Klein, the psychoanalyst who in the 1920s broke revolutionary new ground by highlighting the important and frequently terrifying nature of the relationship of the small infant with the mother. According to Klein, and to others who followed in the study of the psychology of the very small infant, envy is involved in the earliest stages of this dyadic relationship between the infant and the mother. It is pre-Oedipal, and thus distinct from the post-Oedipal feeling of jealousy, which is concerned with the good possession two others are thought to possess between them. Envy, the more primitive feeling, is concentrated on the good possession, attribute or capacity of one other person.[3] Within the initial mother/child relationship, the mother will inevitably be experienced in a variety of ways: as the source of good (when good things are provided), as the source of what is painful (when good things are withheld), and not least, as all-powerful. What envy leads to is an attitude of confusion or ambivalence - on the one hand in expression of hate or denigration for the possessor of the envied quality (or for the envied quality itself), but also the desire not to destroy what is envied, which may lead, by way of defence, to an idealisation of the envied object or the envied possessor. Above all, it leads to lack of clarity in the mind of the person who experiences it, because of the awareness of the destructiveness of envy itself.

What I have said so far about envy may not seem to connect obviously in the first instance with Unamuno, let alone the eponymous character of *La tía Tula*. It is the case, however, that envy is an emotion which clearly interested Unamuno and which, on the evidence of both his fictional works and his essays, he understood well. He recognized both the degree to which those suffering from envy believe themselves to be persecuted[4], and the contrasting reactions it produces of denigration and idealisation[5].

The destructiveness of envy is at the centre of *Abel Sánchez* (1917), and is presented in controversial manner, since Unamuno in his 1928 prologue to the second edition of that novel argues for this most deadly of the deadly sins being considered as angelic, at least in the case of Joaquín. It is 'una envidia trágica, una envidia que se defiende, una envidia que podría llamarse angélica'[6]. Unamuno makes no explicit reference to envy in the work which we might regard as the sister novel to *Abel Sánchez*, *La tía Tula* (1920), and instead suggests in the prologue to the latter that it is a novel about 'sororidad' and the work of civilization. Despite this emphasis made by Unamuno, critics have tended to focus on *La tía Tula* as a novel concerned with 'maternidad' (albeit a deflected form of maternity). As Ribbans points out, however, the prologue has every appearance of being composed *a posteriori*, and certainly well after the original idea for the novel (which dates from 1902), so that there is strong reason for concentrating on the issues about maternity in the text itself, rather than on Unamuno's later elaboration of the meaning and function of aunts in domestic life, as set out in the prologue.[7] The particular point of interest of the prologue is perhaps that, insofar as it softens the image of Tula presented in the novel, it provides an example of the backtracking, idealising aspect of envy which seeks to mitigate its own destructive urge.

La tía Tula (1920) is one of Unamuno's middle-period novels, but as indicated, it was originally conceived in 1902. It is thus a novel whose roots go back to the time of publication of *Amor y pedagogía* and is a novel of particularly long gestation.[8] As Ribbans points out, the idea of the story in the first place was of a young woman who combines a disgust at sexual relations with a strong maternal instinct. He highlights the positive and the negative aspects of the woman's feelings, that is, the rejection of sexual relations, and, on the other hand, the yearning for children.[9] An alternative view of the polarisation in Tula, however, is to see her as both desiring motherhood, and yet spoiling it, simultaneously idealising it, and preventing it from achieving its own full existence, whether in herself, or in others, in those women she obliges into motherhood.

The novel centres, at the level of plot, around birth, marriage and death, or perhaps, more properly put, around death, marriage and birth. Two sisters, Rosa and Tula, live independently (though under the tutelage of their uncle, a priest), and Tula, the elder, acts as the driving force to bring about the marriage of Ramiro to her sister. She subsequently and successfully arranges two further marriages, of Ramiro to Manuela, the *Hospiciana* maid, after Rosa's death, and of Ramirín, the oldest child of Ramiro and Rosa. In the course of the novel five children are born, and are taken under the maternal/auntly wing of Tula, and by the end a further one/two are expected as the outcome of the pregnancy of Caridad, wife of Ramirín.

All this activity of marriage and birth instigated by Tula is, however, carried out in an atmosphere disturbingly dominated by death, with little or no respite. After Rosa's death (consequent upon the birth of her third child) there is little space before Ramiro is obliged by Tula to marry Manuela, the *hospiciana* (who is expecting his child). Ramiro dies during Manuela's second pregnancy, and Manuela herself dies shortly after giving birth. Much later, Tula herself dies as Ramirín's wife draws close to giving birth to what Tula fantasizes will be twins. In addition to this, there is constant awareness through the novel of the degree to which the process of pregnancy and birth is something which appears to sap the strength of the women involved, and the deaths of Rosa and Manuela testify to the dangers of childbirth itself.

Centrally placed (by herself) in the activity of marriage and birth, is Tula as orchestrator and decision maker, and we can see her as performing two functions. She is the woman who provokes pregnancies, a function she owns to, if not in terms of it as an activity in which she has an investment. But in her own eyes, or rather, in the self she presents to public view, and from which she pronounces beliefs about her role in the family she creates, she has another function, which is declared without reticence to Ramiro and his two wives: she sees herself as providing the moral fibre, the guarantor (or, one is tempted to suggest, the guarantrix) of purity and innocence in situations she seems to feel are on the brink of disaster - a disaster which would consist, it appears, of the contamination of the children by witnessing the sensuality and physical love between their parents. This function is presented by her to the rest of the world as a positive one.

Questions are raised by this enigmatic text. A first one concerns Tula's own attitude to motherhood and herself. Does she actually desire motherhood, or only the children? And what does she understand by motherhood anyway? A simple answer to the first question is that what she wants is children, but not at the price of having sexual relations with men. That is, she disowns the physical responsibility for motherhood. Although we are given little information about her dislike of men (other than her belief that they are 'brutos', and creatures to which she does not wish to submit), we are given plenty of information about the physical dangers involved for women in the bearing of children, a process which is demonstrably liable to be fatal. The other information which emerges from the text is that the marriage relationship, and certainly the marriage relationship as perceived by Tula, is one which subjugates women to men, a subservience that Tula herself is anxious to avoid from the start. Again, she avoids this situation for herself, but acquires the children that might be the by-product of it.

At this initial stage, we might note that a split takes place in Tula. She desires children, but not the physical contact which produces them. This leads to her second function, in which she makes a virtue of her own inhibitions about physical warmth. That is, she aims to banish visible evidence of love between the parents from the *hogar*. At one level this simply has the damaging effect of the removal of warmth from the home, so that the domain of the natural mother is effectively spoiled. But there is another damaging effect resulting from her adopted role as observer to the couples in the home, and which spoils more directly the experience of motherhood. Thus in the period of increased sensuality which follows on the birth of Rosa's first child, Tula is vigilant to maintain the 'innocence' of the first child, 'sustrayendo al niño, ya desde su más tierna edad de inconciencia, de conocer, ni en las más leves y remotas señales, el amor de que había brotado' (II. 1056).[10]

At one level it is clear that Tula creates a triangular situation between herself, Rosa and Ramiro, a triangle which might lead us to suppose that one of the emotions involved is jealousy (jealousy of her sister's possession of Ramiro).[11] But there are two observations to be made here. First, that Tula herself comments on her position as observer in the marriage. Rosa requests her presence, and while Tula initially argues the traditional case that the newly-wed couple need time to themselves, she quickly responds to Rosa's persistent urge that she should join them by agreeing that the couple indeed need her as witness to their happiness (II. 1052). This observation, however, seems instantly to bring shame in its wake: thus Ramiro, when Rosa shows affection, 'parecía como avergonzado ante su cuñada'. It is as though Tula introduces shame into the marriage by her activity as witness, spoiling for Ramiro and Rosa the activity of sexual love and its consequence, the bearing of children. Thus Tula's sense of disgust at the thought of sexual relations is lodged with others, and furthermore is used by her so that their experience of sexuality is to some degree spoiled by her observation, her look, as it were, of moral reproach.[12] Unable herself to tolerate the combination of motherhood with a positive experience of sexuality, she makes it impossible for the substitute mother, Rosa, to do so.

Thus what appears to be involved here is not jealousy but envy, that is, not jealousy of Rosa's possession of Ramiro (a possession Tula rejects, since it entails a contact she would rather not have), but envy of Rosa's involvement in the activity of motherhood and the bearing of children. If we follow through the theory of envy, we can see how Tula is led to what amounts to the activity of spoiling the pleasure of Ramiro and Rosa by her watchful gaze, and her constant incitement to more and more child-bearing activity, despite the physical dangers and pains that this involves for the parents. Thus at the birth of Rosa's first child, Tula is in fine form, having transferred elsewhere the physical activity of bearing children, and, it would seem, with a less than total regard for the suffering of the mother: 'nadie estuvo más serena y valerosa' (II. 1054). There is a level of detachment which permits her to do this: it appears her mind is fixed only on the possibility of children to come, rather than on the possible death of her sister in their production. Thus her suppressed thought which entertains the idea that there might be other mothers, even if Rosa should die (II. 1057). In Chapter VI, by the birth of the third child (to prove fatal to her), Rosa has become clearly aware of the physical dangers of child-bearing.

There is the question of whether the avoidance of motherhood is linked in Tula to the avoidance of subservience to men. There is no doubt that Tula avoids such subservience, but only for herself and is more than willing to make other women occupy this position of subservience. She classes all men as 'brutos', a term which seems to indicate not simply that they are linked with the physical and the sexual, but also, and it may be that this is effectively more important, because socially they have been given the upper hand. Thus her comment that she likes having the power of choice, rather than being the one to be chosen (II. 1059). It is indicated that Tula wishes to be subservient to no-one, in that later she is to declare that she could not be a nun, since 'no me gusta que me manden' (II. 1069). When an analogous conversation occurs in the final chapter between Manuelita and Rosita, the former's comment that Rosa might choose the nunnery 'por no servir a los hombres' (II. 1111) is followed by an after-comment that might reveal underlying motives of Tula: 'ni a las mujeres'. That is, despite taking on the guise of indefatigable worker bee, Tula's aim was perhaps to avoid serving either men or women.

While one might argue that Tula is not gender-specific in her avoidance of subservience, it is the case, given the social situation of the novel, that in her independence she is avoiding the limitations imposed on a woman. In connexion with this, we might note that it has been considered that her stance of non-submission is essentially a feminist one.[13] Particularly in her confession with Padre Alvarez (Chapter XII) this is an interpretation which suggests itself, with her strenuous objection to the possibility that she might be considered to be the 'remedio' for the sensuality of Ramiro. As she bridles and declares 'No, me estimo en más' (II. 1080), one feels that her reason for not marrying is more connected with personal pride, rather than her earlier public contention that she does not wish the children to have a 'madrastra'. Furthermore, it is significant that this confessional exchange inevitably takes place with Tula in a position of physical submission to the confessor, since she is on her knees throughout, having thus to observe a submission in some areas of her life that she is keen to avoid in others.

There are, of course, problems in viewing Tula as the mouthpiece of feminism, not least being her high-handed treatment of other women, already mentioned. I would suggest that the interpretation that Tula's activity is motivated by envy rather than by feminist independence produces a more coherent understanding of her, particularly given that other examples of her 'feminism', when examined, are problematic. She expresses anger, for example, at the possibility that she might be an 'animal doméstico' to Don Juan (II. 1092), but seems perfectly happy to treat Manuela in this way (Chapters XIII and XIV). The notion of 'sororidad' floated by Unamuno in the prologue to the novel seems far distant from the feminist notion of a supportive sisterhood, in which women might defend one another from roles of submission to men. Furthermore, her confession (when it is safe, since he is on his deathbed) to Ramiro that she has been motivated by fear of men (II. 1088) suggests her attitude of independence as being no more than a massive defence against her feeling of vulnerability.

We might note, incidentally, that Tula is unwilling to relinquish her own potential activity of motherhood. This is revealed by her hot indignation at Don Juan's suggestion that she might be unable to bear children (II. 1091) and her dismissal of him 'por puerco' for implying such a thing. Given that she still desires 'real' motherhood, we can see extra edge in her desire to impose it on others in a way that spoils it as an experience. Thus her imposition of the duty - rather than the pleasure - of feeding the children as evinced in the case of Manuela (II. 1094). This can be understood as the envious reaction to her own incapacity to do so (II. 1061, 1094-5), and is further expressed in her defensive feeling of horror and loathing for those who can bring themselves to be wet-nurses. We can see the mechanism which explains Tula's lack of sympathy for other women if we understand the split she tries to impose: she off-loads her own contact with the physical life onto other women, in no uncertain manner, and then treats it with scorn.

More interesting still, however, is the way Tula has to destroy or diminish even the capacity of the Virgin to incarnate the ideal of motherhood she might emulate. It would appear that the Virgin managed to achieve all that Tula herself desired, and as Tula says, she herself would like to leave the world without the knowledge of 'cosas que el saberlas mancha' (II. 1103). It is, however, evident to Tula herself that she is in a different state from that of the Virgin, since she does not have total innocence of knowledge: she has had to make an effort to preserve herself from it, which constitutes a state of less than innocence. She moves quickly from a position which seems to express envy of the Virgin 'Quiero irme de este mundo sin saber muchas cosas ... Porque hay cosas que el saberlas mancha ... Eso es el pecado original, y la Santísima Virgen Madre nació sin mancha de pecado original', to a position which implies her own superiority over the Virgin (thus destroying the ideal she has glimpsed but seen as impossible): 'No, no lo sabía todo; no concocía la ciencia del mal ..., que es ciencia ...' (II. 1103).

The discussion above of the relationship between envy and motherhood in *La tía Tula* has so far been restricted to what occurs within the text. Other issues are raised, however, when we move outside the boundaries of the text, and consider the question of Unamuno's curious treatment of motherhood in this novel in the light of his approach to the theme in other works, and in the light of what appears to be his general valuation, in philosophical terms, of things which are associated with the feminine and the maternal. That is, although we could simply read this novel as Unamuno's examination of a single obsessive case (and he is at pains to underline the degree to which Tula is both driven and distressed), we can also place it in the context of a broader philosophical view in which the treatment of the feminine is, to say the least, problematic.

The fact that Unamuno writes both philosophy and novels, and is not at pains to keep the two strictly separate is a first justification for taking a reading along these lines, and in brief, my argument is that we can regard the psychological oddities of Tula, Unamuno's literary product, as an example of his difficulty in assimilating certain qualities and activities which he, according to the other works, appears to find it hard to accept.

The examples of the enviousness of Tula and Joaquín provide a portrayal of a destructive, damaging and ultimately sterile emotional state, which I would suggest can be linked to Unamuno's own awareness of envy in himself, that is to an envy that he is now externalising, and criticising. Unamuno himself recognized how we censure in others those qualities or attributes we possess but wish to disown: 'Es mi envidia, mi soberbia, mi petulancia, mi codicia, las que me hacen aborrecer la soberbia, la envidia, la petulancia, la codicia ajenas'[14], and his treatment of a damaging attitude to motherhood, resulting from feelings of envy, is arguably a case in point. It is also arguably consistent with what appears to be his much more glowing account of the feminine and its attributes elsewhere in his fiction, since as is contained in what I have already indicated about envy, and as Gullón comments, the one who envies will attempt to cover up his traces: 'El envidioso se cree envidiado, y la envidia se disfraza en formas sutiles, hipócritas'.[15]

The presence of splits and opposites such as we can observe in *La tía Tula* (man/woman, maternity/sterility, spiritual/physical, order/disorder) are characteristic of Unamuno's work as a whole, and are polarisations which are not, of course, exclusive to Unamuno alone. Within his novels, the poles of comparison have a tendency to separate along lines established by gender, and gender-linked attributes. Nowhere is this most clearly expressed, perhaps, than in the novel which was published at the time *La tía Tula* was first thought of: *Amor y pedagogía*. Here the opposition is between two exaggerated representatives of the masculine and the feminine - Avito, the positivist, rationalising man, handicapped by his total adherence to principles of mind, and Marina, the dumb, instinctive woman, silently giving birth, and bearing witness in the novel to forces of the earth, of life-processes, and the power and necessity of intuition. There is no doubt that we should see Avito as a man who is less than he needs to be, because of his imprudently total investment in a rigid form of intellectualism, but a less than convincing counter-weight is provided by his wife who appears positively bovine in her helpless acquiescence. Now, as Olson has observed, within the polarisations the masculine-associated qualities 'evoke the discontinuity and conflict of the struggle to differentiate and distinguish the self', while feminine-associated qualities are associated with timelessness, *intrahistoria*, nature, the continuity of pure being.[16] On a first plane of understanding, feminine-associated qualities appear to be qualities desired by Unamuno: *sueño* being superior to *intelecto* or *conciencia*, the capacity to bear children being superior to a sterile existence, creativity being superior to destruction, and to inhibiting definition. If we regard the masculine-associated qualities, we can see how they are linked to what is less than complete, what is unfinished. The relationship between the two might then be characterised not as a simple pair of poles, but as a pair in which the masculine, as unfinished, becomes the desiring subject, and the feminine the desired object, or rather, the object of desire. By putting it this way we can see first how the concept of envy may be introduced (what is desired must be denigrated, as the fox does the grapes, so that it is not too painful to be denied possession), and second, how the idea of desiring subject and desired object immediately places what is feminine into the role of the passive. Since, furthermore, the masculine is associated with the struggle to be, this is implicitly denied as a characteristic attribute of the feminine.

We have already seen from the discussion of Tula's form of mothering that it is less than straightforward: a single-minded process, which envisages nothing odd in the equivalent of a single-parent family, a mothering which appears not to have the individuality of the children at heart, but is prepared to use them as ammunition (or defensive weapons) in a desperate fight for the independence of the woman. The motif of orphanhood is so prominent as to appear to carry meaning: there is no clear or explicit example of a good maternal relationship in the novel. So where there are physical mothers (Rosa, Manuela), their possible activities as mother are kept distant from the text, just as Tula usurps, or perhaps, is made to usurp them. In *La tia Tula* the enviable creativity (in physical terms) of the woman is given neither prominence or effective power in the text. Memories of the mother of Rosa and Tula are frightening and imposing rather than otherwise, and associated with this there is the reluctance to look at roots. The creation of children is an activity which is both desired and achieved by Tula (an act which, according to the analysis above, simultaneously places her in the role of subject, and detaches her from her femininity) yet is associated with a mixture of death and strife. The one period of peace in the novel is that of the years of effective orphanhood, when Tula rules over her collected children (Chapter XVIII onwards), that is, it is associated with the loss of natural parents and the imposition of a substitute mother. Tula's protestations throughout, but particularly at the period when the re-marriage of Ramiro is under consideration, that she is determined that the children should never be subjected to a *madrastra*, and that they have their *madre* in her, are so strident as to make one suppose that she protests too much, and that she herself lacks the conviction that she can in fact provide the maternal presence. The dislocation between Tula's speech and Tula's reality is, furthermore, underlined by Unamuno, by the fact that she protests that what she wants is clarity, and a home that is chaste and pure, whereas he portrays her as achieving it only by separating out everything she does not approve of. Thus Ramiro, the man, is given the capacity to reproach her: '¿Y tú, no te has mirado nunca?' (II. 1070).

What we see, therefore, in this novel so centred on the production of children and the nature and ideal of mothering, is that Unamuno produces no single exemplum of the ideal, but instead on the one hand a series of telluric but essentially helpless physical vessels for the production of children, and on the other a woman who may be clear in her aims, but is far from at peace with them. The final pages in which the remaining family is brought together by Manolita, and her re-iteration of Tula's dominant, abrasive style, demonstrate on the surface that Tula has succeeded in assuring her succession, but there are doubts left for the reader about the quality of both the succession and of the original example. The later addition of the prologue to this novel can be seen, as suggested earlier, as an example of the backtracking, idealising aspect of envy, which seeks to mitigate its own destructive tendencies.

The final, and most crushing way in which Unamuno denigrates the feminine in this novel is in the suppression of information about Tula's inner being, so that we have little or no witness to her struggle, merely to the effects of that struggle, as she fights off those who enquire into it. If we place this novel alongside *Abel Sánchez*, one of the most striking differences is the degree to which we are given access to the protagonist, Joaquín. Tula, however, is placed in the same disturbingly mysterious position as Raquel in *Dos madres* of the *Tres novelas ejemplares y un prólogo*. The mystery about her inner struggle, which I have been characterising as envy on the basis of the external evidence of the text only (that is, on the basis of what Tula does and says to other people) is maintained, so that we have little opportunity to perceive her as a true *agonista*. Since to agonise is proof, to Unamuno, of human worth, and Tula is not allowed by him as author to agonise, we have the final limitation of the feminine within this fictional text, a limitation impelled, perhaps, by the perception of the devastatingly destructive power of the sex which has such enviable qualities.

60

NOTES

1. 'Widowhood in Unamuno's *Dos madres:* The Paradox of the Void and the Uncontained', a paper given to the annual conference of the British Association of Hispanists, Sheffield, March 1990.

2. 'Certes, thanne is Envye the worste synne that is. For soothly, alle othere synnes been somtyme oonly agayns o special vertu, but certes Envye is agaynes alle vertues and agayns alle goodnesses', *The Parson's Tale, The Riverside Chaucer*, general editor L. D. Benson, edited by F. N. Robinson, 3rd edition, (Oxford: Oxford University Press, 1988), 303.

3. See Melanie Klein, 'Envy and Gratitude' (1957), in *Envy, Gratitude and other works 1946-1963,* (London: Virago, 1988), 181.

4. 'La envidia hispánica', *Obras completas*, edited by M. García Blanco, (Madrid: Aguilar, 1966), III. 285, and 'Ni envidiado ni envidioso', *O.C.,* III. 775. All references to Unamuno will be to this edition.

5. 'La envidia hispánica', III. 285.

6. II. 686.

7. Geoffrey Ribbans, 'A New Look at *La tía Tula*', *Revista Canadiense de Estudios Hispánicos*, 11 (2), Winter 1987, 403-20. See this article also for a concise summary of critical attitudes to Tula herself. Rof Carballo, 'El erotismo en Unamuno', *Revista de Occidente*, series 2, n. 19, (1964), 70-96, refers briefly (74) to *La tía Tula* as a novel of 'la envidia femenina', but does not explore the implications of the term.

8. See Geoffrey Ribbans, 'El autógrafo de parte de *La tía Tula* y su significado para la evolución de la novela', *Volumen-Homenaje a Unamuno*, edited by D. Gómez Molleda, (Salamanca: Casa-Museo Unamuno, 1986), 475-493.

9. Ribbans, 'A New Look at *La tía Tula*', 406.

10. Subsequent page reference to *La tía Tula* will be given in the main text.

11. This view is entertained by Juan Rof Carballo, 'El erotismo en Unamuno', *Revista de Occidente*, 75, and by Ricardo Gullón, 'La voluntad de dominio en "la madre" unamuniana', *Autobiografías de Unamuno* (Madrid: Gredos, 1969), 213.

12. See R. Gullón, *Autobiografías de Unamuno*, (Madrid: Gredos, 1964), 212-213, who comments on the degree to which it is likely that Rosa's sexual pleasure is spoiled by Tula's requirement that she have 'hijos para nosotros': 'el lector menos imaginativo puede concebir cómo envenerarían esas palabras a la pobre Rosa, y cómo, unidas a otras y a

tantos indicios inequívocos de su desposesión, la haría sentirse disminiuida por su condición de instrumento'.

13.   See for example, Paciencia Ontañón de Lope Blanch, 'En torno a *La tía Tula*', *Actas del VIII Congreso de la Asociación Internacional de Hispanistas*, II, edited by Kossoff, Amor y Vázquez, *et al*, (Madrid: Ediciones Istmo, 1986) 383-389 (385); A. Sánchez Barbudo, introduction to his edition (1981) of *La tía Tula*, (Madrid: Taurus), 18-24; Geoffrey Ribbans,'A New Look at *La tía Tula*', 414.

14.   'Sobre la soberbia', I. 1204.

15.   Gullón, *Autobiografías de Unamuno*, 117.

16.   Paul Olson, *Critical guide to 'Niebla'*, Critical guides to Spanish Texts Series (London: Tamesis, 1984) 18.

THE FEMALE CANON

EMILIA PARDO BAZÁN:
UN VIAJE DE NOVIOS AND ROMANTIC FICTION

Judith Drinkwater

Un viaje de novios, published in 1881, is Emilia Pardo Bazán's second novel. The scant critical attention which it has been accorded condemns it as a failed realist-naturalist novel, and in one case it is dismissed as being no more than a 'feeble romantic novelette'.[1] The common perception of critics from Alas onwards who have dealt with *Un viaje de novios* in terms of genre and structure is that it is an experimental work, lacking in the proper balance of narrative elements; that it is ridden with 'inhibiciones' of a moral, social or aesthetic nature which vitiate its standing as a realist novel;[2] and that it is marked by what David Henn terms 'a gap between theory and practice' which he sees as characteristic of Pardo Bazán's literary output in the decade 1879-1889.[3]

In general, it would be fair to say that such critics are uneasy about the degree of control, or lack of it, which the author exerts over her text. They are particularly dismissive of the novel insofar as it demonstrates a residue of Romanticism, which they perceive as inappropriate in a work which Pardo Bazán herself claims in the Prologue to be an 'estudio social, psicológico, histórico' in true realist tradition.[4] Always implicit in this criticism is the assumption that this resort to the Romantic is a tendency peculiar to the female writer, to which she turns despite herself and in spite of her professed intent to adhere to the objective, scientific doctrines of realism. Robert

Osborne discerns 'algo romántico en esta novela, algo de melodramático'.[5]
Benito Varela Jacome suggests that 'la persistente tendencia romántica
[actúa] en los impulsos líricos, en las emociones sentimentales, en las
situaciones melodramáticas de las primeras novelas de la escritora coruñesa'.[6]
Mariano Baquero Goyanes devotes considerable attention in his edition of *Un
viaje de novios* to the 'denso lastre romántico' which pervades the novel; the
description of Artegui he cites as an example of 'lo inequivocamente
romántico', 'el más trasnochado romanticismo', and the narrative as a whole
he sums up as 'una visión calificable de romántica', 'de óptica ingenuamente
romántica'.[7] His comments suggest a disdain of the Romantic in literature as
a mode discredited by the privileged genre of the realist novel: its intrusion
into the text is a mark of the writer's naïvete and redundant intellectual
baggage. Varela Jacome also sees the persistence of Romanticism in late
nineteenth-century literature as a disrupting influence, an involuntary
recourse to emotion and melodrama: 'La sensibilidad romántica se mantiene
en escena cerca de cuarenta años; penetra, incontrolada, en la segunda mitad
del siglo [...] los escritores peninsulares difícilmente se despegan de los temas
sentimentales, de las situaciones melodramáticas, de ciertos procedimientos
narrativos de la escuela romántica'.[8] Maurice Hemingway imputes the failure
of *Un viaje de novios* as a feminist work by implication to the tendency to
resort to the worst devices of romantic literature displayed by Pardo Bazán.
Of the work's feminist concerns, he states that whilst these 'are undoubtedly
intended to be serious, the seriousness is undermined by the melodramatic
plot, with its implausible coincidences and hackneyed situations'.[9] Once
again, *Un viaje de novios* is perceived as flawed by its romantic underlay and its
failure to conform to the criteria by which the realist novel is measured.

In a useful corrective to these views that the romantic intrusions in the
text are gratuitous and without any function in the narrative, Noël Valis
discusses a later Pardo Bazán novel, *El Cisne de Vilamorta* (1885), and puts a
different perspective upon the oscillation in the author's early writing between
the realist and romantic modes.[10] *El Cisne*, she argues, is not merely a parody
of literary romanticism, but 'at once a critique of the inadequacies of Spanish
romanticism and a largely unconscious admiration for the mostly unrealized
impulses behind this same literary movement'.[11] Pardo Bazán is seen

alternately to exalt and to ridicule the romantic ideals of the protagonist of *El Cisne*, in particular through her account of the experience of romantic self-consciousness of the main characters gained through their reading and/or writing of romantic literature. Valis notes 'the vacillations of Pardo Bazán as implied author', unable either to dismiss or fully to integrate the romanticism which she is exposing in the text.[12]

In *Un viaje de novios*, Pardo Bazán does not achieve the perspective furnished by the division between author/reader/writer of the romantic text which alerts us to the critique of the mode in *El Cisne*. Nonetheless, Pardo Bazán's exploitation of romantic discourse in *Un viaje*, far from being naïve and unselfconscious, can be read as parodic; and it is the oscillation between the perception of romantic discourse in the novel as serious and the perception of it as parodic which arouses in the reader the feeling of unease shared by the critics cited above. Typical of Pardo Bazán's parodic use of romantic discourse in *Un viaje* is the melodramatic love scene which follows after Lucía has stepped in to stop Artegui committing suicide. He embraces her passionately:

> Creyó ella sentir dos tenazas dulcísimas de fuego que la derritían y abrasaban toda, y reuniendo su vigor nervioso, se desprendió de ellas, quedándose trémula y erguida ante el pesimista. Su alta estatura, su ademán de indignación suprema, la asemajaran a bello mármol antiguo, si la bata de merino negro no borrase la clásica semejanza. (266)

But there is more to Pardo Bazán's playing with romantic discourse in *Un viaje* than the pricking of the melodramatic bubble with the mention of a woollen housecoat. In feminist terms, too, the intertextual references to the discourse of romantic subjectivity and romantic fiction are central to *Un viaje de novios*, and to the situation of both the protagonist, Lucía, and of the writer herself. I would suggest that Pardo Bazán's recognition of the possibilities of romanticism in literature is not, as Valis suggests, 'largely unconscious', but is founded upon a close knowledge of the romantic literature of England, France, Germany and Spain. For evidence of this, one need look no further than the early sections of *La cuestión palpitante* (1882), in which Pardo Bazán asserts that the Romantic movement did not exist merely as a prelude to the age of Realism, but that the romantic aesthetic has been subsumed into and

66

forms an organic whole with the realist vision in literature, to which it contributes its particular perspective. Of the Romantic age she states:

> ¡Tiempos heroicos de la literatura moderna! Sólo la ciega intolerancia podrá desconocer su valor y considerarlos únicamente como preparación para la edad realista que empieza ... existen formas literarias recientes, y ... las antiguas decaen y se extinguen poco a poco [...] Lo cual no quiere decir que se hayan concluido la vaga tristeza, la contemplación melancólica, el soñar cosas diferentes de las que nos ofrece la realidad tangible, el descontento y sed del alma y otras enfermedades que sólo aquejan a espíritus altos y poderosos, o tiernos y delicados ... Sólo es lícito indicar que una tendencia general, la realista, se impone a las letras, aquí contrastada por lo que aún subsiste del espíritu romántico, allá acentuada por el naturalismo, que es su nota más aguda.[13]

This recognition of the romantic capacity to give expression to vague feeling, states of mind beyond 'la realidad tangible', and thus to the inexpressible, or what cannot be spoken, is significant for a feminist reading of *Un viaje de novios*, and for an understanding of the novel's 'feminist concerns'.

I shall assume for the purposes of my argument that we are dealing with two different manifestations of 'the Romantic' in *Un viaje de novios*, bearing in mind that it has been said that there are as many definitions of the term 'romantic' as there are critics who have written on the subject.[14] On the one hand, I shall refer to romantic subjectivity in literature as it appeared in Europe in the early-to-mid 1800s, with its emphasis on the individual's self-consciousness, desires, passions, and intellectual and creative potential; and on the other to the romantic forms of literature exemplified in Spain by the *folletín* or *novela por entregas* which was so popular with the female reading public of the late nineteenth century, and which demonstrates the trivialization of romantic subjectivity: passion becomes sentiment, tragedy becomes melodrama, and so forth. In the context of the *folletín*, the female protagonist is framed within the discourses of the patriarchal literary economy, and is thus cast outside subjectivity, as a non-subject, outside the signifying systems which empower the male and oppress or alienate the female. Pardo Bazán subverts the patriarchal forms of romantic literature through her treatment of the Romantic hero and of the *folletín*; the extent to which she capitulates to the pressures of the patriarchal system by conforming, and having her female protagonist conform, to the standards of acceptable conduct established by a censorious male society, is a matter which will be considered presently.

I am indebted in my understanding of the relationship between romantic discourse and the portrayal of female 'otherness' as it occurs in *Un viaje de novios* to a recent survey of the tradition of women romantic writers in Spain, Susan Kirkpatrick's *Las Románticas*, which traces the emergence of female writers and poets in the period 1830-1850.[15] She sets their work side by side with that of Larra, Espronceda and Rivas in order to demonstrate the markedly gendered approach to the romantic subject which emerges in the literature of those years. She goes on to observe the appropriation of romantic discourse, with its emphasis on self-consciousness, emotion and creativity, by such writers as Gertrudis Gómez de Avellaneda and Carolina Coronado. After 1850, with the mass publication of the *folletín*, this celebration of a female romantic subjectivity disappears, and instead women writers 'sell out' to the female cultural norm of the *ángel del hogar*, the domesticated, obedient, caring, nurturing and self-sacrificing dependent female whose qualities represent the debasing of the desires, emotions, noble and independent spirit, and similar inherent characteristics of the individual which are so much a part of the romantic ideal.

Kirkpatrick characterizes the gendered romantic subject, always inevitably male, and his other, woman, in the following terms:

> The Promethean rebel, fired by never-satisfied desire, was almost a polar opposite of the selfless, compliant, passionless feminine ideal, while the Solitary's cultivation of his isolation and difference directly contradicted the domestic angel's commitment to familial interrelationship ... the female appears as a signifier for nature ... Even when a woman figures in the text as a subject, insofar as she represents the other to whom the poem is addressed, she is silent, characterized by her receptivity and her absorption in nature ... In elaborating a literary discourse of subjectivity, Spanish Romanticism reflected the prevailing view of women. They figured in most Romantic texts as objects of desire or as symbols through which male fears or aspirations were represented and were constantly excluded from the fullness of feeling and imagination incorporated in the Romantic self.[16]

Insofar as the representation of Lucía and her would-be lover Artegui are concerned, this characterization holds true. Lucía is the symbol of the aspirations of her father, a shopkeeper who wishes his daughter to marry into a higher social class, and of her husband, who hopes to bolster his social pretensions with her considerable dowry. Her first meeting with Artegui occurs on a train: as she sleeps, innocent and unconscious, she becomes the object of contemplation of the as yet unnamed *viajero*. Several pages are devoted to his study of her physical charms, and the vocabulary used in the course of this first encounter suggests an underlying sexual motive in Artegui's conduct toward Lucía, who thus becomes an object of desire: 'La imagen más adecuada para representar a Lucía era la de un capullo de rosa muy cerrado, muy gallardo' (123); '¡Y ahora! - pronunció Artegui con la brutal curiosidad de unos dedos que abren a viva fuerza un capullo de flor' (122); 'Parecía el día de otoño sofocante jornada estival, y el polvillo del carbón, disuelto en la candente atmósfera, ahogaba ... de cuando en cuando penetraban en un túnel' (126). Lucía marries in order to please her father, and to get the inevitable over and done with:

> Siempre deseé casarme a gusto del viejecito, y no afligirlo con esos amoríos y esas locuras con que otras muchachas disgustan a sus padres ... Yo me asombraba de eso de enamorarse así, por ver pasar a un hombre ... Y como al fin nada se me daba de los que pasaban por la calle, y al Sr. de Miranda ya lo conocía, y a padre le gustaba tanto ... calculé ¡mejor! así me libro de cuidados. ¿No es verdad? Cierro los ojos, digo que sí y ya está todo hecho. (122)

Artegui, on the other hand, is the epitome of the Romantic hero, an intellectual and free thinker, world-weary and possessed of a deep resentment against society, moved by hidden passions and obsessed by the forces of evil:

> Tenía las facciones bien dispuestas, pero encapotadas por unas nubes de melancolía y padecimiento, no del padecimiento físico que destruye el organismo, pega la piel a los huesos, ... sino del padecimiento moral, mejor dicho, intelectual ... Eran todas sus actitudes y ademanes como de hombre rendido y exánime. Algo había descompuesto y roto en aquel noble mecanismo, algún resorte de esos que al saltar interrumpen las funciones de la vida moral. Hasta en su vestir percibíase la languidez y el desaliento que tan a las claras revelaba la fisonomía. (117)

In contrast to Lucía's passive acceptance of the system to which she is subject, Artegui complains of the suffering in the world, rejects the consolations of religion and asserts his right to dissent from certain social forms if he so wishes, and announces that he is one of only a few 'que conocemos ... el triste misterio del vivir' (143). He lives in spheres beyond Lucía's sheltered environment: he gives her lessons in astronomy, showing off his knowledge of worlds beyond this one, lists his travels throughout Europe, the States and the East, recounts his experiences as a doctor in the Carlist Wars. Obsessed though he is by evil, Artegui possesses life-saving powers through medicine: Sardiola, a soldier whose life he saves, serves Artegui as his manservant in Paris, following him like a faithful dog. Lucía, however, becomes trapped in the asphyxiating environment of her marriage, and is expected to follow her husband's orders and whims. When entrusted with the care of the consumptive and ungrateful Pilar Gonzalvo, she can only watch her charge waste away in the grip of the deadly disease; at one point in the narrative, even this dubious satisfaction is under threat from her husband:

> En su mente germinaba un concepto singular de la autoridad conyugal: parecíale que su marido tenía derecho perfecto, incontestable, evidente, a vedarle todo género de goces y alegrías, pero que en el sufrimiento era libre y que prohibir el padecer, el velar y el consagrarse a la enferma, era duro despotismo. (220)

Denied pleasure, Lucía is also denied the refuge in suffering found by the romantic hero; she is deprived, too, with Pilar's death, of any lasting reward for her caring.

Artegui is therefore depicted as representing the forces of action and desire; Pardo Bazán's extravagant description of him, and his own overblown, melodramatic language, can be read as parody, but in another sense suggest the liberatory side of romanticism; the romantic hero can throw off social shackles and indulge in his own independence from convention. Lucía embodies nature and silence, according to the pattern suggested by Kirkpatrick; at times, she is portrayed as nature subject to the male principle, at others as nature which stifles romantic desire with blind instinct and abundance. The first of these associations of Lucía with nature occurs at the moment when Artegui declares his belief in evil; a storm breaks over the couple:

> Poderoso gemido exhalaba la llanura al percibir los
> signos precursores de la tormenta. Dijérase que el mal,
> evocado por la voz de su adorador, acudía, se
> manifestaba tremendo, asombrando la naturaleza toda
> con sus anchas alas negras, a cuyo batir pudieran
> achacarse las exhalaciones asfixiantes que encendían la
> atmosfera. (152)

A later allusion to Lucía and nature comes with her revelation to Artegui that she is pregnant; he reels at the blow delivered by this 'other': 'Ignacio bajó la frente, abrumado por aquel grito de triunfo de la naturaleza vencedora. Parecióle que era Lucía la personificación de la gran madre calumniada, maldecida por él' (267). The romantic depiction of Artegui, for all that it descends at moments into parody, is more than simply a foil for Lucía's passivity and inability to break out of her situation. It may well be that it is an expression of displaced female desire, as much on the part of the writer as on that of her protagonist, which, as Elaine Showalter has pointed out in a study of the nineteenth-century English novel, is a common feature of women's writing of the period:

> Much of the wish-fulfilment in the feminine novel comes
> from women wishing they were men, with the greater
> freedom and range masculinity confers. Their heroes
> are not so much their ideal lovers as their projected
> egos.[17]

Leopoldo Alas in his review of *Un viaje de novios* in 1881 does in fact accuse Pardo Bazán of being infatuated with her own creation:

> Artegui es un tipo fantástico, engendro de la
> imaginación de una mujer que sabe idealizar y que sabe
> sentir ... Pero, ¿quién sabe si la autora, como Lucía,
> estará enamorada de esta creación?[18]

Alas's tone is patronizing, and his analysis of the reaction to Artegui arguably erroneous, but he has recognized the romantic hero as a powerful figure in Pardo Bazán's novel. I would suggest that Artegui as romantic hero represents for the writer, as for Lucía herself, the freedom of movement and feeling which is denied them; he is set up as a desiring, speaking subject against whom the female is defined, but whose model she cannot adopt.

The development of the debased form of romantic fiction woven into *Un viaje de novios,* the *folletín,* is well-documented by Alicia Andreu in *Galdós y la literatura popular.*[19] The same critic's edition of and introduction to Faustina Saez de Melgar's *La Cruz del Olivar* (1868) furnishes a concrete understanding of the elements which went to make up the typical *folletín* centred on a female protagonist.[20] *La Cruz del Olivar* is a fairy tale in a Spanish setting: the baby daughter of a noble family, abandoned by the roadside when her family flees attackers, is adopted and reared by peasants. A local *marqués* falls in love with the girl, but propriety and class-consciousness act as a restraint in their mutual attraction. Finally, it transpires that the girl is in fact of noble birth, and marriage and a happy ending ensue. All this is made possible by the girl's chastity, modesty, sense of honour, etc. The ingredients which go to make up *La Cruz del Olivar* are common to one of several stock plots in these Mills and Boon of the nineteenth century: a poor girl makes good by adhering to virtue and religion, and is rewarded by marriage to a wealthy and honourable man. The *folletín* as a whole provides a vision of the ideal woman 'firmly rooted in a moral code whose base is composed of a series of social and pseudo-religious virtues and precepts oriented towards submission, obedience, and resignation before the status quo'.[21] Lucía's trajectory in *Un viaje de novios* corresponds only inversely to that of the heroine of *La Cruz del Olivar*, since her youth, innocence and virtue meet only with boorishness in the person of her husband, illness and death in the case of Pilar, and ultimately disgrace when she renounces her love for Artegui in the name of religion. It is this failure to conform to the happy ending of so many *folletines* which exposes the weaknesses of a cliched genre: virtue is not rewarded, and adherence to social norms in Lucía's case brings the censure of society upon her as harshly as if in fact she had chosen to leave Spain with Artegui. Pardo Bazán set *Un viaje de novios* clearly within the framework of the *folletín*, presenting it in the guise of an exemplary romantic tale or fairy tale. The heavy didacticism of its ending ties it in with the tradition of moralizing which was a feature of so much of the popular literature of the middle years of the century.[22] The end of the novel is presented to the reader in intimate tones of warning by the narrator, who speaks of the 'triste ejemplo de Lucía, tradicionalmente conservado y repetido a las niñas casaderas' (278); whilst the tale is set in contemporary Spain, the story of Lucía and her disgrace is already a part of popular mythology, her fate inevitably the fate of women of her class and condition. The narrator herself refrains from appending a moral to Lucía's case; instead, she rehearses the moral conclusions drawn by the gossips of León: '[hubo] quien censuró al maduro pisaverde que buscaba novía de pocos años; quien al padre vanidoso y majadero que sacrificaba a su hija por afán de hacerla dama; quien a la niña loca que...' (277-278). But despite the narrator's professed unwillingness to select one of or to add to the list of moral lessons to be learned from the case, the reader is left in no doubt that: 'en lo que resta de siglo no habrá desposados leoneses que osen apartarse de su hogar un negro de uña' (278).

The presence of archetypes throughout *Un viaje de novios* reinforces the closed nature of the narrative and enhances the reader's perception of events as being fixed outside time and social setting and on the plane of the exemplary and inexorable. In the opening scenes of the novel, which depict the departure of the newly-weds' honeymoon train, the bride is presented as the 'tipo eterno de la forma femenina, tal cual la quisieron natura y arte' (64): she represents the immutably female, and will suffer the common destiny of all women. *Novia* and *novio* at this point in the narrative are nameless, identified only as the archetypal representations of their kind. The gulf between the male and female is evident in the separateness of the groups who accompany the *novia* and *novio* after the wedding: 'Se notaba allí que el séquito de la novia lo componían hembras, y sólo individuos del sexo fuerte formaban el del novio' (63). A further allusion to social myth suggests the fate in store for Lucía: like the virgin and martyr whose name she bears, and with whom she is explicitly associated in the textual reference to an engraving which hangs on her father's bedroom wall, 'una estampa de la bienaventurada santa Lucía, que enseñaba en un plato dos ojos como huevos escalfados' (79), she will eventually suffer (social) death, having rejected a man who brutalizes her and impugns her honour. Yet, ironically, her act of self-sacrifice when she rejects Artegui in favour of a correct religious stance will make her far from 'bienaventurada'. Already in the opening scene, the transformation which Lucía will undergo when she is delivered over to the world of men is clear: 'La novia, que con el traje de camino se les figuraba otra mujer, diversísima de la conocida hasta entonces' (64).

These insistent references to myth and archetype in *Un viaje de novios* render it difficult for the reader to separate the text from the many others written for the moral edification of a nineteenth-century female reading public. The comments of recent critics would suggest that, by and large, they accept Lucía's self-abnegation, and interpret Pardo Bazán's purpose at the end of the novel, particularly in view of her Catholic leanings, to be that of delivering a moral lesson to her audience. Fernando Barroso is an example of this:

> Si el desastre que se cierne sobre ellos [Lucía y Artegui] se evita es por la fidelidad al deber y al buen ejemplo que Lucía había recibido en su ambiente familiar. Así el adulterio no llega a realizarse. Dos almas de buena calidad, la cristiana de Lucía y la escéptica de Ignacio, se apartan del camino del deshonor.[23]

Teresa Cook similarly applauds the moral stance adopted by Lucía:

> Al final de la novela, Lucía se enfrenta con la alternativa: puede huir con el hombre a quien ama, con quien se entiende. Su religiosidad no le permite dar este paso, por lo que con gran entereza rehusa a lo que pueda ser su felicidad humana, rehusa al amor por Dios ... Al final de la novela, cuando Lucía parece haber perdido todo, se vislumbra un rayo de esperanza en el hijo que ha de venir. La maternidad es salvadora.[24]

About the comments on the nefarious effects on society of the foreign custom of the honeymoon, David Henn remarks:

> While the final sentence here is quite possibly said tongue in cheek, nonetheless, in the preceding statements there is an accurate, although somewhat restricted, revelation to the reader of the author's principle thematic concern in this novel. Thus a little preaching has been undertaken, in a roundabout way, at the end of the work.[25]

Perhaps we should accept that Pardo Bazán does take refuge in religious belief at the end of the novel, through a conviction that however innocent Lucía is of her husband's accusations of adultery, she must accept the fact of her marriage and suffer the consequences of its breakdown, taking refuge in the consolations of motherhood. The details of the text do not, however, bear out such an interpretation: Lucía's social annihilation as a consequence of the position she adopts is made clear: '... la llegada de Lucía Gonzalez, sola, triste, desmejorada y encinta, a la casa paterna. Inventáronse mentiras como castillos para explicar el misterio de su vuelta, el retiro en que se dio a vivir' (277). The priest tells her that the child she is bearing will be an eternal reminder of the suspicions which surround her conduct: 'Le castiga a usted

Dios en lo que más quiere; en ese angelito que no vino aún al mundo' (276). Alternatively, it may be that Lucía's rejection of Artegui and subsequent obedience to the advice of her spiritual confessor is simply a sop on the part of Pardo Bazán to a male hierarchy and to an 'immasculated' female readership for whom any other conclusion would constitute a violation of the bounds of propriety.[26] If this is the case, Pardo Bazán is indeed capitulating to the social conservatism of her times regarding the proper conduct of women, and is as much a victim of social convention as is her protagonist, since having demonstrated the injustice of Lucía's position, she then proceeds to condemn her to disgrace and reclusion. That Pardo Bazán may have sought to placate her critics with at least the appearance of a conventional ending is quite possible in the light of the later hostile reception of novels like *Insolación*, where the depiction of the female protagonist's social mores was considered in dubious taste. More radically, it seems to me that Pardo Bazán's presentation of Lucía's downfall is deliberately ironic, an indictment of the social myths which circumscribe the protagonist's existence. In this context, the romantic intrusions in the text serve the ironic function of indicating the impossibility of female attainment of the romantic ideal of freedom, the affirmation of individual autonomy, the breaking free of social bonds, the satisfaction of desire. Indeed, the writer's own statement in a letter to Narciso Oller in 1883 points to her awareness of precisely this conflict between woman and social conventions in the novel:

> A mí se me figuró aplicar el principio realista de los medios ambientes y estudiar el desarrollo de una pasión romancesca en el alma de Lucía, pasión provocada por el espectáculo de la naturaleza ... y por el aislamiento en que la dejaba la sociedad.[27]

I would argue, then, that Pardo Bazán's recourse to the romantic mode in *Un viaje de novios* is not due to defective narrative technique, nor to unconscious impulse, but that it marks the first step on the path to the denunciation of the condition of women in Spain which Pardo Bazán later states plainly in her essays on women in Spanish society.[28]

NOTES

1. John Rutherford, in J. Rutherford and F. W. J. Hemmings, 'Realism in Spain and Portugal', in *The Age of Realism*, ed. F. W. J. Hemmings (Harmondsworth: Penguin, 1974), 289.

2. Emilia Pardo Bazán, *Un viaje de novios*, ed. Mariano Baquero Goyanes (Barcelona: Labor, 1970), 14.

3. David Henn, *The Early Pardo Bazán. Themes and Narrative Technique in the Novels of 1879-89* (Liverpool: Francis Cairns, 1988), 219.

4. *Un viaje de novios*, ed. Baquero Goyanes, 58. All further references to this edition are included in the text.

5. Robert Osborne, *Emilia Pardo Bazán* (Mexico: Andrea, Colección Studium, 1964), 17.

6. Benito Varela Jacome, *Estructuras Novelísticas de Emilia Pardo Bazán* (Santiago de Compostela: Cuadernos de Estudios Gallegos, CSIC, 1973), 16.

7. Baquero Goyanes, 14; 39; 41; 40; 41.

8. Varela Jacome, 15.

9. Maurice Hemingway, *Emilia Pardo Bazán: The Making of a Novelist* (Cambridge: Cambridge University Press, 1983), 11.

10. Noël M. Valis, 'Pardo Bazán's *El Cisne de Vilamorta* and the Romantic Reader', *MLN*, 101 (1986), 298-324.

11. Valis, 298.

12. Valis, 307.

13. Emilia Pardo Bazán, *La cuestión palpitante*, in *Obras completas* (Madrid: Aguilar, 1973), 3 vols., Vol.3, 564-647, 588-589.

14. Lillian R. Furst, *Romanticism* (London: Methuen, 1976), 1.

15. Susan Kirkpatrick, *Las Románticas. Women Writers and Subjectivity in Spain, 1835-1850* (Berkeley, Los Angeles, London: University of California Press, 1989).

16. Kirkpatrick, 23.

17. Elaine Showalter, *A Literature of Their Own. British Women Novelists from Brontë to Lessing* (London: Virago, 1978), 136.

18. Leopoldo Alas, review of *Un viaje de novios* from *La literatura en 1881*, in Sergio Beser, *Leopoldo Alas: Teoría y crítica de la novela española* (Barcelona: Lara, 1972), 271-279, 277-278.

19. Alicia Andreu, *Galdós y la literatura popular* (Madrid: SGEL, 1982).

20. Alicia Andreu, 'Un modelo literario en la vida de Isidora Rufete', *Anales galdosianos*, Anejo 1980, 7-15.

21. Kirkpatrick, 73.

22. There is considerable discussion of the *folletín* as a didactic and moralizing genre in Juan Ignacio Ferreras, *La novela española en el siglo xix (hasta 1868)* (Madrid: Taurus, 1987).

23. Fernando J. Barroso, *El naturalismo en la Pardo Bazán* (Madrid: Playor, 1973), 60-61.

24. Teresa A. Cook, *El feminismo en la novela de la Condesa de Pardo Bazán* (La Coruña: Diputación Provincial de La Coruña, 1976), 24-25.

25. Henn, 180.

26. The term 'immasculated', which refers to a female reading public educated to read according to male values, is borrowed from Judith Fetterley, *The Resisting Reader* (Bloomington: Indiana Univeristy Press, 1978).

27. Letter to Narciso Oller, 25 February 1883, cited by Hemingway, footnote 18, Chapter 1.

28. These essays are collected in Emilia Pardo Bazán, *La mujer española y otros artículos feministas* (Madrid: Editora Nacional, 1976).

PERCEIVING THE FAMILY:
ROSA CHACEL'S *DESDE EL AMANECER*

Abigail Lee Six

Desde el amanecer is Rosa Chacel's account of the first ten years of her life, in the course of which she moved from her father's home town of Valladolid to Madrid, where her mother's family was based. She depicts the change of lifestyle that this entailed as traumatic, but not because of any culture shock arising from the contrast between life in the provinces and the capital; nor yet from the separation from paternal aunts and grandmother in Valladolid, of whom she had been fond. The emotional upheaval is focused instead on the encounter between the author and her maternal grandmother. This happened to coincide with the sudden absence of her father, who had gone to Valencia, supposedly to set up a new family home there and then be joined by his wife and daughter. In the meantime, they were to stay in the maternal abode in Madrid.

There is nothing surprising, one might say, about a little girl's negative reaction to a new grandparent, especially when thrust upon her at the same time as a completely alien household and a father's not fully understood and seemingly indefinite departure. This is not the subject of the present analysis. What does merit investigation, however, is the way in which Chacel characterizes her relationship with different members of her family, according to particular sense perceptions; moreover, there would seem to be some interest in how this intersects with the question of gender.

I shall start by briefly surveying some feminist theory, on sight first and then on sound, the two senses predominant in Chacel's depiction of her family. This should provide a basis from which to consider her experience, as she recounts it in *Desde el amanecer*. By this means, I hope to show that her perception of her various relatives appears to assign them to genders that can transcend their physiological sex.

As far as sight is concerned, theorists are careful to distinguish between two types of looking: first there is the voyeuristic variety whereby one can look without being seen; second, there is mutual or reciprocal gazing, as when mother and baby smile at each other. A considerable and ever-growing body of research exists on the first kind of gaze, for this is an area investigated by film theorists. Whilst recognizing many important differences, they observe that common to the experiences of watching a film, looking at still photography, or for that matter, peeping through a key-hole, is the central fact that one can see without being seen. As Annette Kuhn puts it: 'The voyeur's pleasure depends on the object of [the] ... look being unable to see him: to this extent, it is a pleasure of power, and the look a controlling one.'[1] This type of gaze is associated with masculinity, a quality not, however, necessarily possessed exclusively by men. Kuhn later comments on a softcore pornographic photograph of a woman taking a bath:

> The photograph speaks to a masculine subject, constructing woman as object, femininity as otherness. This does not mean that female spectators cannot, or do not, engage in a "masculine" way with photographs like this, nor does it mean that women cannot adopt a position of voyeurism. Masculinity is not the same as maleness, even if it may be conventional in our society to construct it so. (31)[2]

Contrasting with this way of looking is the reciprocal gaze, associated with femininity. E. Ann Kaplan draws the distinction unequivocally: 'Some recent experimental (as against psychoanalytic) studies have shown that the gaze is first set in motion in the mother-child relationship. But this is *mutual* gazing, rather than the subject-object kind that reduces one of the parties to the place of submission' (336, Kaplan's emphasis). Julia Kristeva finds the mother-child look significant too, linking it with the infant's progression from narcissism to auto-eroticism: 'Mais c'est lorsque ces points épars et drôles se projettent - synthèse archaïque - sur ce support stable qu'est le visage de la mère, destinataire privilégiée du rire vers trois mois, que le narcissisme de la symbiose initiale mère-enfant glisse vers l'auto-érotisme'.[3]

Feminist theory seems broadly to accept that language is fundamentally male-oriented and many writers have considered the question of how this affects women, leaving them, it is argued, with a choice between either keeping silent, or using a language that is inadequate to their needs, or trying to create some sort of new language.[4] Another, perhaps more unusual area of feminist enquiry concerns itself less with language and investigates voice. Words may, after all, be spoken with a man or woman's voice or stand silent on a page; the physical quality of sound produced by male and female speakers is therefore a distinct matter, even though it is bound to overlap with language to a certain extent. Here too, it emerges that women are at a disadvantage:

> Listeners hear lower pitched voices as more confident and dominant than higher pitched ones ... Higher pitched voices are heard as less competent ... or even less truthful and generally less 'potent' ...
> Whilst a man can aspire to a voice quality which attracts many socially desirable connotations (bigness, sexually experienced, and authoritative) a woman will be faced with compromises. The vocal attributes which signal authority and competence, for example, conflict with those that signal desirable features of femininity and female sexuality.[5]

In the light of this theoretical material, let us now consider how Rosa Chacel depicts her childhood perception of various members of the family, attempting to evaluate the extent to which her account confirms, or conversely, undermines these views.

Her relationship with her mother is unequivocally associated with sight: eye contact between them and the child's contemplation of the mother's face. She recounts, for example, an episode from the early days in Valladolid, when she had been tearful because her parents had gone to the opera, leaving her to spend the night in the care of one of her much loved paternal aunts, Eloísa. When questioned as to what the matter was, 'le expliqué: Es que estaba pensando cómo será ahora aquella carita ... ¿Qué carita?, dijo [Eloísa]. La de mi madre, contesté. Yo no sentía no ver la ópera, sino no ver su efecto en la cara de mi madre'.[6] Although it is tempting, because the anecdote concerns a mother-daughter relationship, to consider this as a mark of feminine solidarity and rapport between Rosa Chacel and her mother, it cannot de denied that the type of looking at issue here is the voyeuristic variety, for to watch someone watching an opera is to look without being seen. This, we are told by feminist scholars such as those quoted earlier, is a masculine trait, even if women are capable of it. And when we look back in *Desde el amanecer*, the claim seems indeed to be borne out, for in the first pages of the book, the author writes that it was her father who taught her to use her eyes in this way. Explaining how he had doggedly shown her a photograph of herself with her two parents and taking her finger had repeatedly pointed out "'Papá, Mamá, nena'", she concludes that this had not only taught her to speak at an early age, but also to look:

> Lo que hizo, sin saber, pero con tan decisivo trazo en mi destino, fue enseñarme a mirar. *Me hizo mirar*, podría decir; estableció un istmo o un cable conductor con mi brazo extendido hasta la imagen, haciendo que mi índice tocase tres puntos, tres breves contactos, que junto a mi oído se convertían en palabras, como si cada una de las tres voces fuera el ruido del roce de mi dedo en el papel. (14, Chacel's emphasis)

The father then, initiates the infant simultaneously into looking in this subject-object masculine way and using language, that other masculine domain, in order to name what is thus viewed.

Indeed, throughout the text, Rosa Chacel describes herself as a child who looked long and hard at those around her, and perhaps precisely because an under-ten-year-old tends not to be taken too seriously, she seems hardly to have been looked at herself at all. Her position then is, for the most part, a classic manifestation of that of the unseen gazer. She tends to locate herself on a plane above the objects of her contemplation, her relatives: 'Las personas mayores, mis tíos en primer lugar, eran campos de experimentación en los que me ejercitaba, pero moviendo los peones a mi gusto, sin hacerles participar a ellos en el juego, como si los mirase desde arriba' (243). Such a scientific attitude - what Annette Kuhn calls 'investigation-by-scrutiny' (31) - is what makes Chacel's stance a masculine one by Kuhn's criteria.

However, not only the scientist's but also the artist's gaze is felt by feminists to be voyeuristic, presenting problems for the would-be woman artist. Susan Gubar argues: 'Woman is not simply an object ... She is an art object: an icon or doll, but she is not the sculptor' (293) and Gubar goes on to consider the resultant anxiety experienced by women who seek to assume the normally male role of artist. Rosa Chacel, a woman writer who also attended art school and wanted to be a sculptor, appears not to feel this anxiety, even though she is well aware of practical difficulties for women in the creative arts.[7] She speaks of a male model whom she sculpted, in the objectifying manner associated with masculinity by feminists: 'Era un tipazo muy atlético, muy campesino. Hice una cabeza que era bastante bonita' (*Sinrazón*, 31). However, her comments on creating a work of art are only superficially masculine in approach; even though she uses the trope of sexual contact between artist and creation, the idea of possession is replaced by one of mutual gazing and reciprocal pleasure:

> Cuando la obra [de arte] tiene ya volumen - es ya como una respuesta o una mirada - se establece una *relación* erótica entre ella y el artífice ... El artista no sólo hace con su amor la obra, sino que con la obra hace el amor; en el sentido del goce y hasta del coloquio amoroso. (193, Chacel's emphasis)

The artefact then, looks back at its maker for Chacel, echoing perhaps the other visual facet of her relationship with her mother, not the one where she wished to look unobserved at her mother's face as she watched the opera, but the one she describes, for example, when recounting the degeneration of their contact after the move to Madrid: now, she says, 'mi madre y yo no intercambiábamos miradas - y tal vez fuera ése el modo que habíamos adoptado de entendernos con los ojos; no mirarnos, establecer un silencio de miradas que equivalía a decir: más vale no hablar' (270); 'un silencio de miradas': an arresting phrase, which forcefully expresses the eloquence of their former exchanges of looks.

The reason for this breakdown in visual communication between them is imputed to the maternal grandmother, prior to the move to Madrid, a fantasy figure who had starred in Chacel's mother's stories of her Caribbean childhood, and whose domineering and unglamorous reality now seemed to falsify and devalue the tales, thereby also condemning the mother of deception. However, this factor in the child's antipathy towards her grandmother is less central than the assertion by the author that she took an instant and seemingly irrational dislike to her grandmother's voice. Indeed, she often calls her grandmother simply *la voz*, as if to convey that this was her very essence. There seems to be a certain connection between the language she used (which will be considered presently) and the physical timbre of her speech, but the emphasis is squarely placed on *how* she spoke and what this meant, rather than on what she said:

> Su timbre está ahí, ante mí, no ya recurrente o como una grabación, sino concreto como un tetraedro, como algo que se abarca al primer golpe de vista y queda explicado. Su timbre está ahí delante y veo - no oigo - todos sus componentes que, por supuesto, ni se ven ni se oyen ... Está la prosa de lo sensato y conveniente, la fuerza - no la autoridad - de lo habitual, la ventaja del mando hasta en lo superfluo, la vanidad, la ignorancia, el convencionalismo resabiado. En la misma medida ... el sino, la determinación fatal, la acción de fuerzas lejanísimas de poder gigantesco, inesquivable. Todo esto en *la voz*. (220, Chacel's emphasis)

With the benefit of hindsight, Chacel explains what it was about *la voz* that made her loathe it and its owner: 'Por primera vez después de cincuenta y tantos años, veo que en aquel tono no había maldad ... El tono era solamente la voz de la ausencia. Ausencia de lo que mi amor esperaba, de lo que yo no sabía cómo iba a ser, pero que ante la presencia que aparecía vi en seguida que no era así' (217). Thus, we may conclude that rather than being two separate elements contributing to this hatred, the disillusionment relative to the image shared by mother and daughter in Valladolid, on the one hand, and the voice quality on the other, are part of the same phenomenon; the voice is the emblem of disappointing reality.

Interestingly, for a feminist study of Chacel's relationship with her grandmother, the words used by *la voz* to which the child took greatest exception are both appellations of women and both inappropriate in purist terms. These are, on the one hand, the use of *señorita*, applied to her, a nine-year-old and not yet literally a *señorita*; and on the other, the Caribbean use of *niña* as a form of address used by servants to the grandmother herself (when reminiscing on one occasion, she imitates their calling her 'niña Julia' ([292]). Graddol and Swann's observations about English usage are pertinent here:

> The use of *girl* to refer to an adult is ... variable ...

> If the usage is reciprocal (e.g. when a group of women call one another *girls*) this indicates familiarity or friendliness. If the usage is non-reciprocal - when a boss refers to a secretary as *girl* - this may indicate the superior status of the boss. If this explanation is correct, *girl* and *boy* would be functioning as markers either of solidarity or power - in a similar way to terms of address (in English) or the use of the 'familiar' or 'polite' pronoun forms in languages such as French. (117-118)

But this is a straightforward overtone, whereas the Spanish usage noted by Chacel is inverted, so that calling someone not yet entitled to the term, *señorita*, becomes subtly offensive, and calling someone *niña* when she has long since ceased to be one, becomes grotesque: 'Me parecía inaudito, disparatado y obsceno que le llamasen eso a mi abuela y ¡sobre todo! que ella se atreviese a repetirlo. Volví a sentir, por aquella frase, la pérdida de nuestras Antillas, pero la pérdida más cruel de todas las pérdidas: la de la fe en su anterior existencia' (292). Hence, voice, words, and the dismantling of the Caribbean fantasy, are all inter-dependent, combining to form the immense resentment that was Chacel's when she met her grandmother.

Nevertheless, she also indicates another cause for disillusionment: namely, the effect on her mother of the grandmother's authoritarian style. Although she had expressed disappointment at her mother's passivity in the face of her father's aggression, she takes far greater exception to the same reaction to the grandmother's tyranny. Let us compare the two. When the father harangued the mother as they walked along the street and she failed to defend herself, but gradually tore her fan to pieces instead, Chacel commented: 'Yo esperaba que mi madre contestase claro y rotundo, pero no ... El sentimiento de enajenación me lo inspiraba más mi madre, que quedaba apabullada ante su violencia, que no sabía hacerle frente y se desahogaba rompiendo un objeto inerte, como si patalease en su impotencia para responder' (35). Later in *Desde el amanecer*, she alluded to 'mi desprecio por lo blando, por lo feminino impotente' (48) and commented that 'yo quería ser igual que mi madre, pero tal como yo *creía* que mi madre *debía* ser y *podía* ser. No frágil y feminina y llorosa, sino majestuosa, fuerte, intrépida' (98-99, Chacel's emphasis). Years later in Madrid, however, the mother now bends to her own mother's opinion that Rosa ought to be made to plait her own hair; at *la voz*'s decree, the mother 'callaba; ... obedecía

porque ante su madre no se atrevía a ser madre. La hija prevalecía en ella'
(220). But the reaction is much more emotive here than in the case of
Chacel's comments on her parents' relationship with each other, for here she
conceives 'un odio, ... la decisión de no perdonar' (221), whereas she claimed
not even to have taken the parental rows seriously:

> No me impresionaba porque sentía bajo todo ello la
> comedia ... No es que yo quedase indiferente: quedaba
> inmensamente apenada, pero con una aceptación que
> consistía en mi falta de crédito a la causa. Era algo
> como lo que deben de sentir los hijos de los alcohólicos
> cuando ven venir a su padre dando tumbos: ¡Vaya por
> Dios, hoy también! ... [sic] Cuando empezaba el huracán
> yo sólo pensaba: Vamos a ver cuánto dura. (181)

Now, if the loathing for the grandmother is targeted on her voice, the
child's war against her is fought almost solely in silence and by means of
mutual gazing. A far cry from the benevolent mother-baby eye contact, this
aggressive version of visual communication is nevertheless equally well
understood by the two females concerned and suggests that the feminine
reciprocal look need not be exclusively associated with love and warmth.
Indeed, echoes of superstitions concerning women's ability to cast the evil
eye, or the Gorgon Medusa's petrifying stare, for example, might fit into this
pattern of eye contact as a feminine speciality, just as well as the loving,
empathetic mutual gaze. The grandmother has a gaze as well as a voice,
'*mirada* que se había jurado con la mía guerra sin cuartel y que no se dejó
engañar por las apariencias' (221, Chacel's emphasis). Chacel summarizes
the nature of the battle thus:

> Nunca hubo un roce entre ella y yo, nunca le di motivo
> para reñirme como se riñe a una niña: en nuestra lucha
> silenciosa, yo estaba a su altura y el hecho la
> escandalizaba tanto que procuraba disimular su
> escándalo. La lucha no era esgrima; no había juego
> descubierto: era un choque lanza en ristre a cada
> momento, en el que yo nunca fui desarzonada ...
> Yo la miraba y ella sentía que habíamos chocado ...
> Y todo esto, de mirada a mirada. (234-235)

As far as sight is concerned, then, *Desde el amanecer* can be read as
supporting the distinction between the voyeuristic and the mutual gaze, as
supporting too the association of the former with masculinity, with scientific
scrutiny and with the artist's use of models (literal or figurative). In this

regard, Chacel must be seen as having a masculine element in her character, learnt in infancy from her father. Also borne out by the text is the link between the reciprocal look and femininity, with the silent communication conducted thus between the author and her mother, as well as the fierce visual fight between the child and her grandmother. What this concrete example of a female's testimony adds to the theory is more than verification, however; it demonstrates a danger that women theorists would do well to heed, namely, that the feminine should not be equated by them - however tacitly - with benevolence and masculinity with malevolence. To make the point that women can have masculine qualities and men feminine ones, does not solve the problem, as *Desde el amanecer* shows. Chacel's supposedly masculine desire to gaze at her mother's face while she watches the opera, for example, seems innocuous compared with her feminine aggressive eye contact with her grandmother.

When we turn to consider the portrayal of voice in the text, a more comfortable position for feminism seems at first to be posited: the masculine qualities of aggressivity, authoritarianism, and victimization are condemned through the portrayal of the grandmother, even though she happens to be a woman, physiologically. This idea is conveyed through the reduction of the person to the voice, a voice that is masculine not only in its words, which alternate between issuing orders or patronizing the female sex, but also in its tone.[8] And yet, a minor character in the text is given an extremely positive weighting owing to what the author perceives as the very masculinity of his voice: 'Tenía una voz que no era ni excesivamente grave, ni excesivamente sonora, ni infrecuente para la acústica por ningún concepto, pero excepcional, absolutamente excepcional, por su masculinidad. Era una voz posesiva, también cobijadora, protectora: era tan palpable como una mano, tan envolvente como una bocanada de calor y, al mismo tiempo tan verídica, confiante, fiel. Bueno, masculina (101).' Thus, we are forced to concede that on this count too, Chacel cannot be hauled aboard the bandwagon proclaiming masculinity evil and femininity fundamentally good.

In conclusion, it would seem that *Desde el amanecer* intersects with feminist theory, providing, as it does, concrete testimony that supports the linkage between both the objectifying gaze and the voice of authority with masculinity on the one hand; and the linkage between both the eloquent reciprocal gaze and aural silence with femininity. It further confirms the assertion that these qualities of masculinity and femininity are not confined respectively to males and females, through both the depiction of the grandmother and the self-portrait of the author. But where it departs from feminist theory (and indeed, the opposing phallocratic view too) is in its refusal to align these categories with positive and negative, with soft and hard, with warm and cold. Instead, the reader is faced with a chiaroscuro effect, subtler and less comfortable perhaps than neat theories, but which rings truer in its complexity.

NOTES

1.   Annette Kuhn, *The Power of the Image: Essays on Representation and Sexuality* (London and New York: Routledge & Kegan Paul, 1985), 28.

2.   E. Ann Kaplan makes the same point: 'The [voyeuristic] gaze is not necessarily male (literally), but to own and activate the gaze, given our language and the structure of the unconscious, is to be in the masculine position.' 'Is the Gaze Male?', in *Desire: The Politics of Sexuality*, ed. By Ann Snitow, Christine Stansell, and Sharon Thompson (London: Virago, 1984), 321-338 (331).

3.   Julia Kristeva, *Polylogue*, Tel Quel (Paris: Editions du Seuil, 1977), 481.

4.   Examples: 'Woman's experiences cannot be spoken in a man-made language without gaps and discontinuities.' Paul Julian Smith, *The Body Hispanic: Gender and Sexuality in Spanish and Spanish American Literature* (Oxford: Clarendon, 1989), 38.
      'The model of the pen-penis writing on the virgin page participates in a long tradition identifying the author as a male who is primary and the female as his passive [i.e. silent] creation.' Susan Gubar, '"The Blank Page" and the Issues of Female Creativity', in *The New Feminist Criticism: Essays on Women, Literature and Theory*, ed. by Elaine Showalter (London: Virago, 1986), 292-313 (295).
      'For Lacan, woman cannot enter the world of the symbolic, of language ... [Woman's] relation to language is a negative one, a lack. In patriarchal structures, thus, woman is located as other (enigma, mystery), and is thereby viewed as outside of (male) language.' E. Ann Kaplan, 321.

5.   David Graddol and Joan Swann, *Gender Voices* (Oxford: Blackwell, 1989), 32 and 38.

6.   Rosa Chacel, *Desde el amanecer*, Literatura Contemporánea, 55 (Barcelona: Seix Barral, 1972), 50. Unless stated to the contrary, this is the text from which quotations of Chacel are taken, and henceforth cited in parenthesis.

7.   'Si no he triunfado no ha sido más que por eso: por ser gorda y mal vestida. Nada más ... Ahí viene lo de ser mujer. Los hombres no han sufrido eso, pero las mujeres, sí. Un hombre gordo y mal vestido podría haber triunfado desde un principio. Pero una mujer, no.' Alberto Porlán, *La sinrazón de Rosa Chacel* (extended interview with her), De palabra, 5 (Madrid: Anjana, 1984), 86. A further reference, given within the text of the article, will abbreviate the title to Sinrazón.

8.   'In Western culture we are ready to believe ... that a harsh voice is correlated with more aggressive, dominant, authoritative characteristics, and a breathy voice with more self-effacing,

submissive, meek personalities.' J. Laver, 'Voice quality and indexical information', *British Journal of Disorders of Communication* (1968), 3, 43-54 (49-50), cited in Graddol and Swann, 34.

ON THE THRESHOLD:
CIXOUS, LISPECTOR, TUSQUETS

Stephen M. Hart

The epistemological problem faced by the twentieth-century female writer is epitomised in Rosario Castellanos's arresting poem 'Meditación en el umbral':

No, no es la solución
tirarse bajo el tren como la Ana de Tolstoi
ni apurar el arsénico de Madame Bovary
ni aguardar en los páramos de Avila la visita
del ángel con venablo
antes de liarse el manto a la cabeza
y comenzar a actuar.

Ni concluir las leyes geométricas, contando
las vigas de la celda de castigo
como lo hizo Sor Juana. No es la solución
escribir, mientras llegan las visitas,
en la sala de estar de la familia Austen
ni encerrarse en el ático
de alguna residencia de la Nueva Inglaterra
y soñar, con la Biblia de los Dickinson,
debajo de una almohada de soltera.

Debe haber otro modo que no se llame Safo
ni Mesalina ni María Egipciaca
ni Magdalena ni Clemencia Isaura.

Otro modo de ser humano y libre.

Otro modo de ser.[1]

It is striking how many of the examples of female experience adduced in Castellanos's poem in her search for 'another way of being' are drawn from the world of literature: Flaubert's Emma Bovary, Tolstoy's Anna Karenina. The threshold Castellanos is describing clearly has as much to do with our conception of women in literature, or literary women, as with women in everyday life. Indeed, it is only relatively recently that women's writing has ventured across the threshold of the literary canon. In the not too distant past women writers, with a few exceptions, were dismissed by their male contemporaries. Indicative of this approach is the comment made by the North-American novelist, Nathaniel Hawthorne, in a letter he wrote to his publisher in 1855: 'America is now wholly given over to a damned mob of scribbling women, and I should have no chance of success while the public taste is occupied with their trash - and should be ashamed of myself if I did succeed'.[2] Little has changed, the cynic might say, in 135 years. Even nowadays the work of women writers seems to be less worthy of academic scrutiny than the work of male writers. During the period 1986-1988, for example, only 9.9% of published scholarship on modern Spanish literature was concerned with women's writing. For modern Spanish American literature and modern Brazilian literature respectively, the comparable figures were 5.5% and 13.3%.[3] It was due to this ostracization that the need was felt by women writers to search for, in Castellanos's words, 'another way of being', by writing a new canon into existence. What better way of doing this than by writing in a new language, one which was specifically feminine?

The concept of 'écriture féminine' grew, rather surprisingly, out of the union of psychoanalysis and feminism. Freudian theory is, of course, anathema to the traditional discourse of feminism which sees Freud's obsession with the phallus, penis-envy, female lack and hysteria as an apt illustration of his sexual credentials.[4] But gradually the discourse of what came to be known as psychoanalytic feminism emerged. Nancy J. Chodorow has identified three strands within this new discourse which are object-relations and interpersonal psychoanalytical feminism, and Lacanian psychoanalytic feminism.[5] The present essay will be specifically concerned with the third type of discourse as identified by Chodorow. An early example of Lacanian psychoanalytic feminism was the pioneering work carried out by

Juliet Mitchell, who employed psychoanalysis to uncover the hidden (in the sense of unconscious) agenda of patriarchy in our society.[6]

In the years immediately before his death Freud was intensely preoccupied with a question which he suspected was unanswerable. The question was superficially a simple one: 'What does a woman want?'[7] Jacques Lacan felt inspired to carry on where his master left off, and in his seminar 'Dieu et la jouissance de la femme', the French psychoanalyst attempted to address this issue. Lacan's answer, if it could be called an answer, was, predictably enough, controversial: 'The woman can only be written with The crossed through. There is no such thing as The woman since of her essence - having already risked the term, why not think twice about it? - of her essence, she is not all'.[8] In the course of that seminar Lacan also drew attention to his own belief in the undeniably phallic nature of the Symbolic order and the words which are rooted in that order, since woman is 'excluded by the nature of things which is the nature of words' (Feminine Sexuality, 144). Other of Lacan's insights likewise betray phallocentrism. In his account of the growth of human personality, for example, Lacan invariably invokes a paternal metaphor; thus the break in the relation between mother and child is presided over by the phallus. Lacan's concept of the 'nom du père' as a site within which paternal authority as well as the language system is centred likewise suggests that the Symbolic order itself is androcentric (Feminine Sexuality, 38). It is not surprising therefore that Lacan should speak of women as 'excluded by the nature of things which is the nature of words'.

These were the fruits of Lacanian knowledge that the body of psyochanalytic feminism could not digest whole. Luce Irigaray, for example, in her study Ce sexe qui n'en est pas un (1977) argued that Lacan's androcentric discourse 'like all the others - more than all the others? - that he reproduces in applying their logic to the sexual relation, perpetuates the subjection of woman'.[9] What has been specifically excluded from the discourse of psychoanalysis, Irigaray argues, is the female body. A similar critique of Lacan's standpoint was voiced by the Argentine novelist Luisa Valenzuela who promoted 'un lenguaje femenino en absoluto emparentado con aquellas azucaradas palabras con las que hemos sido recubiertas a lo largo de siglos' (88).[10] The Lacanian notion of the gliding of the signifier did not exclude, she went on to argue, the possibility of a feminine language: 'El célebre deslizamiento del significado por debajo del significante - hoy tan vital como lo fue en su momento el encuentro fortuito del paraguas con la máquina de coser - no es necesariamente el mismo para cada individuo, y con mayor razón para individuos de distinto sexo' (89). By identifying with women - and especially witches - who in the past have suffered under the dictatorship of men, Valenzuela sought to create a 'lenguaje hémbrico' (91), which itself echoes Irigaray's notion of women-speak ('parler femme'). When this central issue of the relationship between woman and language subsequently emerged in the pioneering work of Hélène Cixous, the role of the body had become a central metaphor. Cixous turned the knowledge of psychoanalysis on its head, starting from the basic supposition that a 'feminine language' of necessity exists.

But what is meant by the phrase 'feminine language'? The science of sociolinguistics has established that, in many societies, the speech of men and women differs; the more striking cases for which there is evidence pertain to non-European cultures. In Zulu, for example, a wife is not allowed to mention the name of her father-in-law, or his brothers, and she might be put to death if she broke this taboo. Likewise in some Amerindian languages the word a woman will use to denote her brother will be different from that used by a man. One of the more striking examples of different sexes speaking different languages came, rather appropriately, given the subject of this study, from the New World. When Europeans first arrived in the Lesser Antilles and made contact with the Caribs who lived there they discovered that the men and women spoke different languages. As a contemporary report from the seventeenth century suggests:

> The men have a great many expressions peculiar to them, which the women understand but never pronounce themselves. On the other hand the women have words and phrases which the men never use, or they would be laughed to scorn. Thus in their conversations it often seems as if the women had another language than the men.[11]

The surprise of the European observer is not fortuitous, given the fact that the language spoken by men and women in Standard Average European, from the point of view of lexicon, syntax and grammar, is identical. It is intriguing therefore that Cixous should be exploring the concept of a 'feminine language' in the context of a European language that does not readily admit to any such distinction. Cixous's purpose in adopting a term of this kind, however, is not merely syncretistic. One important difference between her concept of 'écriture féminine' and the idiolect spoken by women in non-European cultures concerns Cixous's emphasis on the written nature of her language.

In *La jeune née* Cixous argues that women must 'write their own selves into writing', and in the process divest their writing of its phallocentric stamp by escaping the 'language of the father'. Playing on the double meaning of 'voler' in French, Cixous imagines feminine writing to 'fly' and 'steal' simultaneously: 'It is not pure chance then that woman has something of the bird and the thief, as the thief has something of woman and bird: they pass, fell, enjoy the scrambling of orderly space, of disorientation, changing the place of furniture, things, values, breaking in, out, voiding structures, turning own and ownership upside down ... A feminine text cannot be anything but subversive: if writing itself, it does so by the volcanic raising of ancient, established, encrusted surfaces'. These 'established, encrusted surfaces' are the purview of phallocentrism which must be subverted since, as Cixous goes on to argue, 'if we enter society to become men, we have lost everything'. This new type of discourse devolves from the female body which has been supressed from view under the historic weight of masculine discourse, becoming no more than a 'disquieting stranger' (*La jeune née*, 179). Bringing this 'écriture féminine' into play involves integration with female libido which, according to Cixous, is 'cosmic' (*La jeune née*, 162), transcending the androcentric view of libido.[12] Cixous extends this idea: 'The ideal harmony, reached by few, would be genital, assembling everything and being capable of generosity, of spending. That is what I mean when I speak of *écriture féminine*, that is what I talk about'.

The impact of this notion of 'feminine writing' was felt in Spanish literary circles in the early 1980s. In 1982, for example, Francisco Umbral suggested that 'la nueva novela femenina ... está floreciendo en España', identifying its characteristics as 'realismo, intimismo, historias familiares, marginaciones sociales'.[13] Women writers, however, were split over the issue as to whether their writing was generically different from male writing. Lourdes Ortiz and Adelaida García Morales were unconvinced; Ortiz suggested that 'no existe un lenguaje específicamente femenino'.[14] García Morales argued: 'no creo que haya algo característico de las escritoras muy diferentes a los escritores'. Some writers were more forceful about the differences. Martin Gaite's view was that: 'las mujeres siempre se han volcado en lo concreto, en los interiores (...) viendo sin ser vistos, y, por tanto, al escribir tienen la fuerza del testigo no apreciado'; and Marta Traba argues that 'sí hay un texto o literatura femenina diferente' pointing among other things to its 'insistencia en el emisor'.[15] Rosa Montero takes a mid-way position. Thus, although 'en cuanto arte, la literatura carece de sexo', nevertheless, Montero argued, 'las mujeres viven el mundo de forma muy diferente a los hombres y se ven obligadas a contarlo de forma a menudo radicalmente distinta'.[16] Some women writers go even further. When questioned on this issue in an open discussion on the modern Spanish novel held at the MLA conference in Washington in December 1989, Marina Mayoral and Carme Riera both said categorically that, not only is feminine language different, but language itself is feminine and men have been trying to conceal this truth since time immemorial. During a *Feria del Libro Feminista* held in Barcelona in June 1990, the Uruguayan writer Cristina Peri Rossi argued: 'Las mujeres tenemos demasiados derechos prohibidos. Y yo quería subirme a los árboles, usar pantalones, fumar, e imaginar historias ...'. As Elizabeth Ordóñez has suggested, this group of writers 'desire nothing less than to escape being spoken of and to become the subjects of their own discourse'. As Carme Riera proposes pithily: 'dejando de ser habladas comencemos a hablar'.[17]

It is clear that Cixous's theory of feminine writing cannot be applied indiscriminately to all writing composed by women. The work of the Chilean novelist Isabel Allende, for example, in its emphasis on plot and the delineation of character, falls outside the purview of 'écriture féminine'. Perhaps more importantly, Allende's fiction presents feminism as an ideology which is restricted to the female sex and therefore simply an extension of femaleness rather than a revolutionary world-vision. In *La casa de los espíritus* (1982), for example, in a highly essentialist gesture, Allende presents the knowledge of feminism as locked into gender. Esteben Trueba's violent assertion of his dominance is part and parcel of his sex, just as feminism is the natural growth of Clara and her mother before her. By consistently translating political conflict into universalist sexual archetypes in *La casa de los espíritus* Allende turns a potential political allegory into a naturalist symbol. Allende's metaphors, therefore, deconstruct the overt level of political commitment to feminism which lies like a patina on the surface of the text. The text's metaphors refer back to a biologically sexualized universe which sterilizes any putative politically revolutionary message.

One strategy used to differentiate women's from men's fiction is to compare and contrast the mythical sub-texts present in each of the two genres. Whereas novels written by men tend to allude - albeit ironically - to Greek myths and folklore (one thinks of the Ulysses narrative underpinning Martin-Santos's *Tiempo de silencio* and the Orestes narrative in Cela's *La familia de Pascual Duarte*), women's fiction tends to allude more readily to fairy tales. Fairy tales - especially the Cinderella story - are a recurrent motif in female development novels written by women in post-civil-war Spain.[18]

If one were to choose the work of one writer as an example of 'écriture féminine' it would necessarily be Clarice Lispector (1925-1977). Cixous has indeed proposed the work of the Brazilian authoress as the epitome of 'écriture féminine', and has freely admitted the extent to which Lispector influenced her own writing after she first read Lispector in 1977. Critics have pointed to various similarities in the work of both writers: their joint espousal of fluid, open texts, their rejection of the phallocentric prison of binary oppositions, and their expression of a singularly feminine libidinal desire. Both writers are intent on 'writing the body'; Cixous's contention, when describing her own work that 'Je suis là où ça parle' (translated by Fitz as 'I am where it/id/the female consciousness speaks') might serve as an epigraph to Lispector's work.[19]

Lispector's first novel *Perto do coração selvagem* (1944), published when she was just nineteen years old, treats themes which would remain the hallmark of her work for years to come: the preoccupation with specifically feminine experience, the sexual repression of women, the concern with capturing the fluidity of existence, and philosophical anguish. The protagonist of the novel is, in Giovanni Pontiero's words, 'a conventional suburban wife with unconventional thoughts'.[20] Her dilemma seems simple enough: 'How was she to tie herself to a man without permitting him to imprison her? And was there some means of acquiring things without those things possessing her'? (29) In order to break free from the bonds of phallocentrism, Joana strives to break down the binary logic which separates mind from body. She uses bodily metaphors to describe thought: 'She was pervaded by long, integral muscles. Any thought descended through those smooth tendons only to tremble there in her ankles whose flesh was as tender as that of young fowl'(97).[21] In particular, Joana's interior monologues focus on a specifically feminine knowledge which is born from the body:

> How curious that I'm unable to say who I am. That is to say, I know perfectly well, but I cannot bring myself to say it. Most of all, I'm afraid of saying it, because the moment I try to speak, not only do I fail to express what I feel, but what I feel slowly transforms itself into what I am saying. Or at least, what makes me act is not what I feel but what I say. I feel who I am and the impression is lodged in the upper part of my brain, on my lips - especially on my tongue - on the surface of my arms and is also coursing inside me, deep down inside my body, but where, precisely where, I cannot say. (19)

Joana's sense of identity is lodged, as she suggests, 'especially on my tongue'. This is typical of the novel as a whole. Beneath the linear movement of the plot the text expresses a desire to body forth that sense of linguistic identity which is specifically feminine, and which cannot be defined since it has 'a quality of primary matter, something that might define itself but never came to be realized', or, as Joana puts it, 'the mystery in itself' (131). It is characteristic that this new knowledge is associated not only with the feminine, but also with the world of words. For Joana's quest involves a radical re-thinking of the (man-made) laws of language: 'Is "never" man or woman? Why is "never" neither son nor daughter? And what about "yes"'? (15) Joana's search for a new language is implicit (and complicit) in her search for femaleness. Joana is often *talking* with a mysterious *mulhjer de voz* (literally, 'woman of the voice'), whose ideas, as Earl E. Fitz points out, 'have a powerful if uncertain effect on Joana'.[22] As she asks herself at one point: 'Where was the woman with the voice? Where were the women who were merely female'? (21)

Generally, the voice of womanhood is characterised by its absence. What the narrator desires 'still has no name' (64) and is expressed as 'strange gibberish coming from her lips'. (75) At certain Joycean moments of 'epiphany', however, this deeper awareness of the body emerges in a new language, equivalent to what Cixous has called 'avant-langage':

> Then she invented what she must say. Her eyes closed, submissive, she uttered in a whisper words born at that moment, hitherto unheard, still tender from creation - new and fragile buds. They were less than words, merely disconnected syllables, meaningless, lukewarm, that flowed and criss-crossed, fertilized, were reborn in a single being only to separate immediately, breathing, breathing ... (127)

To emphasise its separateness from man-made language, this new linguistic world is inscribed within a neologism, 'Lalande', which encapsulates an Amazonic world from which men are excluded. Octávio's husband is desperate to find out what he is missing:

> - Tell me again what Lalande means - he implored Joana. It's like angel's tears. Do you know what angel's tears are? A kind of daffodil, the slightest breeze bends it backwards. Lalande also means the sea at dawn, before anyone has set eyes on the shore, before the sun has risen. Each time I say: Lalande, you should hear the fresh and salty sea-breeze, you should walk the length of the beach still covered in darkness, slowly, stark naked. In a word, you will feel Lalande ... (157)

This amazonic world is a pre-conscious world which conflates the divine ('angel's tears') and the physical ('daffodil'), a landless sea which the daylight of phallocentric civilisation has not yet lit up. In attempting to body forth this 'brave new world', Lispector, true to the spirit of 'écriture féminine', brings about 'the volcanic raising of ancient, established, encrusted surfaces'.[23]

Many other female writers, both in Latin America and Spain, have addressed some of the issues raised by Cixous, particularly in relation to the issues of gender and identity. But one other writer deserves special mention in this context and she is the Spanish novelist, Esther Tusquets (b. 1936). While it cannot be said that Tusquets's work embodies 'écriture féminine' to quite the same degree that Lispector's does, the notion of a feminine writing is invoked at certain key junctures in Tusquets's novels. Her first novel, *El mismo mar de todos los veranos*, published only a few years after the demise of the Franco regime in 1978, created a literary scandal, mainly because of its frank treatment of female sexuality and lesbianism. At one point in the novel, Elia begins speaking to her lover, Clara, in a new language which has some of the characteristics of Cixous's concept of 'écriture féminine':

> en los breves momentos en que mis labios se separan un poco de sus labios, la arrullo con palabras increíbles, tan extrañas, palabras que no he dicho a ningún hombre, que no dije ni siquiera nunca a Jorge, ni siquiera a Guiomar cuando era chiquita y no había adquirido todavía estos ojos duros de mujer que sabe, palabras que ignoraba yo misma que estuvieran en mí, en algún oscuro rincón de mi conciencia, agazapadas, quietas y al espera de ser un día pronunciadas, ni siquiera pronunciadas, sino salmodiadas, cantadas, vertidas espesas y dulcísimas en una voz que tampoco reconozco aunque debe ser forzosamente la mía, tantos años ocultas esta voz y estas palabras en un centro intimísimo y secreto, para brotar al fin en esta oscuridad grana, en este cubil con aroma a mar y a cachorro'. (138)[24]

Similar to Cixous's conception of 'écriture féminine' quoted above, this new voice transcends binary categories, such as between self and other; it is perceived as emerging simultaneously from a secret space *within* the self ('centro intimísimo y secreto'), and also from without ('una voz que tampoco reconozco'). Tusquets's text, however, gives a further twist to Cixous's notion of 'écriture féminine' since she uses its metaphors to express lesbian sexual desire, echoing Monique Wittig's theory of writing.[25] A description of this female voice which appears later on in the novel also emphasises its alterity:

> empiezo a musitar también yo palabras muy extrañas, palabras que tampoco tienen sentido y que tienen sentido y que pertenecen a un idioma no aprendido, y recuerdo que ya me pasó otra vez con Clara algo semejante, pero esta vez yo no quiero detenerme, porque las palabras surgen en una embriaguez sin fin, y sé que han caído todas las barreras y se han bajado todas las defensas'. (157)

A particularly significant feature of this passage is the suggestion that the language Elia has just begun to speak is 'no aprendido', which we must interpret as not learned from the phallocentric language men use. In this novel, indeed, the men do not speak.[26] As this particular passage continues it becomes clear that the new language spoken by women is associated with the body rather than the mind:

> este lenguaje no nace en el pensamiento y pasa desde allí hasta la voz hecha sonido: nace hecha ya voz de las entrañas y la mente lo escucha ajena y sorprendida, ni siquiera ya asustada o avergonzada, porque estamos repentinamente al otro lado - mucho más allá - del miedo y la vergüenza, y es evidente y claro que en cualquier instante yo tendré que morir, porque la ternura me ha traspasado como cien alfileres de diamante, la ternura me ha pisoteado y arrollado a su paso como el más terrible de los ejércitos en marcha, y me voy deshaciendo, disolviendo, desangrando en palabras, tan dulcemente muerta'. (158)

Composed of pain and tenderness, this 'avant-langage' spoken by the body is a feminine voice on the other side of words. The mind cannot understand its import: 'la mente lo escucha ajena y sorprendida'. As we can see, Tusquets borrows her metaphors from Cixous's notion of feminine writing, expanding it to encompass the full spectrum of sexual desire.

In their different ways both Clarice Lispector and Esther Tusquets embody many of the crucial concerns underlying feminine writing. What is intriguing, however, is the fundamentally silent or absent nature of 'écriture féminine' as figured in their work. At no point in their respective works does the female language speak out. It is constantly alluded to, it makes sporadic and tantalizing appearances, but is never brought fully out of the closet. The presence of female language is reported, but not spelled out, and reported speech by definition implies an absent speaker. Tusquets, for her part, describes the new language that her love bids her to speak without spelling out its words, while Lispector leaves us with a neologism 'Lalande' which hints at a new language and a new world of difference, which is enclosed - silent and absent - within the master text, another way of being as yet unsaid.

NOTES

1. Rosario Castellanos, *Meditation on the Threshold* (New York: Bilingual Press, 1988), 48.

2. Elaine Showalter (ed.), *The New Feminist Criticism: Essays on Women, Literature, and Theory* (London: Virago, 1987), 81-104 (101).

3. To give a rough indication of the critical prominence of women's writing the lines devoted to that subject were divided by the total number of lines of a given section and then expressed as a percentage. The percentage annually for the '1936 until the Present Day Section' for Spanish literature, for example, were as follows: 1986 (5.9%), 1987 (10.5%), 1988 (13.3%); for twentieth-century Spanish-American literature, the corresponding figures were: 1986 (5.5%), 1987 (5.3%), 1988 (5.8%); for modern Brazil: 1986 (18.6%), 1987-88 (8.1%); see the respective sections in vols. 48-50 of *YWMLS*. The very high percentage for the modern Brazilian literature section corresponding to the year 1986 was mainly due to the large number of works published on Clarice Lispector that year. These figures can only be approximate since the coverage on which the contributions are based is necessarily selective.

4. An example of this more traditional feminist approach can be found in Kate Millet, *Sexual Politics* (London: Virago, 1970), esp. 176-203.

5. N. J. Chodorow, *Feminism and Psychoanalytic Theory* (New Haven: Yale University Press, 1989), 184-198.

6. See Juliet Mitchell's essay 'On Freud and The Destruction Between the Sexes' (1974), reprinted in *Women: The Longest Revolution*, 221-232; as well as her later study *Psychoanalysis and Feminism* (Harmondsworth: Penguin, 1982, first published in 1974), which attempts to integrate the knowledge of Lacanian psychoanalysis with the discipline of feminism. In this work she argues on behalf of Freud against the adoption of the psychoanalytical theories of Wilhelm Reich and R. D. Laing, arguing that a 'rejection of psychoanalysis and of Freud's work is fatal for feminism'; xv. In the process she challenges Simone de Beauvoir and Kate Millett, among others, on their rejection of Freudianism; see *Psychoanalysis and Feminism*, 305-318, and 351-355.

7. 'L'inconscient freudien et le notre', in *Les quatre concepts fondamentaux de la psychanalyse* (Paris: Seuil, 1973), 21-30 (29).

8. 'God and the *Jouissance* of The Woman', *Feminine Sexuality: Jacques Lacan and the "école freudienne"*, edited by Juliet Mitchell and Jacqueline Rose (London: Macmillan, 1982), 137-148 (144).

9. *This Sex Which is Not One*, translated by Catherine Porter (Ithaca, New York: Cornell U.P., 1985), 104.

10. Luisa Valenzuela, 'Mis brujas favoritas', *Theory and Practice of Feminist Literary Criticism*, edited by Gabriela Mora and Karten S. Van Hooft (Ypsilanti, Michigan: Bilingual Press, 1982), 88-95.

11. Quotation and examples are drawn from Peter Trudgill, *Sociolinguistics: An Introduction to Language and Society* (Harmondsworth: Penguin, 1974), 79-80. Trudgill furthermore mentions that the anomaly between the speech of the men and the women in the case of the Lesser Antilles tribe cited may have been caused by the invasion of a foreign tribe (the Caribs) and their subsequent extermination of the male population of the Arawak people. I do not intend to give the impression that there are no distinctions in the speech of men and women in Standard Average European languages. Differences clearly do exist although they are more subtle; see Francine Wattman Frank, 'Women's Language in America', *Women's Language and Style*, edited by Douglas Butturff and Edmund L. Epstein (Akron, Ohio: University of Akron, 1978), 47-61.

12. In an interview with Verena Andermatt Conley, Cixous elaborated on this point, taking Freud's model of the oral, anal and genital phases as a spring-board in order to argue that feminine writing is built on genitality; see Verena Andermatt Conley in *Hélène Cixous: Writing the Feminine* (Nebraska: University of Nebraska, 1984), 138. In his earlier writings on infantile sexuality Freud isolated two pregenital sexual organisations, the oral-cannibalistic and the sadistic-anal. In 1925 his research led him to add a third stage which he called the phallic stage; see *The Basic Writings of Sigmund Freud*, translated by A. A. Brill (New York: Random House, 1938), 597-598.

13. *El País* (9 January 1982); quoted by Fernando Valls,'La literatura femenina en España: 1975-1989', *Insula*, 512-513 (1989), 13.

14. *El País* (17 June 1982), and *ABC* (11 May 1986); quoted by Fernando Valls, 'La literatura femenina en España: 1975-1989', *Insula*, 512-513 (1989), 13.

15. Marta Traba, 'Hipótesis sobre una escritura diferente', *Quimera*, 13, XI (1981); both citations quoted by Fernando Valls, 'La literatura femenina en España: 1975-1989' *Insula* 512-513 (1989), 13.

16. Quoted by Fernando Valls, 'La literatura femenina en España: 1975-1989', *Insula*, 512-513 (1989), 13.

17. The statement by Peri Rossi is quoted in Rosa María Piñol, 'Nueve autoras de distintas culturas coinciden en asociar escritura y libertad', *La Vanguardia* (23 June 1990). Other quotations may be found in Elizabeth J. Ordóñez, 'Inscribing Difference: "L'écriture féminine" and New Narrative by Women', *Anales de Literatura Española Contemporánea*, 12:1-2 (1987), 45-58 (53, and 48).

18. Emilie Bergmann, 'Reshaping the Canon: Intertextuality in Spanish Novels of Female Development', *Anales de Literatura Española Contemporónea*, 12:1-2 (1987), 141-156, studies this motif in Laforet's *Nada*, Matute's *Primera memoria*, Moix's *Julia*, Martín Gaite's *El cuarto de atrás*, and Rodoreda's *La plaça del diamant.*

19. Earl E. Fitz succinctly summarizes the main similarities between Cixous and Lispector in his article 'Hélène Cixous's Debt to Clarice Lispector: The Case of *Vivre L'Orange* and "l'écriture féminine"', *Revue de Littérature Comparée*, no. 1 (1990), 235-249 (235-37). See also Claudine Fisher, 'Hélène Cixous' Window of Daring through Clarice Lispector's Voice', in *Continental, Latin-American and Francophone Women Writers*, edited by Eunice Myers and Ginette Adamson (Lanham, MD: University Press of America, 1987), 21-27. For a good discussion of the 'writing the body' theme, see Ann Rosalind Jones, 'Writing the Body: Towards an Understanding of *l'écriture féminine*', *Feminist Studies*, 7:2 (Summer 1981), 247-306. On the role of this concept in modern Spanish fiction see Elizabeth J. Ordóñez, 'Inscribing Difference: "L'écriture féminine" and New Narrative by Women', *Anales de Literatura Española Contemporánea*, 12:1-2 (1987), 45-58 (47). For a discussion of the motif of writing the body in the work of Rosa Montero see Elena Cascón Vera, 'Rosa Montero ante la escritura femenina', *Anales de Literatura Española Contemporánea*, 12:1-2 (1987), 59-77.

20. *Near to the Wild Heart*, translated and with an afterword by Giovanni Pontiero (Manchester: Carcanet, 1990), 189. All subsequent textual references are to this edition.

21. At times Joana's body seems to have a will of its own. After the passage in which Joana hears that her aunt intends to send her away to boarding school, we read: 'Joana's hands fidgeted, independent of her will. She observed them with mild curiosity and forgot them almost immediately. The ceiling was white, the ceiling was white. Even her shoulders, which she had always thought of as being so remote from herself, throbbed with life and began to tremble. Who was she?' (47)

22. Earl E. Fitz, *Clarice Lispector* (Boston: Twayne, 1985), 71.

23. The word 'Lalande' as it appears in the original Portuguese text is pure invention. To Portuguese ears it would sound quite foreign, as indeed it does to English ears. I am grateful to Dr Giovanni Pontiero for his advice on this matter. For further discussion of Lispector's work see Earl E. Fitz's general study *Clarice Lispector*, quoted in note 22; *Revista Iberoamericana*, 126-127 (1984) is a special number devoted to Lispector's work. Other important studies are: G. Pontiero, 'Testament of Experience: Some Reflections on Clarice Lispector's *A Hora da Estrela*', *Iberoamerikanisches Archiv*, 10 (1984), 13-22; Daphne Patai, 'Clarice Lispector and the Clamor of the Ineffable', *Kentucky Romance Quarterly*, 27 (1980), 133-149; Valerie C. Lastinger, 'Humor in a New Reading of Clarice Lispector', *Hispania*, 72 (1989), 130-137. See also the bibliographies in Fitz, *Clarice Lispector*, 140-155; and in

Giovanni Pontiero's essay 'Clarice Lispector: An Intuitive Approach to Fiction', in *Knives and Angels: Women Writers in Latin America*, ed. Susan Bassnett (London and New Jersey: Zed Books Ltd., 1990), 74-85 (79-85).

24.   All references are to *El mismo mar de todos los veranos* (Barcelona: Lumen, 1979), 3rd edition. As far as I am aware there has been, to date, no book-length study of Tusquets's works. Important contributions are: Mary S. Vásquez, 'Tusquets, Fitzgerald and the Redemptive Power of Love', *Letras Femeninas*, 15:1-2 (1988), 10-21 (15). See also her article 'Image and Linear Progression Toward Defeat in Esther Tusquets' *El mismo mar de todos los veranos*', in *La Chispa '83: Selected Proceedings*, ed. Gilbert Paolini (Baton Rouge: Louisiana State University, 1983), 307-313. Mirella d'Ambrosio Servodidio 'Perverse Pairings and Corrupted Codes: *El amor es un juego solitario*', *Anales de la literatura española contemporánea*, 11:3 (1986), 237-254. See also her article 'A Case of Pre-Oedipal and Narrative Fixation: *El mismo mar de todos los veranos*', *Anales de la literatura española contemporánea*, 12:1-2 (1987), 157-174. Janet N. Gold, 'Reading the Love Myth: Tusquets with the Help of Barthes', *Hispanic Review*, 55 (1987), 337-346 (343). Catherine Bellver, 'The Language of Eroticism in the Novels of Esther Tusquets', *Anales de la literatura española contemporánea*, 9:1-3 (1984), 13-27. Robert C. Manteiga, 'El triunfo del Minotauro: ambigüedad y razón en *El mismo mar de todos los veranos* de Esther Tusquets', *Letras Femeninas*, XIV:1-2 (1988), 22-31. Gonzalo Navajas, 'Repetition and the Rhetoric of Love in Esther Tusquets' *El mismo mar de todos los veranos*', *Nuevos y novísimos: Algunas perspectivas críticas sobre la narrativa española desde la década de los 60*, edited by Ricardo Landeira and Luis T. González-del-Valle (Boulder, Colorado: Society for Spanish and Spanish-American Studies, 1987), 113-129. Geraldine Cleary Nichols, 'The Prison House (and Beyond): *El mismo mar de todos los veranos*', *Romantic Review*, 75 (1984), 366-385 (379).

25.   See Monique Wittig, *Le Corps lesbien* (Paris: Minuit, 1973). For a discussion of the difference between the theories of Cixous and Wittig, see Dianne Griffin Crowder, 'Amazons and Mothers? Monique Wittig, Hélène Cixous and Theories of Women's Writing', *Contemporary Writing*, 24:2 (Summer 1983), 117-144.

26.   *El mismo mar de todos los veranos* is indeed notable for its absence of men; there are a few negative references to Elia's husband Julio, a few scenes recalling Elia's father (and notably the scene when he bought his wife a basket of roses; 173-176), but these pale into insignificance when compared with the preponderance of references to Elia's daughter, mother, grandmother and lover. The world of Tusquets's fiction is not only dominated in a physical sense by women, but the language of men is by the same token banished from that world.

THE SEXUAL REPRESENTATION OF POLITICS
IN CONTEMPORARY HISPANIC FEMINIST NARRATIVE

Catherine Davies

In a much disputed 1986 article Frederic Jameson states categorically that 'all third-world texts are necessarily allegorical' and are to be read as national allegories. These texts, he suggests, redress the radical split - the result of capitalist reification - between the private and the public, between individual libidinal experience and collective socio-political experience so that 'the private individual destiny is always an allegory of the embattled situation of the public third-world culture and society'. An individual's story involves, 'overtly and consciously', that of the collectivity. He illustrates his argument with a political allegory which is *almost* overt and conscious belonging to a not-quite-third-world nineteenth-century Spain: *Fortunata y Jacinta*. Here Juanito Santa Cruz is seen as the Spanish nation-state incarnate, torn between Fortunata (read 1868 Revolution) and Jacinta (1873 Restoration).[1] It could be argued that Fortunata also stands for the nation-'pueblo' let down by a worthless bourgeoisie, as similarly Ana Ozores of *La Regenta* - the nation torn between the Church (de Pas) and middle-class corruption (Mesía), or Amparo of *Tormento* - the nation torn between the Church (Polo), middle-class corruption (los Bringas) and the salutary influence of the colonies (Agustín). In these novels, woman is equated with the maleable, potentially dangerous and irrational forces of the 'madre patria'/'pueblo' shaped by man. Jameson's point is that the realist novels of the Spanish 'periphery' can be read as personal *or* collective dramas and so tend to confirm the public/private fissure rather than dissolve it. But he seems to do little more than restate one of the most characteristic tropes of the European realist novel: namely 'the double inscription of sexual and social difference' explained by Cora Kaplan as the point at which 'female sexuality became the displaced and condensed site for the general anxiety about individual behaviour' provoked by republican and liberal political philosophy.[2]

Replying to Jameson's article, Aijaz Ahmad raises a further objection; the article is itself an obtrusively 'gendered' text, 'For it is inconceivable to me that this text could have been written by a ... woman without some considerable statement ... of the fact that the bifurcation of the public and the private, and the necessity to re-constitute that relation where it has been broken, which is so central to Jameson's discussion of the opposition between first-world and third-world cultural practices, is indeed a major preoccupation of ... women writers today on both sides of the Atlantic'.[3] This would seem a valid point of departure; by no means to disregard Jameson's useful notion of political allegory - expounded at length in *The Political Unconscious* - but to appropriate it in a consideration of women's contemporary fiction in an arguably Hispanic third-world.[4]

The texts studied are indeed national allegories but predicated by women writers on *women's* personal dramas. They are: *La hora violeta* (1980) by the Catalan Montserrat Roig (b. 1946) and the novella 'Cuarta versión' (1982) by the Argentinian Luisa Valenzuela (b. 1938). I shall also refer briefly to the latter's short story 'Cambio de armas' from the collection of the same name, to the Spanish novelist Rosa Montero's (b. 1951) *Crónica del desamor* (1979) and to the Chilean Isabel Allende's (b. 1942) *De amor y de sombra* (1982). All the authors are or have been journalists and have made statements regarding their varying degrees of feminist and political commitment.[5] In these fictions, the experiences of the female protagonists and their intimate relationships with men tell the reader something about the immediate political situation and crises of the countries in which the stories are set (Spain, Argentina and Chile). But at the same time the personal dramas function as allegories of the inner workings of patriarchy and of gender conflict expressed from a feminist point of view. The split between the personal and the political will indeed be challenged, if not dissolved, on these two fronts (the feminine and the quasi-third-world) which both lie outwith and yet are essential to patriarchal first-world formations.

In these narratives (unlike the nineteenth-century ones mentioned earlier) woman represents herself. The texts deal with women for whom self-awareness becomes concomitant with political-awareness as they contend with authoritarianism or re-position themselves with regards to left-wing politics at moments of acute national crisis: in Spain the difficult transition period following Franco's death (1975-79), in Argentina the regime of the military Junta (1976-1983) and in Chile the years of repression following Pinochet's coup of 1973.[6] The stories are told in the third-person or in free indirect style but can be considered semi-autobiographical, particularly when substantiated by comments given by the authors in interviews.[7] The semi-autobiographical lends itself to 'desdoblamiento' - a technique especially appropriate to the 'novela de concienciación', and this is found particularly in the Roig and Valenzuela texts (less so in Montero's) which are more effective because of the complex metafictional involvement of the author.[8]

La hora violeta, set in Spain in 1979 shortly after Suárez's victory in the first general elections within the new constitution (although these are never mentioned) is an allegory tracing the 'desencanto' and disarray amongst the Left - the former Franco opposition - after the legalization of the Communist Party in 1977. Without the monolithic dictatorship, the Party loses its oppositional identity in the remapping of the political scenario and re-grouping of power blocks. Spain is 'un país enfermo, neurótico, que nunca acaba de constituirse' in which, says one of the characters, 'el clima somos nosostros' (19).[9] At this level the novel reopens for debate the binary individual/society and the interaction of personal and collective freedom, the key issue being 'cómo podemos hacer compatibles el amor a la humanidad y el amor a las personas' (191).

But the individuals who ask this leading question are women, situated outside the boundaries of power, and through them the novel represents not only shifts from authoritarianism to liberalism in Spain but a serious challenge to the fundamental tenets of patriarchal ideology itself. The two protagonists, Norma the writer and Natàlia the photographer, both members of the PCE, are clearly constructs of a divided authorial self. Disillusioned in love, they subject their sexual relationships to thorough scrutiny (Norma is about to separate from her husband and Natàlia to end an affair with a married man) and in so doing undergo a process of self-awareness. As they realize the profound contradictions in their partners' behaviour and outlook (both men are Communists of the 'vieja guardia' whose self-sacrifice for the Cause does not begin at home) Norma and Natàlia relinquish their political commitment to Marxism, social realism in their work and the precise and reasonable language of the hegemonic voice; they drop the masks donned for a collective enterprise and turn their attention to their own fragmented female subjectivity. Yet this is by no means a clear-cut conflict between Marxism and Feminism. Having abandoned one form of liberation discourse, and unable to revert to traditional roles, the two women find themselves in limbo as the feminist strategy, unable to account for heterosexual desire or animosity among women, proves insufficient. Their most urgent conundrum is how to dissolve the boundaries between the public and the private, the patriarchal exterior and the feminine interior, 'la lucha por convertir en uno solo el amor colectivo y el amor individual' (267). How can the freedom of individual women and their loving, sexual relationships with men relate to the perfect society?

The novel suggests that democracy, a new 'pluralism of subjects', needs to be reinvented and that the basis of this Utopian project of wish-fulfilment is, in the final instance, the female body.[10] In this way the contemporary feminist view that 'Gender is obviously a division of power ..., and the female body the locus of power politics' complements what has been described as 'a perspective in which the imagery of libidinal revolution and of bodily transfiguration once again becomes a figure for the collective community, the unity of the body must once again prefigure the renewed organic identity of associative or collective life'.[11] Yet women, says Norma, are 'perdidas en miles de partículas, hechas a través de los hombres, repartidas entre los genios, ¿qué queda de nosotras?' (18). For them the powerlessness resulting from the outer effects of social oppression and the inner of sexual repression are one and the same thing. This is what Norma's strange dream indicates. In it she caresses another woman on a beach and a dead Franco rises from the

waves to admonish her: 'El dictador nos prohibía que hiciésemos el amor ...
Franco está dentro de mí ... Surge cuando menos lo espero, está al acecho
como una fiera, a punto de saltar sobre mí ... pero no tiene rostro. El dictador
ya no tiene nombre ...' (106): Franco represents phallocentrism, ubiquitous in
time and space, to which Norma is submitted over and above her immediate
political situation. No immediate solutions are envisaged in the novel. The
women sense, as Jon Cook argues in another context, that liberating sex is
merely the 'bad faith' of a radicalism unable to achieve its social and political
objectives.[12] They consider love between heterosexual women as a possible
direction; hence Norma's laborious reconstruction from diary notes of
Natàlia's mother's loving relationship with her friend Kati during the Civil
War, 'ellas creyeron que podían engañar el destino de su sexo. ¿No es toda
una esperanza?' (18); this diachronic 'desdoblamiento' through generations
forms the axis of the novel and affords an example of women's reconstruction
of history, to save everything left out, condemned or idealized by men (17).

It is the break with the PCE, 'Dios, el Padre', which is indicative of a
continuing project. The Party, once the 'gran útero dentro de la
clandestinidad' (55) has now moved into the open world of the word and so is
of no use for women. Like Germinal (the Communist who destroys himself
rather than compromise), women prefer not to 'crecer' (191) but remain in
the world of desire, feelings and dreams. They should 'grow up' but have yet
to find their language. 'Convivencia', then, at home and in society is mere
compromise. But while men continue to express power through heterosexual
relationships, an offshoot of their 'necesidad física marxista' (15), and women
continue to join the common enterprise 'por la vagina' (64) ending up
fragmented, true communication between men and women - in bed and in the
world - would seem to be, at best, only through mutual self-destruction. The
one overriding conviction to which the author returns repeatedly, and which is
best illustrated in the final scenes when the down-trodden Agnès asserts her
independence, is that self-exploration, self-representation and a breaking out
of the male paradigm constitute a first crucial step for women restructuring
their bodies, their desires and society from scratch despite the 'terror a
encontrarse vacía' (251). As Natàlia tells Norma, 'Sólo cuando te hayas

sabido mirar a ti misma aprenderás a mirar lo que te rodea. Tal vez entonces sabrás amar a la humanidad y a las personas al mismo tiempo' (252).

Rosa Montero's novel is less optimistic. Set in the same 'supuesta democracia' (42) of the late seventies, it is an accumulation of negatives, mapping the profound 'desgana' and inertia experienced in Spain by the Left in general and its women in particular after 1975.[13] One of the female characters when breaking-up with her boyfriend feels 'el mismo agotamiento de cuando abandonó el PCE' (62). Political and sexual ideals are razed to the ground while sexual relations, whether they be homosexual, traditional or casual bring no pleasure because political and sexual liberation within existing structures lead nowhere. Ana, the protagonist, explicitly rejects Wilhelm Reich; 'hemos mitificado el orgasmo que nos esclaviza a todos' (241) and cultivates a fantasy of romantic love with her boss who also proves to be no more than another grey mediocrity. Again, as a priority women must redefine and reconstruct themselves and, above all, their own sexuality in order to avoid the 'sexualidad machista que esclaviza hoy a hombres y mujeres' (243).

If (frustrated) desire is the informing principle in *La hora violeta* and *Crónica del desamor*, in 'Cuarta versión' it is fear. In this story, set in a menacing Buenos Aires some months after Videla's coup of March 1976, the actress Bella allows herself to become ensnared in a sexual relationship with a foreign ambassador which leads to her death. Again the metafictional mode and 'desdoblamiento' suggest semi-autobiographical content, substantiated by Valenzuela's own comments in 1982.[14] Her personal political involvement, she says, is 'bastante explícita' in the collection *Cambio de armas*; hence the censorship problems she encountered (both governmental and self-imposed) with regard to its writing and publication. 'Cuarta versión' is once more a national allegory: Bella is equated with a tragic Argentina on a number of occasions: 'Este país es Bella rodeada de mucha gente' (55) says Pedro the Ambassador, and she is shot by the military storming the Embassy.[15] At this level, Pedro might represent foreign interests which, under the guise of protection, lure Argentina to catastrophe. But the text's structure is more complex. As Sharon Magnarelli points out, the erotic story pieced together from Bella's dispersed papers for the fourth time is itself a clear metaphor for a subtext which is highly political but incomplete - Bella's involvement with and the plight of political refugees. In the words of the author/narrator: 'Lo que más me preocupa de esta historia es aquello que se está escamoteando, lo que no logra ser narrado. Lo escamoteado no es el sexo, no es el deseo ... Aquí se trata de algo que hierve con vida propia ... Los asilados políticos' (21). Attention is focused on Bella's role as political activist (precisely because it is silenced), particularly on the resulting developing insight of herself, her sexual relationship and the immediate political context. From a position of indifference, '¿Qué tengo que ver yo con la política?' (8) and lack of self-awareness, 'cabeza de pizarra por dentro y de cobre relumbrante por fuera' (14) Bella becomes enmeshed in a situation which destroys her, and the catalyst in this sea-change is Pedro. Through him the story reveals the insidious workings of power which complement the more obvious indictment of military repression.

Pedro's 'sutil red de encantamiento' (26) is his sexual attraction made all the more allusive by his confessions and constant word-play with Bella. These 'pantallas verbales' (34), a form of verbal exclusion experienced only by Bella, delude her. So when she enters the Embassy, the 'puertas del infierno' (12), she is beset by fear not of the political dangers but of the personal involvement this entails. Half way through the story, when the political situation turns critical, Bella responds by going to bed with Pedro, 'Pero no pudo despedirse. Pedro la fue gradualmente envolviendo en sus palabras' (30). The protection he affords her is highly ambiguous; like the military protection of the Embassy, and the Regime's protection of family values it is a mere facade for aggression. Bella, then, is threatened from outside and from within, from the world of the public and her own desires created by man. 'Esta parece ser la historia de lo que no se dice' (22) says the narrator, referring not only to the political subtext but to the feminist one: woman's oppression and eventual destruction by man. It is no surprise that Bella should dress up as Caesar and reproach Pedro (Brutus) for killing her, albeit 'dulcemente' (41); that as she makes love with him she should feel suffocated, inarticulate, dissatisfied, or that she should sense that the 'arenas movedizas' which surround her 'me atrapan. Me abrazan' (47). There is no asylum. In the story it is unnamed, hence unspecific, and stands for patriarchal collusion with violent oppression.

The outcome of the short story 'Cambio de armas', again an allegory of the military violation of Argentina, is more positive from a feminist point of view. The 'concienciación' of the protagonist involves simultaneously a reconstruction of her self (recovering from amnesia), awareness of her lover the General 'sinnombre' (representing violent patriarchal abuse) and cognizance of the immediate political situation.[16] A re-encounter with her subjectivity is gained through feelings or images (not words) released during the sexual act which is seen as the expression of power, pain, torture and female submission. These, say the General, are his weapons. The girl's weapons are her body and her subconscious ('el pozo') which, resisting and reconstructed like a rifle-sight, are turned against the abuser when least he expects it, so accomplishing her original mission as a political activist.

What these narratives are denying is Jameson's view that the priority of sexual oppression over social class is a false problem. However, they do seem to concur with his view that the radical feminist project 'is perfectly consistent with an *expanded* [mine] Marxian framework' insofar as the transformation of late capitalism, associated with 'recent political kinds of repression', must be accompanied by the annulment of the archaic, patriarchal structures of alienation which it subsumes.[17] Masculinist ideology and capitalism are interdependent as far as women are concerned.[18] But a prior, fundamental step is the one indicated by these semi-fictions: a redefining of gender identity and the reconstruction of female subjectivity and desires by women.

Allende's *De amor y de sombra* is somewhat different. Despite being the narrative with the clearest political content, the most detailed descriptions of the horrors of military repression, underground resistance and social inequality, it is the least harrowing. This is mainly to do with Allende's treatment of the heroine Irene Beltrán, a middle-class journalist who becomes politically involved through her work and through a sexual relationship with Francisco Leal, the son of Spanish Civil War exiles; Irene 'no pudo resistir la tentación del abismo' (128) of both personal and political commitment.[19] She and Francisco realize that they have 'iniciado una inexorable travesía' (192), that they have crossed 'una frontera invisible y entrado en una nueva y terrible dimensión' (195) in their newly acquired consciousness of themselves and of their society. Political awareness certainly leads Irene to question received opinions, the traditional role of women and her relationship with an army captain, but not her self as a unified female subject. She does not challenge the patriarchal ideology with which she complies and which forms her identity. More importantly, the third-person traditional narrative frustrates insight into the psychological and impedes a consideration of Irene as 'sujet en procès'. Hence the novel borders on sentimental mass-market romance. Irene - her lover's ideal woman, constructed from childhood readings and adolescent dreams - overcomes her difficult circumstances with help from two men and a homosexual, solves the riddle of the 'desaparecida' Evangelina's death, fulfills her desires and finds happiness in true love - albeit in exile. All the main characters are heroes; even the implausible captain who sacrifices himself for her. Love and freedom conquer the shadows of repression and violence. Family organization, exemplified by the Leals, not only remains intact (contrary to the other novels discussed here) but becomes the kernel of mutual support.[20] Yet Allende states, 'el golpe militar partió mi vida como un hachazo' and that she wrote the novel to exorcize from her mind the newspaper report of the horrific finds in the Longuén mines in 1978.[21] It is true that a very self-possessed Irene brings about the reconciliation between the radical political activist and the army captain. Optimism and political realism are commonly recognized as characteristic of the post-Boom novel attempting social criticism through mass-market strategies. Perhaps, then, this is how the novel should be read: as a fantasy of Utopia, an imaginary resolution, brought about by a mythically unified female self.[22]

116

NOTES

1. Frederic Jameson, 'Third-World Literature in the Era of Multinational Capitalism', *Social Text*, 15 (1986), 65-88. By allegory he means a fluctuating series of equivalences and by third-world, all that is neither capitalist first-world nor socialist bloc. In this article Jameson refers to Latin Amerca as a 'special case' within the Third World. I consider the Spain of the 'transición' similarly quasi-third world. See Jean Franco's guarded comments on Jameson's article in *Plotting Women. Gender and Representation in Mexico*, (New York: Columbia U.P., 1989), 221-222. With regard to anthropological deconstructions of the arbitrary dichotomy domestic/public (as well of the equally pernicious Western construct of selfhood) see Henrietta L. Moore, *Feminism and Anthropology*, (Cambridge: Policy Press, 1988), 21-30.

2. Cora Kaplan, 'Pandora's box: subjectivity, class, sexuality in socialist feminist criticism' in *Making a Difference. Feminist Literary Criticism*, edited by Gayle Greene and Coppelia Kahn, (London: Methuen, 1985), 146-76, 165-66. Of course, nineteenth-century writers were fully aware of the technique they were using. Galdós writes in the prologue to the third edition of *La Regenta* (1901), 'En ella [Ana Ozores] se personifican los desvaríos a que conduce el aburrimiento de la vida en una sociedad que no ha sabido vigorizar el espíritu de la mujer ... el problema de Doña Ana ... no es otro que discernir si debe perderse por lo clerical o por lo laico. El modo y el estilo de esta perdición constituyen la obra, de un sutil parentesco simbólico con la historia de nuestra raza', *Obras Completas*, vol. VI (Madrid: Aguilar, 1951), 1450.

3. Aijaz Ahmad, 'Jameson's rhetoric of Otherness and the National Allegory', *Social Text*, 17 (1987), 3-25, 24.

4. Frederic Jameson, *The Political Unconscious. Narrative as a Socially Symbolic Act*, (London: Methuen, 1986). See Catharine A. Mackinnon, 'Feminism, Marxism, Method and the State: An Agenda for Theory' in *Feminist Theory. A Critique of Ideology*, edited by Nanerl O. Keohane, Michelle Z. Rosaldo, *et al* (Brighton: Harvester, 1982), 1-30; 'To say that the personal is political means that gender as a division of power is discoverable and verifiable through women's intimate experience of sexual objectification, which is definitive of and synonymous with women's lives as gender female', 21.

5. I take feminism as questioning how women are inserted into the social context. See the interviews given by Allende and Valenzuela in Magdalena García Prieto, *Historias íntimas. Conversaciones con diez escritoras latinoamericanas*, (Hanover: Ediciones del Norte, 1988), 1-26 and 215-50 respectively. See Montserrat Roig, *Mujeres en busca de un nuevo humanismo*, (Barcelona: Salvat, 1981) and the interview she gives in Geraldine C. Nichols, *Escribir, espacio propio: Laforet, Matute, Moix, Tusquets, Riera y Roig por sí mismas*, (Minneapolis, Institute for the Study of Ideologies and Literature, 1989), 147-85. Also, Miguel

Bayón, 'Mujeres escritoras: la mirada que va desde el rincón', *Cambio 16*, 24 de noviembre 1986, 149-52.

6. See María del Carmen Feijoo, 'The Challenge of Constructing Civilian Peace: Women and Democracy in Argentina' and Patricia M. Chuchryk, 'Feminist Anti-Authoritarian Politics: The Role of Women's Organizations in the Chilean Transition to Democracy' in Jane S. Blanquette, *The Women's Movement in Latin America. Feminism and the Transition to Democracy*, (London: Unwin Hyman, 1989), 72-94 and 149-84 respectively. Also, Jo Fisher, *Mothers of the Disappeared*, (London: Zed, 1989); Francine Masiello, 'Cuerpo/presencia: Mujer y estado social en la narrativa argentina durante el proceso militar', *Nuevo Texto Crítico*, 2 (1989), 155-171; M. A. Durán and M. T. Gallego, 'The women's movement in Spain and the new Spanish democracy' in *The New Woman's Movement. Feminism and Political Power in Europe and the USA*, edited by D. Dahlerup (London: Sage, 1986) and Concha Borreguero, Elena Catena et al, *La mujer española: de la tradición a la modernidad (1960-1980)*, (Madrid: Tecnos, 1986); Phyllis Zatlin, 'Women novelists in Democratic Spain: Freedom to Express the Female Perspective', *ALEC*, 12 (1987), 29-44.

7. *Historias íntimas*, op. cit., 15-16, 18, 233 and *Escribir, espacio propio*, op. cit., 157-158.

8. A lengthy study of 'desdoblamiento' in feminine narrative is found in Birute Ciplijauskaité, *La novela femenina contemporánea (1970-1985): Hacia una tipología de la narración en primera persona*, (Barcelona: Anthropos, 1988), 73-81. See also, Concha Alborg, 'Metaficción y feminismo en Rosa Montero', *Revista de Estudios Hispánicos*, 22, 1, (1988), 67-76.

9. All references are to the Castilian translation of the Catalan original, *La hora violeta*, (Barcelona: Argos-Vergara, 1980). For an interesting discussion of eroticism in the contemporary Spanish novel, made possible by the removal of censorship, see Marta E. Altisent, 'El erotismo en la actual narrativa española', *Cuadernos Hispanoamericanos*, 468 (1989), 128-144.

10. The term 'pluralism of subjects' is borrowed from Chantal Mouffe, 'Hegemony and New Political Subjects: Towards a New Concept of Democracy' in *Marxism and the Interpretation of Culture*, edited by Cary Nelson and Lawrence Grossberg (Chicago: Illinois U.P., 1988) 89-104, 100.

11. Linda Hutcheon, *The Politics of Postmodernism*, (London: Routledge, 1989), 154. The female body and female desire cannot escape representation within patriarchal categories, now challenged by feminists (142). The second quote is from *The Political Unconscious*, op. cit., 74.

12. Jon Cook, 'Notes on History, Politics and Sexuality' in *The Left and the Erotic*, edited by Eileen Phillips, (London: Lawrence and Wishart,

1983) 83-112, 110; sexuality becomes a 'surrogate for political practice' ... 'The consequent political paralysis can be compensated for by replaying the archaic goals of Marxism in a semi-private and narcissistic world of the body and its desires'.

13. All references are to *Crónica del desamor*, (Madrid: Editorial Debate, 1979). See Eunice D. Myers, 'The Feminist Message: Propaganda and/or Art? A Study of Two Novels by Rosa Montero' in *Feminine Concerns in Contemporary Spanish Fiction by Women*, edited by Roberto C. Manteiga *et al* (Potomac: Scripta Humanistica, 1988), 99-112.

14. *Historias íntimas*, op. cit., 232-234 and the interview she gave in 1981 included in Sharon Magnarelli, *Reflections/Refractions. Reading Luisa Valenzuela*, (New York: Peter Lang, 1988) 203-236, which deals with censorship.

15. All references are to *Cambio de armas*, (Hanover: Ediciones del Norte, 1987).

16. *Cambio de armas*, op. cit., 113-146.

17. *The Political Unconscious*, op. cit, 99-100, 'sexism and the patriarchal are to be grasped as the sedimentation and the virulent survival of forms of alienation specific to the oldest mode of production of human history, with its division of labour between men and women ...'. Jameson also writes of the 'archaic structures of alienation ... beneath the overlay of all the more recent and historically original types of alienation - such as political domination and commodity reification - which have become dominants of ... late capitalism' (100).

18. Gayle Greene and Coppelia Kahn, 'Feminist Scholarship and the Social Construction of Woman', in *Making a Difference*, op. cit., 1-36, 15.

19. All references are to *De amor y de sombra*, (Barcelona: Plaza y Janes, 1988).

20. For the important interrelation between structures of kinship and state structures, particularly for women, see Henrietta Moore, op. cit., 183-84.

21. *Historias íntimas*, op. cit., 7, 15-16.

22. See *Landmarks in Modern Latin American Fiction*, edited by Philip Swanson (London: Routledge, 1990), 242. As Catharine Mackinnon argues, objectivity or aperspectivity is the male epistemological stance (art. cit. 23-24). Equally Jameson points to the ability of free indirect style to mediate between the psychological and the social unlike the device of an omniscient narrator which implies narrative closure (the story has finished) and the representation of an 'ideological mirage', *The Political Unconscious*, op. cit., 154. Jean Franco, op. cit., 135-136

considers the use of popular romance in Mexican fiction by women both relevant and justified given women's identification with this genre in that culture.

THE DARK CONTINENT

ALFONSINA STORNI:
A FEMINIST READING OF HER POETRY

Evelyn Fishburn

Alfonsina Storni enjoys the well earned acclaim of being one of the first and foremost Latin-American feminist poets. Thus, Beatriz Sarlo places her at the head of a list of women 'que abrieron camino' to whom she dedicates her book *El imperio de los sentimientos* (next in line is Victoria Ocampo).[1] Similarly, Irene Matthews, in a recently published article on Gabriela Mistral, notes that Alfonsina Storni is included in most reviews of literary feminism in Latin America as among a handful of 'attractive standard bearers whose spite, charm and intelligence - differential and iconoclastic - undermine the masculine norm'.[2] Needless to say, this undermining of the masculine norm was not always seen in terms of approval, particularly by contemporary male critics; what is more, in many cases it was simply ignored, sanitized out of existence, and Storni's feminism presented in general terms of a woman writing about marginal women's preoccupations.[3] The point here being made is that whilst Storni's feminism has always been acknowledged, there exists to date no detailed study of the nature of her feminism. While such an exhaustive task would by far exceed the possibilities of the present study, I should like to take a step in that direction and offer a re-appraisal of some of Storni's poetry by focusing on different aspects of femininity in her poetic output.[4]

There is today a general agreement that Storni's poetry matured as it grew from the somewhat neat sentimental, neo-romantic verses of her youth to the more complex poems of her last two collections, *Mundo de siete pozos* (1934) and *Mascarilla y trébol* (1938), a critical position which is reflected in the title of Rachel Phillips's important mongraph *Alfonsina Storni: From Poetess to Poet*.[5] The overall validity of such criticism seems beyond dispute and I seek no quarrel with it; on the contrary, in looking at Storni's feminism, I too, can see a parallel maturing in her emancipation from the masculine norms of her society, and one which would seem to coincide with Elaine Showalter's perception of three main stages in the history of women's writing, namely, the feminine, the feminist and the female.[6] I propose to begin with the least controversial of these, Storni's last stage, corresponding to the female, in which she deals with themes such as sexuality, motherhood and sterility in verses which eschew formal and conceptual constraints. One or two examples must suffice: in 'Pie de árbol' (399 - see Appendix), birthgiving and sexual orgasm are seen in symbiotic relationship: oral sex, flagellation and penetration are deliberately confused with an image of birthgiving, erasing the traditional dichotomy of Mother/Whore.[7] The poem, like all in *Mascarilla y trébol*, is an anti-sonnet, a term coined by Storni to describe her invention of poems which have kept some of the formal characteristics of the sonnet such as fourteen endecasyllabic lines, but not the sonnet's rhyming pattern; similarly, it has kept some of the traditional imagery of sexuality, but none of the constraints of dominant patriarchal thought patterns. In other poems too, the female psyche is free to express its desire and anxiety through bodily images which cannot be categorised according to traditionally gendered attributes. *Tiempo de esterilidad* (396 - see Appendix), written soon before the poet's death, is a poem of endings, with sterility standing for death. It may be interesting to note the unveiled allusion to menstruation and menopause - until very recently taboo subjects - in this decidedly unsentimental view of procreation, where new-born babes are referred to as 'noúmenos fríos revelados/en tibias caras de espantados ojos'. The poem's final liberating sting, however, appears in the playful ambiguity of the last stanza:

Un día de su seno huyóse el río
y su isla verde *florecida* de hombres
quedó desierta y vio crecer el viento.

(emphasis added)

The final image, 'y vio crecer el viento', can be read as an image of annihilation and death or alternatively as a life-giving image, 'el viento' standing for the invigorating breath of presumably female self sufficiency. Such a reading problematises 'florecida de hombres': 'florecer' and all allied derivations are given positive meanings in María Moliner's *Usos del español actual* with explanations such as 'más aplicable a actividades estimables' and 'con referencia a cosas buenas' yet the word also evokes 'florear' and 'floreo' in which the adornment of the flowers passes from being esteemed to superfluous: 'superfluos, que se hacen o dicen sólo como adorno o para hacer alarde de ingenio o maestría', an association which opens up the anti-sonnet to an anti-reading of sterility as a means of transcending oppositional sexuality and a freeing of self with the invigorating wind of liberation. This reading is supported by the upbeat ending of *y vio crecer el viento*. The demythifying image of creation quoted above ('noúmenos fríos revelados/en tibias caras de espantados ojos') allows for a view of Woman no longer confined to her use in procreation but as occupying a central position in a universe transcending sexuality.[8]

Turning now to the 'feminist' aspect of her poetry, Storni presents an ironic when not aggressive picture of man almost throughout her work, hesitantly at first, but increasing in the forthrightness of her attack. She is perhaps best remembered as a feminist for this aspect of her work with poems such as 'Tú me quieres blanca' (120) and 'Hombre pequeñito' (165) finding their way into most anthologies, the first as an example of Storni's rebellion against traditional patriarchal expectations of women and the second as a frontal attack on the mythification of male superiority both in terms of size - 'hombre pequeñito' is surely considered a contradiction in terms within patriarchal discourse - and understanding - 'no me entiendes ni me entenderás'. The collection *Ocre* (1925) abounds in poems in which man is ironised and ousted from a dominant position. One such example is 'Saludo al hombre' (290), where man is first hailed as superior being - 'Con mayúscula escribo tu nombre y te saludo' - a myth from which he is mockingly liberated (Desligado) after having been likened to a suckling babe - 'Mas, no con gesto humilde, instintivo, anhelante,/Tu pecho se deforma en boca del lactante'. In 'Divertidas estancias a Don Juan' (291), Tirso's hero is addressed patronisingly as 'noctámbulo mochuelo' and advised to continue in his eternal sleep, for were he to wake he would find not only his sadistic seduction strategies unsuccessful ('Hoy tu castigante mano/no hallaría fortuna') but most probably replaced by a mirror image: that of a female Don Juan:

> Y hasta hoy alguna artera
> Juguetona mujer,
> Que toma tu manera
> Y ensaya tu poder.

The poem is representative of 'hembrismo', one of the consequences of feminist aggressive self-assertiveness, that is, replacing an aggressive male stereotype with a similar female one.[9] More tender, and more devastating, is Storni's demythification of one of the most unassailable bastions of Latin-American, and perhaps universal machismo, namely, the Navy. In Buque-Escuela (317) the unqualified title leads to expectations of hardiness, bravery and a-girl-in-every-port machismo; instead, the poem subverts such expectations as it subverts conventional verse forms. Using varied metre, irregular stanzas, free verse and stark but unusual imagery, everything related to the Navy is either feminised or made vulnerable. Thus the sea is not tempestuous but 'el plumón blando/de las aguas.' The sailors are presented in contrasting images of manliness and vulnerability:

> Cuellos fornidos
> de cuerda
> prensada.
>
> Ojos tiernos.
>
> Dientes agudos,
> luminosos.
>
> Grandes bocas
> húmedas aún
> de besos maternos,
> abiertas
> pedigüeñas,
> como la de los pichones.

The poem ends with an image of enforced manliness, a haunting vision of how patriarchy has supressed human emotions in its standard bearers:

> ...Máscara de hierro
> sobre las caras...
> y nacía,
> hosca,
> la fila
> sin albedrío.

The 'feminist' phase of Storni's poetry does not focus only on demythologising the male, but also in appropriating for women the right to need, feel, and express their own sexuality. It is the phase, in Showalter's words, of protest and of advocacy of minority rights and values, including a demand for autonomy.[10] In a shocking inversion of roles, the female gaze is focused erotically upon an unknown man:

> Viaja en el tren en donde viajo. ¿Viene
> del Tigre, por ventura?
> Su carne firme tiene
> la moldura
> de los varones idos, y en su boca
> como prieto canal
> se le sofoca
> el bermejo caudal... (Uno, 348)[11]

This active demand for sexuality constitutes the theme of 'Femenina' (278), a poem which is of particular interest because it establishes a dialogue with a poem by Baudelaire, No XXXII from 'Les Fleurs du mal'. I have chosen 'Femenina', clearly not one of Storni's best poems and disadvantaged when placed next to Baudelaire's inspirational poem, to illustrate not only the achievements but also the limitations of Storni's feminism at this stage. Placing the two sonnets side by side (see Appendix), it is obvious from Storni's reductive paraphrase that the complex interplay between the two female representations in the French poem has either escaped her or failed to interest her, since only the 'affreuse juive' is recalled.[12] Storni's poem hinges upon a comparison and a contrast, each introduced by the word 'pero'. The comparison is daring: the female persona of Storni's poem is set against the male persona of Baudelaire's in that both have similar needs. A likeness is established between the two unsatisfactory sexual partners: both are cold, she being 'serpiente fría' and he 'gélido lago' and dangerous, she, 'en el daño genial'; he, 'oscuro de ambiciones'. But that is where the comparison in 'Femenina' ends; the rest is contrast. 'Femenina' betrays the strong phallocratism of society in Storni's time where men are essentialized in their sexuality, their emotional claims silenced and their physical needs seen as almost mandatorily satisfied by the sexual act: 'Hombre al cabo, lograbas un poco de placer.' This line is placed in direct contrast to the poet's own sexuality, claiming dependence for its fulfilment upon an emotional need: to be the recipient of an accompanying 'un poco de generosidad'. The point here being made is that in 'Femenina', a title that draws attention to the feminist aspects of Storni's poetry, two conflicting attitudes prevail: one, which sees the title as ironic in that the poem's voice clamours for a very unfeminine right to sexual satisfaction, and the other, in which the irony of the first is subverted or cancelled, because, finally, the poem's voice remains trapped in a neat binary opposition of traditional gender expectations.

In this backwards journey of Storni's poetry, we turn now to her first collection of poems, those which she herself all but repudiated and which earned her the critical stricture 'poetisa de mal gusto' from Beatriz Sarlo, not to argue in any way for the artistic merit of these works, this being in any case outside the scope of this study, but to focus once more upon different aspects of Storni's feminism.[13] As most critics have noted, Storni's earliest collection, written at the time when she established herself in defiant independence as a single parent, responsible for her own and her child's upkeep, surprises by its seeming abject conventionality in both aesthetic and thematic terms. Poems such as 'Resurgir', with its sugary plea for 'la casita con hiedras y un pedazo de cielo' or 'El Recuerdo', plaintive and indulgent, or the embarrassing self-abasement of 'Plegaria de la traición', every stanza repeating the motif of suffering and forgiveness of '¡Entra traidor! y vénceme, sofócame', belie the daring, emancipated lifestyle of their author. As Rachel Phillips points out, 'we are not mistaken in feeling that Storni's life and work are out of harmony certainly until 1925. She was a young woman leading a life consciously different from that prescribed for her sex, and yet she wrote as women had always written'.[14] Apart from these and other poems which quite rightly earn her the rebuke of 'poetess', there are a number of poems in which the rebelliousness of the later Storni can be detected, though this has seldom been the case.

The collection *El dulce daño* (1918) reflects in many ways the indulgent sweetness of its title: as Rachel Phillips has aptly observed, the poet here is annoying because she represents a helpless, passive, female awaiting life-giving arousal from a protective male lover.[15] 'Nocturno' (97) is a poem in paired verse which seems to epitomise the attitude described above. The couplets rhyme with regular, consonantal or rich rhymed monotony while they describe a stereotyped situation:

> Oh ven, que entre tus manos haré almohada,
> Para apoyar mi testa desolada.
>
> Te esperaré en nuestro banco
> Y por gustarte vestiré de blanco.

The poem continues to express a nostalgic death-wish and would not be worthy of further comment were it not for a dissonant note in the last few couplets,

> Y soy una y soy mil; todas las vidas
> Pasan por mí, me muerden sus heridas
>
> Y no puedo ya más; en cada gota,
> De mi sangre hay un grito y una nota.

This is the only example of enjambement in the poem, a touch of unconventionality matched by the content of the lines. At one level, these can be read as the tacit 'yo' symbolising the suffering of all women, but in the light of Storni's feminism another reading offers itself: one that sees the specular, phallocratic union between male and female represented by the closed couplets disrupted by the final enjambement as noted above and 'soy una y soy mil' interpreted as a defiant attestation of female polyeroticism. The claim I am making here is bold, but freed by Pierre Menard, the celebrated author of Don Quixote, to read in ever-renewed contexts, I propose to see in these lines a response to Helène Cixous's call for woman to 'write herself'.[16] In 'Soy una y soy mil' and in 'me muerden sus heridas' Storni can be seen to be 'dynamising the false theatre of phallocentric representation', allowing a true glimpse of 'a woman's body, with its *thousand and one thresholds* of ardor once, by smashing yokes and censors, she lets it articulate the profusion of meaning that runs through in every direction.[17]

In *Irremediablemente* (1919), the last of the early collections of poems, there is a section on 'Momentos humildes - amorosos pasionales', consisting mainly of poems about abject women adoring superior males. 'El hombre sereno' is a case in point: 'Entre los hombres pasa dadivoso y prudente/porque todo lo sabe.' From an artistic point of view it is perhaps one of Storni's weakest, with boring, predictable rhymes such as 'sereno'/'sirena', fully embodying the triviality of the content. But, bearing in mind the dilemma of how to reconcile the author's life-style with her poetry, a less conformist reading suggests itself: one which accords with Irigaray's strategies of subversion from the margins via laughter and parody and which would make visible in 'El hombre sereno' a strong caricature of prevalent gendered myths.[18] It would, of course, be ludicrous to claim that Storni's contemporaries were consciously roused to subversion by poems such as the one quoted above; what can be suggested is that, as Sarlo has pointed out in her analysis of porteño society at that time, in order to be accepted and reach a wide female audience Storni had to write within certain narrow constraints, but these did not prevent her from using humour in different forms to dis-establish accepted myths.[19] I do not think her contemporaries always understood this. The male critic Fernández Moreno only saw in these early poems the public's preference of 'aquel modo inicial "sobrecargado de mieles románticas"', a preference he seems to put into practice in his reading of 'Capricho' (87 - see Appendix).[20] This is a poem about a woman asking her lover to love her without worrying about her recent tears. Fernández Moreno, in accordance with his patriarchal expectations, foregrounds the penultimate stanza to prove Storni's acceptance of female weaknesses and as confirmation of women's intellectual inferiority:

> Así somos, ¿no es cierto? Ya lo dijo el poeta:
> Movilidad absurda de inconsciente coqueta
> Deseamos y gustamos la miel de cada copa
> Y en el cerebro habemos un poquito de estopa.

A less blinkered reading might have focussed not upon the second last but on the last stanza, the one that dis-establishes all that has come before in a surface reading of the poem, and picked up its underlying irony, noting the mocking note 'Oh, déjame que ría ...' with its final dismissive injunction: 'Espínate las manos y córtame esa rosa.'

I should like to end this exploration of re-readings of Storni's poetry, particularly her early poetry, as seen through the prism of theories on feminism with a reading of 'La que comprende' (232 - see Appendix) from *Languidez* (1920). This is a poem about a pregnant woman's plea to the Lord that her child should not be female: '¡Señor, el hijo mío que no nazca mujer!' It would appear not only to conform to but to be a willing acquiescence of patriarchal domination. Traditionally it has been understood as such, even by as insightful a feminist critic as Irene Matthews, who quoted it in contra-distinction to Gabriela Mistral's celebration of the special relationship between mothers and daughters. Matthews asserts that 'Storni's image is of a socialized fate, the child already trapped into a negative, subservient sexuality'.[21] And of course, such a reading is correct. The poem is structured upon a set of binary oppositions: there are two stanzas of four verses each which mirror each other in that the rhyming pattern of the first stanza is reversed in the second, ae/a/ae/a becoming ea/e/ea/e; the black-haired woman kneels in front of a white Christ figure and the oppositional and hierarchical division of gender is emphasized in the last line, where 'Señor' is counterbalanced not by 'Señora' but by 'mujer'. Yet within such a dominant patriarchal framework there are dis-establishing forces at play. A central disruption seems to take place, in that the 'Señor' constructed in this poem has certain telling qualities in common with the implied 'Yo' of the poem. 'La de mediana edad' can be seen as echoing Christ's age on the cross; her 'tristeza' is matched by his agony (agonizante); the power of patriarchy which seems to crush her is matched by the 'duro leño' which forms the backdrop to his suffering. The figures are further linked by an allusion to bleeding (sangrando): Christ's blood, redemptive of mankind, can be seen as a symbol of renewal and birthgiving, much as women's shed blood is linked to fertility and birth. Ultimately, there seems to be a transcending of the oppositional barriers between the kneeling woman and Christ. Who is 'La que comprende'? The two figures are not separate: it is she who understands the subservient position of women fused with a feminised Christ (that most female of men, in Luce Irigaray's words[22]), whose compassionate understanding transcends his power.

As in most of Storni's poetry, the dominant note in 'La que comprende' is Patriarchy and the poem returns, in true classical fashion, to the home key, but, to continue the musical metaphor, the development section is full of atonal disruptions, call them babbles or pulsations, which undermine the authority of the dominant mode.[23] The purpose of this study has been to make some of these pulsations audible.

APPENDIX

PIE DE ARBOL

No sé cuando...Por una arboladura
como ésta yo trepaba acelerando
y a cuatro manos descendía a tierra
la lengua alegre de jugosos frutos.

Y vi una caballada por el aire
de negra crin y a látigos de fuego
azuzar sus turbiones de tormenta
y yo chillé con voz no articulada.

Y huía; y con los otros, apretados
en un montón de bestias temerosas
nos detuvimos quietos y encogidos.

Y sacudió la tierra el paso rudo
de una mole animal que se metía
por un túnel abierto en la espesura.

TIEMPO DE ESTERILIDAD

A la Mujer los números miraron
y dejáronle un cofre en su regazo:
y vió salir de aquel un río rojo
que daba vuelta en espiral al mundo.

Extraños signos, casi indescifrables,
sombreaban sus riberas, y la luna
siniestramente dibujaba en ellos,
ordenaba los tiempos de marea.

Por sus crecidas Ella fue creadora
y los noúmenos fríos revelados
en tibias caras de espantados ojos.

Un día de su seno huyóse el río
y su isla verde florecida de hombres
quedó desierta y vio crecer el viento.

FEMENINA

Baudelaire: yo me acuerdo de tus Flores del mal
En que hablas de una horrible y perversa judía
Acaso como el cuerpo de las serpientes fría
en lágrimas indocta, y en el daño genial.

Pero a su lado no eras tan pobre, Baudelaire,
De sus formas vendidas, y de su cabellera
Y de sus ondulantes caricias de pantera,
Hombre al cabo, lograbas un poco de placer.

Pero yo, femenina, Baudelaire, ¿qué me hago
De este hombre calmo y prieto como un gélido lago,
Oscuro de ambiciones y ebrio de vanidad,

En cuyo enjuto pecho salino no han podido
Ni mi cálido aliento, ni mi beso rendido,
Hacer brotar un poco de generosidad?

LES FLEURES DU MAL (XXXII)

Une nuit que j'étais près d'une affreuse Juive,
Comme au long d'un cadavre un cadavre étendu,
Je me pris a songer près de ce corps vendu
A la triste beauté dont mon désir se prive.

Je me représentai sa majesté native,
Son regard de vigueur et de grâces armé,
Ses cheveux qui lui font un casque parfumé,
Et dont le souvenir pour l'armour me ravive.

Car j'eusse avec ferveur baisé ton noble corps,
Et depuis tes pieds frais jusqu' à tes noires tresses
Déroulé le trésor des profondes caresses,

Si, quelque soir, d'un pleur obtenu sans effort
Tu pouvais seulement, ô reine des cruelles!
Obscurcir la splendeur de tes froides prunelles.

CAPRICHO

Escrútame los ojos, sorpréndeme la boca,
Sujeta entre tus manos esta cabeza loca;
Dame a beber, el malvado veneno
Que te moja los labios a pesar de ser bueno.

Pero no me preguntes, no me preguntes nada
De por qué llorée tanto en la noche pasada;
Las mujeres lloramos sin saber, porque sí:
Es esto de los llantos pasaje baladí.

Bien se ve que tenemos adentro un mar oculto,
Un mar un poco torpe, ligeramente estulto,
Que se asoma a los ojos con bastante frecuencia
Y hasta lo manejamos con una dúctil ciencia.

No preguntes, amado, lo debes sospechar;
En la noche pasada no estaba quieto el mar.
Nada más. Tempestades que las trae y las lleva
Un viento que nos marca cada vez costa nueva.

Sí, vana mariposas sobre jardín de Enero,
Nuestro interior es todo sin equilibrio y huero.
Luz de cristalería, fruto de carnaval
Decorado en escamas de serpientes del mal.

Así somos, ¿ya lo dijo el poeta:
Movilidad absurda de inconsciente coqueta
Deseamos y gustamos la miel de cada copa
Y en el cerebro no habemos un poquito de estopa.

Bien, no me preguntes. Torpeza de mujer,
Capricho, amado mío, capricho debe ser.
Oh, déjame que ría ... ¿No ves qué tarde hermosa?
Espínate las manos y córtame esa rosa.

LE QUE COMPRENDE

Con la cabeza negra caída hacia adelante
Está la mujer bella, la de mediana edad,
Postrada de rodillas, y un Cristo agonizante
Desde su duro leño la mira con piedad.

En los ojos la carga de una enorme tristeza,
En el seno la carga del hijo por nacer,
Al pie del blanco Cristo que está sangrando reza:
—¡Señor, el hijo mío que no nazca mujer!

NOTES

1. Beatriz Sarlo, *El imperio de los sentimientos* (Buenos Aires: Catálogos, 1985). Also, Helena Percas, in *La poesía femenina argentina* (Madrid: Ediciones Cultura Hispánica, 1958) uses Storni as a yardstick, dividing the first part of her study into 'La poesía femenina anterior a Alfonsina Storni'; 'Alfonsina Storni y la generación del 16' and 'Poetisas contemporáneas de Alfonsina Storni'.

2. Irene Matthews, 'Woman as Myth: The "Case" of Gabriela Mistral', *Bulletin of Hispanic Studies* LXVII (1990), 57-69.

3. For a curious exception, see Enrique Anderson Imbert, who, writing on feminine literature in *El realismo mágico y otros ensayos* (Caracas: Monte Avila Editores, 1976) admires Storni's unique understanding of 'las problemáticas relaciones de la mujer con el hombre' (169). Interestingly, whilst Anderson expects conventional feminine behaviour and cannot accept Storni's lack of soft, passive qualities as a person (No me impresionó como mujer ... Me pareció áspera, chabacana, mordaz.'), he praises her as a poet for precisely those independent aspects of her poetry which showed a female subtlety and sensitivity which owed nothing to the dominant male poetic imagination (174; Anderson's comments, however, are brief, anecdotal and unsubstantiated). The most exaggerated misogynist commentary is quoted, albeit disapprovingly, by C. A. Andreola, in *Alfonsina Storni: vida talento, soledad* (Buenos Aires: Plus Ultra, 1976) 208-209: '"*Mundo de siete pozos*" es un poco concupiscente. Un poco también fue (ella) siempre...horroriza un tanto, que personas crecidas y algo níveas ya, se pongan a decir de un hombre, con evidente mal gusto: "Nunca lo vi en traje de baño" [reference to 'Balada arrítmica para un viajero' in Alfonsina Storni, *Obra poética completa* (Buenos Aires: Sociedad Editora Latino Americana, 1964) 341-344, hereafter cited in text with page number]. Eso es turbia delectación, pornografía pura, y más todavía se lo piensa cuando se lee el resto".' For a selection of contemporary criticism of Storni's poetry, consisting mostly of bland generalisations, see María Teresa Orosco, *Alfonsina Storni* (Buenos Aires: Imprenta de la Universidad, 1940) 253-274.

4. This point is acknowledged by Gwen Kirkpatrick, in 'Alfonsina Storni: "Aquel micromundo poético"', *MLN*, 99(2), (1984) 386-392; this excellent article examines subversive erotic imagery in Storni's later poetry.

5. Rachel Phillips, *Alfonsina Storni: From Poetess to Poet* (London: Támesis, 1975). See, too, Janice Geasler Titiev, 'The Poetry of Dying in Alfonsina Storni's Last Book', *Hispania* 68(3) (1985 Sept) 467-473 and G. Kirkpatrick, op. cit.; for the dissenting views of Augusto González Castro, Roberto Giusti and Manuel Ugarte see M. T. Orosco, op. cit. 268-271.

6. Elaine Showalter, *A Literature of Their Own* (London: Virago Press, 1978) 13. Showalter argues that these three major phases singled out in the history of women's writing are common to all literary subcultures; she makes the further point that the phases overlap and that, indeed, 'one may find all three phases in the career of a single novelist'.

7. The interplay between motherhood and sexuality has been discussed, among others, by Luce Irigaray in 'Ce sexe qui n'en est pas un', (Paris: Minuit, 1977) 23-32, reprinted in translation in *New French Feminism, An Anthology*, ed. Elaine Marks and Isabelle de Courtivron (New York: Harvester Press, 1981). See too Julia Kristeva's study of the Virgin Mother in 'Stabat Mater', *The Kristeva Reader*, ed. Toril Moi, (Oxford: OUP, 1986) 161-186.

8. For a wholly pessimistic reading of this poetry, see Tiniev, 471. For a more supportive position, see Kirkpatrick, 391-392.

9. The danger of simply reversing the existing order and replacing one phallocratism for another is mentioned by Irigaray, in *NFF*, 106.

10. Showalter, 13.

11. The irony and subversiveness of this seemingly playful poem can best be judged if considered in the light of Freud's theorization of the gaze as a phallic activity and Irigaray's critique of this theory. For a succinct resumé, see Toril Moi, *Sexual/Textual Politics* (London: Methuen, 1985) 134-136, 180n; for a fuller discussion, see Luce Irigaray, *Speculum of the other woman*, translated by Gillian C. Gill (Ithaca: Cornell University Press, 1985) 46-55.

12. The allusion in Baudelaire's sonnet is most probably to a prostitute called Sarah whom the poet knew before he had met Jeanne Duval. It is possible that it was composed at a time of separation from Jeanne Duval.

13. Beatriz Sarlo, *Una modernidad periférica: Buenos Aires 1920 y 1930* (Buenos Aires: Nueva Visión, 1988) 78. Sarlo's essay is the most intelligent social reading of Storni's feminism (pp. 78-85).

14. Phillips, 9.

15. Phillips, 32.

16. The allusion is to Jorge Luis Borges, 'Pierre Menard, autor del Quijote' in *Ficciones* (Buenos Aires: Emecé, 1956).

17. Helène Cixous, 'The Laugh of the Medusa' in *NFF*, 256.

136

18. Toril Moi, 35-41 and 140-143.

19. *Modernidad*, 84-85.

20. César Fernández Moreno, *Situación de Alfonsina Storni* (Santa Fe: Castellví, n.d.) 18. For a totally insensitive reading of this poem, see Lucrecio Pérez Blanco, *La poesía de Alfonsina Storni* (Madrid, 1975) 259.

21. Matthews, 65.

22. Irigaray, 'La Mystérique', in *Speculum*, 199.

23. Irigaray talks of a woman's babble as an alternative to patriarchal discourse and Kristeva uses pulsations as something that occurs in the pre-symbolic stage of the Semiotic.

DWARFED BY SNOW WHITE:
FEMINIST REVISIONS OF FAIRY TALE DISCOURSE
IN THE NARRATIVE OF
MARIA LUISA BOMBAL AND DULCE MARIA LOYNAZ

Verity Smith

> At some point, the Great Divide took place: they (the boys) dreamed of
> mounting the Great Steed and buying Snow White from the dwarfs; we (the
> girls) aspired to become that object of every necrophiliac's lust - the innocent,
> *victimized* Sleeping Beauty, beauteous lump of ultimate, sleeping good.

Andrea Dworkin, Woman Hating

Over the past few years both feminist critics and women writers have
turned their attention to the fairy tale as a source of imaginatively powerful
and influential cultural myths. Since the publication of Perrault's collection in
1697, these stories have been used to inculcate a set of values into the young
which includes correct behaviour for both genders.[1] These patriarchal values
are turned upside down by Angela Carter in her collection of short stories,
The Bloody Chamber (1979). She rewrites the end of 'Bluebeard' so that it is
the mother rather than the brothers of the heroine who comes to the latter's
rescue, while her version of 'Little Red Riding Hood' takes a very positive
view of sexual love, being quite at odds therefore with the classic fairy tale
which threatens the young girl who strays from the path with devoural. In the
context of contemporary Spanish American fiction, it is probably Luisa
Valenzuela who comes to mind as a revisionist of fairy tale discourse,

particularly in her story 'Cuarta versión', which weaves Sleeping Beauty into its account of Bella's political awakening. But two earlier writers, María Luisa Bombal and Dulce María Loynaz, began this process of critical revision in the 1930s. It is intended here to examine Loynaz's novel *Jardín* and two stories by Bombal, 'Las islas nuevas' and 'La historia de María Griselda', in terms of their contribution to this debate.

1. *JARDIN*

I shall begin with Dulce María Loynaz's experimental novel, *Jardín*, written between 1928 and 1933, but only published in 1951. My reason for giving her pride of place is that, although her excellence as a poet is widely recognised in the Spanish-speaking world,[2] next to nothing is known about her works in prose. I was fortunate in coming across a reference to it in Cintio Vitier's study, *Lo cubano en la poesía* where there is a footnote that reads as follows:

> Dulce María Loynaz merece un estudio aparte. Su poesía en verso y prosa, y sobre todo su importante novela lírica *Jardín*, donde el tema de la mujer y naturaleza (no abierta y telúrica como en *María*, sino alucinante y encerrada entre los muros de la criolla quinta) alcanza una dimensión romántica y religiosa de primera magnitud, tendrán que ser cuidadosamente valoradas.[3]

Intrigued, I tracked down a copy of the novel in the British Library and then on my next trip to Cuba prevailed on a friend to introduce me to her. She was born in 1903 and is now something of a fairy tale figure herself, living in a large, shabby house filled with the heirlooms of her patrician family. (Her father, General Loynaz, whose memoirs Dulce María compiled, fought against the Spanish in Cuba's second War of Independence.[4]) The author received me very cordially on two occasions and I soon gathered that she remains a very committed feminist. She told me among other things that she would have liked to have written a biography of Eva Perón, something which might surprise those who view her as socially aloof. She also told me that the reason for the long delay in publishing *Jardín*, as is the case also with her poetry, is that she lacked self-confidence. It was her second husband, a journalist who wrote a social column for a Havana newspaper, who prevailed on her to approach Aguilar with a view to publishing her work. Closer to the present, a skimpy and poorly edited anthology of her poetry has appeared in Cuba and right now, as though to make amends for earlier neglect and casualness, a scholarly edition of her poetry is being prepared by the poet César López for publication by Casa de Las Américas.

In many ways *Jardín* fits into the pattern of narratives by women discussed by Annis Pratt in her study of 1982, *Archetypal Patterns in Women's Fiction*. This is partly because it comes into the category of a failed *Bildungsroman*, which for Pratt is a characteristic of narratives by women about female, personal growth:

> In the woman's novel of personal development...the hero does not *choose* a life to one side of society after conscious deliberation on the subject; rather, she is radically alienated by gender-role norms *from the very outset*. Thus, although the authors attempt to accommodate their heroes' *Bildung*, or development, to the general pattern of the genre, the disjunctions that we have noted inevitably make the woman's initiation less a self-determined progression *towards* maturity than a regression *from* full participation in adult life.[5]

Other characteristics which *Jardín* shares with the novels discussed by Annis Pratt are, firstly, what she terms 'alienation from normal concepts of time and space' (11), something she views as inevitable in the case of fiction by persons on the margins of day to day life; secondly, the crucial importance in *Jardín* of what Annis Pratt terms 'the green world model', a place from which the woman hero sets forth and a memory to which she returns for renewal. However, *Jardín* departs from this model to the extent that the midlife rebirth journey described in the last section of the novel is given an apocalyptic end.[6] It is not part of Annis Pratt's intention to study fairy tale discourse from a feminist perspective, but in the case of both Dulce María and María Luisa Bombal, the critique of the fairy tale relates closely to the whole question of 'a woman's place' being in the green world.

At this point it would be useful to provide a summary of the events in *Jardín*, something which, in any case, can be kept very brief granted the archetypal nature of the novel.[7] Its protagonist is a child called Bárbara who is in search of her identity. A mirror described on the first page of the novel is said to be hung too high to reflect anything in the room save for a frieze of warriors struggling against dragons ('combates de monstruos, guerreros acometidos por dragones y vuelos de grandes aves negras', 19). Being, as a woman, predictably absent from the mirror, her voyage of self-discovery begins with the perusal of a family album: seven out of a total of eight chapters in the first part contain the term "*retrato*". The only exception is chapter V, 'El cuento (glosa de un cuento pasado de moda)', the author's interpretation of 'The Sleeping Beauty', to which I shall return at a later point. Adults are ignored; the mother disappears behind a door after her son dies; there is no mention of a father; other relatives, uncles in particular, are only figures in photographs.[8] The omniscient narrator describes the child imprisoned by her heavy clothes and bound to the ground by her shoes. She is always photographed, according to the taste of the period (1910), against a studio backdrop which in this case depicts the sea:

> El otro retrato es las misma niña más crecida: son seis
> años escasos ... una sonrisa artificial debajo de un
> enorme sombrero de plumas...y un par de piernecillas
> aprisionadas en sendos zapatos de charol con hebilla y
> lazo...El fondo del retrato es una cortina donde se ve,
> pintado al *crayon*, un precioso mar de olas encrespadas,
> con barcos de vela muy alineaditos. (28)

The child reaches puberty, and this is followed by her "*puesta de largo*", duly photographed for posterity: 'Se siente lástima por la mirada atónita, por el vestido sin pliegues, sin gracia, que sólo la aprisiona como una cárcel más' (62). She then finds a summerhouse in the garden and in it love letters written the previous century by a man to a woman who was her namesake. The letters reveal a possessive, jealous love so all-consuming that the man dies. There are no letters from the woman to her lover; her story is unwritten. In the course of rummaging through this woman's belongings, the adolescent cuts herself on a crystal perfume bottle. Then she encounters a scientist on a beach (this episode appears to invoke *Robinson Crusoe*) and he takes her away to marry and to civilize her. The chapters that describe modern civilization (World War One and the twenties) are flawed because their tone is strident and hectoring. As a lyric poet, Dulce María is here assuming a social voice which does not ring true; the rhetoric is cliché-ridden and unconvincing. The voice Dulce María's circumstances allowed her to develop was a more traditionally feminine one: capable of passion, certainly, and also of irony, but decidedly private. Disillusioned with the outside world, Bárbara returns to the garden of her youth. The house has been demolished and the garden has reverted to a jungle. A 'green man' in the shape of a fisherman leads her to the garden. There they are killed when a wall with a dragon carved on a stone block falls on top of them. Only a lizard survives this apocalyptic scene.[9]

Clearly this is the work of a feminist pioneer in Spanish American literature and also of a considerable artist. A vanguard writer of the twenties, Dulce María dispenses with the conventions of realism to create a complex, intriguing work with a number of suggestive elements. Of these I have selected one on this occasion, but I am fully aware of the need to return to *Jardín* and attempt to do it justice in an article devoted entirely to it.

Turning now to Dulce María's version of 'The Sleeping Beauty' (Part I, chapter V), it is clear that since all the other chapters in the opening section are concerned with the adolescent's search for identity, here too identity is being sought, this time by reference to a cultural myth. However, Dulce María does not debunk the tale as one might expect in the case of a contemporary feminist. This is partly because, as Cintio Vitier noted, her work conveys a strong religiosity which involves a rejection of materialism and an advocacy of communion with nature in a way which makes her work not so much "romantic", as Vitier writes, but rather very relevant to an age as concerned as ours with ecological problems. Like Bruno Bettelheim and Marie Luise Von Franz, both of whom have studied the tale of 'The Sleeping Beauty', Dulce María advocates periods of quietude or spiritual withdrawal in which the individual can dream and grow in ways which cannot be discerned on the surface. Dulce María expresses this point in 'El cuento' as follows:

> ... ella/la bella durmiente/es inmortal e inmutable como la Belleza. Ella no puede morir; duerme otra vez, acaso a la sombra de los rascacielos, murallas de cemento armado que le vedan al mundo ... ¿quién vendrá a despertarla dentro de nosotros mismos, dormida tras de la selva que va creciendo? (52)

Bettelheim, in his Freudian study of the fairy tale, *The Uses of Enchantment*, likewise takes a positive view of apparently static periods in adolescence, but he disagrees with feminists on the question of sexual stereotyping in the classic fairy tale:

> Recently it has been claimed that the struggle against childhood dependency and for becoming oneself in fairy tales is frequently described differently for the girl than for the boy, and that this is the result of sexual stereotyping. Fairy tales do not render such one-sided pictures. Even when a girl is depicted as turning inward in her struggle to become herself, and a boy as aggressively dealing with the external world, these two *together* symbolize the two ways in which one has to gain selfhood: through learning to understand and master the inner as well as the outer world.[10]

Bettelheim supports his arguments by referring to tales derived from 'Cupid and Psyche' in which it is the sleeping male who is observed by the female. From this rather slender evidence he draws the following conclusion:

> This is just one example. Since there are thousands of fairy tales, one may *safely guess* that there are *probably* equal numbers where the courage and determination of females rescues males, and vice versa. (226-27). The italics are my own.

Unlike Bettelheim, Marie Louise Von Franz takes for granted that in a society that gives primacy to rational forms of knowledge, the role allocated to women will be a restricted one. In her published lectures, *The Feminine in Fairy Tales*, she offers a Jungian interpretation of, among other stories, that of 'The Sleeping Beauty' and makes the following observation about the godmother who curses the infant Aurora:

> If a god is forgotten, it means that some aspects of collective consciousness are so much in the foreground that others are ignored to a great extent. The archetype of the mother-goddess has suffered that fate in our civilization.[11]

In her third lecture Von Franz elaborates this point by saying that nature and her dark side were in harmony until, roughly, the twelfth century, but that at this juncture there was a failure to understand that a further evolution was necessary. What had once been right developed into a neurotic attitude (35). This is precisely the lesson learned by Bárbara in the modern world and it explains why she has to return to her garden even though, for her, it is too late.

One further aspect of *Jardín* belongs to myth and fairy tale. This is the recurring image of the dragon which Vitier interprets in terms of the dragon of Revelation, a reading with which it is hard to quarrel, given the novel's apocalyptic end. But the dragon has other connotations in the novel. Traditionally, in myth and fairy tale, the dragon guards the treasure; blocking the forces of renewal and the consummation of the sacred wedding. Here, though, the dragon, like the spindle in 'The Sleeping Beauty', is given phallic connotations and is associated with penetration. The child hallucinates when she is ill and imagines that one of the dragons on the frieze has attacked her, biting her chest (27). In the same scene the doctor's thermometer becomes a threatening needle: 'Las caras tristes se inclinan más y más...La aguja de cristal tiembla en los dedos y cae al suelo, quebrándose en briznas de estrellas...'(27). The shattering of the scientific instrument points to a desire for freedom from masculine control, present also when the child shatters her porcelain doll by throwing it out of the window into the beckoning garden (41).

2. '*LAS ISLAS NUEVAS*' (1935) and '*LA HISTORIA DE MARIA GRISELDA*' (1946)

María Luisa Bombal's fiction has won some attention from scholars and translators over the past few years, principally in the Anglo-Saxon world. But granted its quality and relevance to feminist lines of critical enquiry, there is still a good deal of research to be done, particularly since some of her works remain unpublished.[12] In terms of narrative strategies, Bombal's fiction is more innovative than Loynaz's. Her approach to narrative is similar to Rulfo's in that it shares his determination to achieve extreme economy of style: Bombal, too, dispenses with introductory or explanatory passages, uses a lot of dialogue and interior monologue, and changes the relation of character to space by subordinating the latter to the viewpoint of the individual narrator. She also writes in a fragmentary or discontinuous manner, leaving gaps to be filled by the reader's imagination. Both the stories I have selected involve not only fairy tale discourse, but the female protagonist in relation to the green world and, specifically in the case of 'Las islas nuevas', to what Pratt calls the rape-trauma archetype. These stories, like *Jardín*, act as reminders that magic realism was being practised in Spanish America by women writers (as also by men) long before the Boom. Their work is also a reminder that Latin Americanists should abandon that critical tunnel vision which expresses itself as an obsession with the so-called Boom and turn their attention to other directions, including a more comprehensive study of the continent's earlier literature.

Yolanda, the protagonist of 'Las islas nuevas', is a semi-mythical character. She is unaffected by linear time since she does not age physically; when first described she seems to uncoil herself like a snake as she rises from her chair to be introduced to the male protagonist, Juan Manuel.[13] She is tall and very slender, but her movements are gawky because her feet are disproportionately small for her height. She has the long tresses that either link or tie down the typical Bombal heroine to the primeval world; she has a stunted wing on her right shoulder and is associated throughout the story with a gull.

One of the fairy tales by the Brothers Grimm examined by Von Franz is that of the 'The Six Swans' in which six brothers are turned into swans. When they are restored to their original form, one is left with a wing instead of his left arm from his period of enchantment. For Von Franz this physical feature should not necessarily to be understood as a deformity, but, instead, as a reminder of the spiritual world: 'The archetypal basis must remain a mystery, which the best interpretation cannot solve; it has its wing in the other world and can never be quite pulled over into this one.'(137) However, in 'Las islas nuevas' the polarization is not so much a physical/spiritual one but, instead, of prehistory/history with its usual gender connotations. An outcast in an androcentric society, Yolanda is condemned to solitude and to the terror of dreams that drag her back into the abyss of primeval time. In what is for understandable reasons one of the most frequently cited passages in Bombal's fiction, Yolanda describes the setting of her dream to Juan Manuel in the following terms:

> Estaba en un lugar atroz. En un parque al que a menudo bajo en mis sueños. Un parque. Plantas gigantes. Helechos altos y abiertos como árboles. Y un silencio...no sé cómo explicarlo..., un silencio verde como el del cloroformo. Un silencio desde el fondo del cual se

aproxima un ronco zumbido que crece y se acerca. La
muerte, es la muerte. (158-159)

Like the protagonist of Cortázar's 'La noche boca arriba', Yolanda fears that
one day she will not re-awaken from her dream world.

The setting of Yolanda's dream echoes an earlier episode in the story
which also serves as an illustration of what Annis Pratt describes as the rape
trauma. In the first chapter of her study, 'The Novel of Development', Pratt
considers the plot line of Greek myths involving the relentless pursuit by a
male of an unwilling woman, as in the myth of Daphne and Apollo. She then
describes the backdrop normally associated with this form of pursuit:

> The pursuit narrative in mythology often involved a
> green-world locale, an island, "well" or grotto, invaded by
> men who rape the beneficent women residents -
> followed by an account of the destruction and theft of
> the area's natural value.(25)

The relevant episode in Bombal's story concerns the new islands which break
through the surface of a lake and are then invaded by a group of hunters who
plunder their natural wealth. Subsequently these islands, which belong to the
world of Yolanda's unconscious, are sucked back into the water. There is no
community of women on them, of course, but the islands' associations with the
feminine and the virginal are made abundantly clear as the hunters ransack
them:

> Y avanzan aún, aplastando, bajo las botas, frenéticos
> pescados de plata que el agua abandonó sobre el limo.
> Más allá tropiezan con una flora extraña: son matojos de
> coral sobre los que se precipitan ávidos. Largamente
> luchan por arrancarlos de cuajo, luchan hasta que sus
> manos sangran.(144)

Yolanda's dream world and its projection in the physical world, the 'islas
nuevas', describe woman's plight in an androcentric society. It is worth noting
that her stunted wing is on the right shoulder, the side generally associated
with masculine characteristics. I agree with Gabriela Mora's interpretation of
this stump ('muñón' in the original version).[14] For her, Yolanda is a siren-like
creature with part fish (her inadequate feet), part serpent (the pull of telluric
forces) and part bird. She is an incomplete being, a being in the making
because she has not been able to develop those character traits regarded as
masculine. (She shows emotional dependence on Juan Manuel and is unable

to use the green world as a locus for rebirth.) Thus the feminine experience of the primeval world is in complete contrast with the description of it in masculine, scientific discourse: the text-book version of Juan Manuel's son which conveys wonder rather than horror (171).

I should like to turn now to the second story which also examines the destructive effects of cultural myths about women. Among other things, María Griselda incarnates the dark aspects of the feminine nature goddess who, according to Von Franz's argument, will seek revenge if she is not allocated her proper place within a given culture. Her physical features and colouring contrast with those of Silvia, whose blonde, baby-doll good looks are precisely those regarded as desirable in Western society where the prevailing canon of beauty is the Anglo-Saxon or Nordic one.[15] María Griselda, on the other hand, has narrow green eyes and long dark hair. She withdraws into a nature described as wild and threatening, where, as thwarted green goddess, she takes out her rage on nature itself:

> ... Y Rodolfo le contaba que, con la fusta que llevaba siempre en la mano, María Griselda se entretenía a menudo en atormentar el tronco de ciertos árboles, para descubrir los bichos agazapados bajo sus cortezas, grillos que huían cargando una gota de rocío, tímidas falenas de color tierra, dos ranitas acopladas.(21)

Elements from different fairy tales are introduced in a fragmentary way, as though it were part of the author's intention to destroy the power of fairy tale discourse by making it disjointed and incoherent.[16] Thus the title refers to Patient Griselda; the presence of a frog that appears to have fallen in love with María Griselda recalls 'The Frog Prince', while other references relate the female characters to the story of Snow White.

The last of these are the most important since the story is an extended metaphor about the deadly effect, as much on the self as on others, of perfect beauty. This is the tale of Remedios la Bella in another register, since here too beauty condemns María Griselda to total isolation. Her beauty caused her to be rejected by her family and to view herself as a genetic aberration since 'nunca se pudo encontrar el rasgo común, la expresión que la pudiera hacer reconocerse como el eslabón de una cadena humana'(36). Thus figuratively, like Snow White, she is parentless from an early age. Sharon Magnarelli considers the significance of the motherless female protagonist of classic fairy tales (Rapunzel, Cinderella and Snow White) in her study *The Lost Rib* and reaches the following conclusion:

> To have no 'real' mother during one's fairy tale childhood seems to generate two significant and related encumbrances: first, the child grows up without ever learning successfully how to interact with other people; and, secondly, and as a consequence of this, the adolescent is doomed to solitude, loneliness, and a lack of both human companionship and communicativeness.[17]

Magnarelli's argument might have been written with this story by Luisa Bombal in mind. In addition, María Griselda's beauty, by challenging the prevailing canon of beauty, cuts her off from society. Like the nakedness of Remedios la Bella, her green world beauty has no proper place in society, and thus can express itself only as a malefic influence. It manifests itself only in Silvia's suicide or the destruction of María Griselda's doves by her husband in a fit of blind rage.

Conclusion

Dulce María Loynaz and María Luisa Bombal were contemporaries. As Latin American women of their generation with a literary vocation, they were assisted by a common background of considerable privilege and cultural refinement. This helped them to write boldly and to introduce a (proto)feminist critique into their work. What they were not able to do in the context of their period was to anticipate a time of greater freedom for women which would justify their taking the further step of writing *her* version of the fairy story and giving it a happy end.[18] Within the archetypal patterns studied by Annis Pratt, their heroines get as far as withdrawing into the green world, but they are unable to take the final, transformative step: the rebirth that makes the woman whole.

NOTES

1. Particularly useful to those interested in a socio-historical approach to the classic fairy tale is the study by Jack Zipes, *Fairy Tales and the Art of Subversion* (London: Heinemann, 1983).

2. Dulce María Loynaz was a candidate for the Cervantes prize in 1987. This eluded her, but in the same year she was awarded the Cuban *Premio Nacional de Literatura*. In the English-speaking world I am aware of only one article of recent publication which notes her importance as a woman poet. See Miriam Díaz Diocaretz,"'I will be a scandal in your boat": Women poets and the tradition' in *Knives and Angels*, edited by Susan Basnett (London: Zed Books Ltd., 1990).

3. Cintio Vitier, *Lo cubano en la poesía* (La Habana: Instituto del Libro, 1970), 378.

4. See Enrique Loynaz del Castillo, *Memorias de la guerra* (La Habana: Editorial de Ciencias Sociales, 1989).

5. Annis Pratt, *Archetypal Patterns in Women's Fiction* (Brighton, Sussex: The Harvester Press, 1982), 36. The page numbers for all further citations from this study appear in the article itself at the end of the quotation. I have used the same method in the case of all the texts quoted with some frequency in this article.

6. All quotations from *Jardín* are taken from the only edition of this novel to date, that published by Aguilar (Madrid, 1951).

7. Clearly, my concentration here on the novel's archetypal characteristics does not preclude the possibility of other readings such as a biographical one. Dulce María Loynaz told me of the pain caused her in childhood by her parents' divorce, something which created scandal and grief granted both the period in which the event took place (around 1910) together with the fact that theirs was a distinguished family of practising Catholics. In addition, relevant to the character of the jealous lover in *Jardín* is her first husband who was neurotically and destructively jealous of her poetic gift.

8. *Jardín* begins wth a *'Preludio'* in which the author makes clear her intention to ignore the conventions of realist fiction. The opening paragraph reads as follows:

    > Esta es la historia incoherente y monótona de una mujer y un jardín. No hay tiempo ni espacio, como en las teorías de Einstein. El jardín y la mujer están en cualquier meridiano del mundo - el más curvo o el más tenso - . Y en cualquier grado - el más alto o el más bajo - de la circunferencia del tiempo. Hay muchas rosas. (9)

9. On page 2 of her study, *Writing the Apocalypse* (Cambridge: Cambridge University Press, 1989), Lois Parkinson Zamora makes an observation that is most pertinent to *Jardín*: 'Novelists who employ the images and narrative perspectives of apocalypse are likely...to focus less on the psychological interaction of their characters than on the complex historical and/or cosmic forces in whose cross-currents those characters are caught'.

10. Bruno Bettelheim, *The Uses of Enchantment* (Harmondsworth, Essex: Penguin Books Ltd., 1978), 226.

11. Marie Louise Von Franz, *The Feminine in Fairy Tales* (New York: Spring Publications, 1972), 25.

12. For a list of Luisa Bombal's unpublished works see Marjorie Agosin (et al.), *María Luise Bombal: Apreciaciones críticas* (Tempe, Arizona: Bilingual Press, 1987), 266. The list includes two plays in English and a story whose title is likely to intrigue feminists, 'Dolly and Jeckyll and Miss Hyde'.

13. All quotations from 'Las islas nuevas' are taken from *La última niebla* (Santiago de Chile: Editorial Orbe, 1970), 129-183. The introductory description of Yolanda is on 135. For Jung's interpretation of the snake and water as maternal attributes see 'Symbols of Transformation' in *The Collected Works of C. G. Jung* (London: Routledge, Kegan, Paul, 1956), vol. 5, 350-351.

14. See '"Las islas nuevas": o el ala que socava arquetipos' on pp. 162-174 of the published papers on Bombal's work quoted in note 12.

15. All quotations from this story are taken from *La historia de María Griselda* (Quillota, Chile: Ed. "El Observador", 1976).

16. I am reminded of the point made by William Rowe in chapter 6 of his *Critical Guide to Rulfo's El llano en llamas*, 'Symbol and Myth'. Here he notes how the myths of the people 'are disarticulated and fragmentary ... because Rulfo's characters do not belong fully to an archaic or a native culture'. See William Rowe, *Rulfo: El llano en llamas* (Valencia: Grant & Cutler Ltd., 1987), 59-60.

17. Sharon Magnarelli, 'Women and the Not-So-Golden Silence' in *The Lost Rib* (London and Toronto: The Associated University Presses, 1985), 64.

18. Women are not the only marginalized social group to have rewritten fairy stories. For information about a homosexual version of 'Little Red Riding Hood' see Abigail Lee, *'La paradigmática historia de Caperucita y el lobo feroz:* Juan Goytisolo's use of "Little Red Riding Hood" in *Reivindicación del conde don Julián'*, *Bulletin of Hispanic Studies*, LXV (1988), 141-51.

WOMEN AND LANGUAGE:
LUISA VALENZUELA'S *EL GATO EFICAZ*

Linda Craig

El gato eficaz, published in 1972, is a subversive, sensuous, visceral *tour de force* which marks Valenzuela's strivings to find a language beyond the bounds of censorship in all of its forms. It is a novel which unblinkingly confronts many aspects of traditional thought, questioning accepted ideas of hierarchies and identity and exploring the legacy of these ideas particularly for women in Western society. As such it is a work which brings into play questions which are at the forefront of contemporary feminist thought.

This strange, fragmented, often surrealist novel defies any attempt at synopsis, given that it has virtually no plot and few, if any, stabilising elements. Indeed, possibly the only coherence to be found in the text exists at a level of play. For, as the narrator says: 'todo lo vivible puede ser jugable' (67). But this is not innocent play, it is a form of play which shuns neither eroticism, violence nor death.

The initial setting is in Greenwich Village, New York, at dawn. And in true Lacanian fashion, the novel would seem to come into being as the result of a lack. For, as the second paragraph begins: 'El le dijo mañana nos veremos y ella de inocente le creyó' (7). But he has gone, for as she says later: 'El le dijo nos veremos mañana y hasta él lo creía. ¿Por qué entonces entró en el improbable baño de los túneles y dejó que otro hombre le sorbiera la vida?' (7) The allusion to a rather sordid underworld and the ambiguous reference either to homosexuality or to death at this early stage in the novel, are indicative of the tone which the novel is going to take. Certainly, whether he has chosen homosexuality or has died, he is lost to her.

In this dangerous, half-lit world, the main protagonists are black 'gatos de la muerte', white 'perros de la vida' and a constantly mutating first person narrator. This narrator at one point describes herself as 'cómplice de un gato de la muerte' (9) and there would seem to be no doubt that, despite her multiplicity, she generally identifies more with the cats than with the dogs. The greater weight given to the cats in the text is echoed in the title.

The novel is divided into eighteen sections, each with a heading. Some of these play with the images of cats and dogs, such as 'Primera visión felina' and 'Esta perra vida', others with what would seem to be particularly strange choices of words, for example 'Abrid paso, señores, que ya llegan las quejas', or 'Paréntesis para 3 variaciones lúdicas', but, in fact, these headings are relevant to the sections that follow them, and they help to open up to the reader what would otherwise be a well-nigh inaccessible text. Within these sections, the narrator presents a world which strains at the very edges of human experience.

This is a world of voyeurs, of lesbians, of wolf-men having sex with passive women and of many other sexual fantasies of grotesque and dismembered images and of murder. The narrator reveals a near obsession with bodily secretions and with the sexual act. It is a no-holds-barred view of the human condition. If Valenzuela was trying, as suggested above, to push back the boundaries of censorship, there can be no doubt that this novel is an important step in that direction. And while the monsters and demonic creatures have a certain baroque flair, the novel has a tightness and control that defy any hint of gratuitousness.

Julia Kristeva, in her work *Desire in Language*, talks of the need to abolish the strong, would-be autonomous 'I', what she describes as the phallic presence, in order to 'reemerge still uneasy, split apart, asymmetrical, overwhelmed with the desire to know...'.[1] She goes on to say that:

> If a solution exists to what we call today the feminine problematic, in my opinion, it ... passes over this ground. I believe two conditions are necessary if this course is to be followed. The first is historical; it was satisfied much more rapidly in socialist countries and is already

> reaching the Christian, bourgeois West. It involves
> throwing women into all of society's contradictions with
> no hypocrisy or fake protection. The second condition
> is sexual ... it involves coming to grips with one's
> language and body as others, as heterogeneous
> elements.[2]

It seems to me that *El gato eficaz* is a novel which contends with and fulfils both of these conditions.

Looking at the second of these condition, at the idea of coming to grips with one's body and language as others, as heterogeneous elements; this possibility would seem to be addressed within this novel in many ways, and one of these can be found in what is its most striking feature, that of the already mentioned mutating narrator. This narrator speaks at times from the position of the third person, but is generally to be found employing the first person singular, addressing the reader directly, writing in an almost confessional form. She would seem, for the most part, to be female, although there is a moment in which she becomes male, where she says: 'me voy a cambiar de sexo. Soy un joven atleta y apolíneo, bastante pornográfico ... me tiro a la piscina desde el trampolín más alto, las niñas me contemplan ... Ay dios cómo me aburro.' (19)

There are echoes of Rimbaud's famous phrase: 'Je est un autre', [3] and this idea is taken further so that 'I' becomes not one other, but a multiplicity of others.

In the course of the text, this slippery, evanescent 'I' is to be found assuming the forms of a cat, a tarantula, and a bat, and leaving the realms of the animal kingdom, she becomes an eye, music, a tree with sap and even a rough, cold hotel wall. Any possibility of a fixed identity is constantly undermined, indeed she talks of 'nosotros los que somos amorfos' (94). And this mutating process applies equally to others, so that at one point the narrator says:

> En Chicuito vi a una vieja convertirse en piedra, a una
> piedra en vieja, a una vieja en piedra, y así como en
> cadena hasta que todas las ruinas fueron seres humanos
> y los seres humanos, ruinas. (28)

At another point, the jazz musician, Herbie Mann, who is dead, is described as having 'entregado su cuerpo a los sonidos' (26).

It is a world in which any strong dividing line between people, animals and objects becomes blurred, as too does the opposition between life and death, since the 'gatos de la muerte' 'mueren de allá para acá, del otro mundo a éste' (12), and between male and female, as can be seen in a subsection called 'Juguemos al fornicón', where the narrator suggests: 'Se juega mejor por parejas y resulta más fácil si los componentes de cada pareja pertenecen a sexos lo suficientemente diferenciados.' (68) Rational values of opposition and of hierachy are, in this, and other similar ways, constantly brought into question.

The idea of play can be found again in moments when the narrator plays with the different possibilities implicit in her multiple personae, thus she can become both watcher and watched: 'tengo ... sed de estar muy sola y observar mi propia imagen por el ojo de una cerradura periscópica' (10), and again: 'desde aquí me observo jugar a ser mirada con mi propia mirada que me guarda cariño' (106). And the game becomes one of chess bringing to mind the dichotomy within the novel between the black cats and the white dogs, in a passage which reads:

> Muevo una pieza, es jaque mate y el muerto soy yo qué
> bueno: he sido también rey y omnipotente. ¿ Perder en
> el instante en que todo se gana? Poco importa: el gane
> es anterior, cuentan las milésimas de segundos que
> preceden la muerte cuando se ha sido rey, peón, torre,
> alfil, íntegra maraña. (67)

But while all of these possibilities exist, the narrator in no way presents herself as being autonomous, she has no position of power from which to move, everything is in play and all identities are equally valid, or indeed, equally false. Her body enters into the same economy, something that she bears witness to when she says:

> Ay, cómo quisiera ir a casa a sacarme la vieja dentadura,
> pero mis admiradores me exigen tantos besos que sin
> dientes se me gastan las encías. Ay, sacarme la peluca,
> estos pechos postizos si sólo mis amantes me dejaran.
> Pertenecer, para serles bien franca, nada ya me
> pertenece. (83)

And language is brought into play too. No more stable than anything else, there are passages in different typesettings, lines written in bold print in capital letters and numerous other variations. As the narrator says: 'Fuego, juego, así soy yo, me ocupo de una letra hasta el mismo dibujo' (67), and later, in a line which undermines any idea of referentiality: 'El papel es trampa, yo soy trampa toda hecha de papel y mera letra impresa' (110).

Returning to Kristeva's conditions for a solution to the feminine problematic, it is clear that *El gato eficaz* has engaged with the idea of coming to grips with one's language and body as 'other', as heterogeneous elements. It has opened up all of these ideas, and while there is no question here of its offering solutions, or any other closure, it has situated the feminine problematic fairly and squarely within the realms of modernity. If modern thought has reached a point at which the strong, autonomous 'I', what Kristeva calls the 'phallic presence', can no longer be sustained, then it has reached a point too at which the general, or what is actually masculine problematic coincides with similar ideas within the field of feminist thought.

The deconstruction of the idea of centre has created a situation in which all is peripheral, and in which, therefore, masculine and feminine have equal value.

There is a line in *El gato eficaz* which reads: 'Puedo fácilmente dividir en dos al mundo' (17), and here it seems, the narrator is pointing out the facile nature of binary oppositions. Thus she is not only drawing the reader's attention to the rigid nature of language which tends to freeze objects in time, creating a veneer of immutability, but also to our way of thinking which constantly creates hierarchies by means of binary oppositions.

It is now almost a commonplace in feminist thought that the concept of binary oppositions is one which works strongly against women in our society. As Hélène Cixous noted, a list of oppositions which includes the basic categories of male/female; masculine/feminine; active/passive; life/death, would equate femininity with passivity and death, leaving no positive space for woman.[4]

El gato eficaz in its entirety would seem to problematize the arbitrary and simplistic limitations of binary oppositions. By going beyond any static notions of identity, the novel problematizes any idea that given attributes might belong to given genders and opens up the field of play to a multiplicity of possibilities.

The idea of play and the disruption of logic so central to this text brings to mind Bakhtin's work on the carnivalesque, as too does the inversion of hierarchies to be found in it. According to Bakhtin:

> Carnival is not contemplated and, strictly speaking, not even performed; its participants *live* in it, they live by its laws as long as those laws are in effect; that is, they live *carnivalistic life*. Because carnivalistic life is life drawn out of its *usual* rut, it is to some extent 'life turned inside out', 'the reverse side of the world'.[5] (emphasis his)

Certainly the world depicted in *El gato eficaz* is a totalizing vision, both the first and third person narrators are involved in that world, and there is no question of the existence of any point of view which might somehow compare this chaotic world with another more stable. Moreover, the idea of 'life turned inside out' brings to mind the line, already mentioned, in the novel which reads, '[los gatos] mueren de allá para acá, del otro mundo a éste' (12).

The inversion of hierarchies implicit in the image of 'life turned inside out' is actually basic to the carnivalesque. Bakhtin describes feast days as being a celebration of the 'lower bodily stratum' which, as he says 'could not express itself in official cult and ideology'.[6] Certainly *El gato eficaz* celebrates the corporeal rather than the spiritual aspects of life, but the idea of a hierarchical system of values is also turned on its head in allusions to 'El sano juicio, sí, el que tienen los otros, del que hablan los libros y que él tan sabiamente ha dejado colgado de una percha' (21), or to 'MI VASTO DOCTORADO', which is described in a bizarre fashion as 'Doctorado en Sombras con tesis de Asesinos'. The traditional scale of values which would accord merit to good sense and to the world of academia is undermined and, in fact, stood on its head.

Much of the work of Bakhtin was brought to the attention of Western Europeans by Todorov and Kristeva, and she has written at some length on the idea of the carnivalesque in literature, of which she says:

> Carnivalesque discourse breaks through the laws of a language censored by grammar and semantics and, at the same time, is a social and political protest. There is no equivalence, but rather identity, between challenging official linquistic codes and challenging official law.[7]

El gato eficaz, with its neologisms and its broken, disrupted language, is subversive both in terms of grammar and of semantics, and it accords well with other aspects of the carnivalesque which Kristeva goes on to describe.

Starting from what she refers to as 'the inability of any logical system based on a zero-one sequence (true-false; nothingness-notation) to account for the operation of poetic language', she develops the idea that the epic and most Realist narrative confine themselves to a space within this zero-one sequence of logic. She suggests, however, that there exists a concept of poetic logic, which transgresses the zero-one sequence, not arbitrarily, but by obeying another law which she describes as zero-two poetic logic. Of this she says 'The only discourse integrally to achieve the zero-two poetic logic is that of the carnival.' And, later: 'Carnivalesque structure is like the residue of a cosmogony that ignored substance, causality, or identity outside of its link to the whole, *which exists only in or through relationship*' (emphasis hers).[8] And while this definition of the carnivalesque is probably not complete in that it ignores the importance of the inversion of hierarchies which Bakhtin himself considered to be an 'essential element',[9] it is nevertheless useful and perceptive.

Kristeva then goes on to conclude that the zero-two sequence implies a constant movement, a becoming, as opposed to the logic of being, which is presumably static. The parallels here between the carnivalesque and *El gato eficaz* are notable, since this is a novel in which nothing is fixed, in which, as has been seen, the imagery and language are in constant flux.

And if carnivalesque discourse is a social and political protest, then one manifestation of this in *El gato eficaz* can certainly be found in the field of sexual politics. At one point the narrator says:

> Ya no es libre, me jacto de decirlo. Libre soy yo despúes
> de haber dejado mi imagen en sus manos y no tener así
> que andar cuidándola como hace la gente que no sabe
> entregarla. Puedo hacer ahora lo que quiera, él cuida de
> mi imagen. (118)

She is celebrating her liberation from her image, her restricting feminine role, and thus pointing out the rigidity and falseness of the roles that society demands of us. This kaleidoscopic narrator who can be active or passive, masculine or feminine, queen or pawn, word or blank page signifies, above all, the limitations of any idea of a fixed identity or of any gender-specific behaviour that such an identity might imply.

In a sense this novel might be seen as Valenzuela's version of Rimbaud's 'Le Bateau Ivre', as in this, her most radical work, she metaphorically cuts herself off from her moorings and sets off on an uncharted journey. And what motivates her to do this would seem to be, above all, this search for a language beyond censorship in all of its forms, and beyond the connotations and myths which so often cloud our perceptions.

The idea of censorship clearly looms large in Valenzuela's thought. Indeed, Sharon Magnarelli, who has recently published a book on Valenzuela's work, includes in it an interview with the writer, which, as its title 'Censorship and the Female Writer - An Inverview/Dialogue with Luisa Valenzuela' suggests, deals almost exclusively with this theme. But while much of her later work, such as *Cambio de armas* and *Cola de lagartija*, written around the time of and subsequent to the terrible political violence of the latter part of the nineteen-seventies in Argentina, is, in fact, much more referential and carries a strong political charge, she has never suffered overt censorship imposed on her by the authorities. What she is actually more preoccupied with is censorship in a broader sense, as she says: 'when I think of censorship, I always think of its multiplicity of faces; it is like a hydra with its many heads.'[10]

Clearly at least one of these heads takes the form of self-censorship, which Valenzuela describes as a 'Freudian negation of reality'. She goes on to say:

> You cannot see things because you do not allow yourself to see them; you are blindfolded. Like horses we have been put into blinkers so that we cannot see much of reality and deal with language. When women could not say what were called, at least in Spanish, bad words - they could not deal with words that were a little too strong - it was a terrible form of censorship.[11]

While she considers that the climate has changed somewhat and that women writers are now allowed to be freer in their use of language, she suggests that: 'even so, I think the structure of our own unconscious mind has not accepted this in some ways - we are not yet very free with language' (206).

The author's remarks bear witness to a constant recognition of the difficulties which arise around the subject of women and language. But it is a subject which, as indicated above, is clearly central to *El gato eficaz*. In the same interview with Magnarelli, Valenzuela remarks:

> The minute the writing flows freely, then you are writing what you didn't know you knew. All these forms of truth somehow come out of what you call inspiration or the unconscious mind, and that is when you break those barriers of censorship, of your own self-censorship.[12]

And she goes on to say that in her opinion, *El gato eficaz* is one of her best books in this sense.

It would seem that the writer has been engaged in the historical aspect of Kristeva's two conditions, that of confronting, from her position as a woman, all of society's contradictions with no hypocrisy or fake protection. This novel is indeed one which transcends the barriers of tradition and in so doing offers an acute perception of the falsity of the generally accepted feminine role.

NOTES

1. *Desire in Language* (Oxford: Basil Blackwell, 1980), 165.

2. *Desire in Language*, 165.

3. This famous line was written by Rimbaud in a letter to his friend Georges Izambard, dated the 13th May 1871. The letter in its entirety can be found in *Rimbaud: Poésies Complètes* (Paris: Le Livre de Poche, 1984), 199-200.

4. There is a brief outline of Cixous' ideas in Toril Moi's *Sexual/Textual Politics: Feminist Literary Theory* (London: Methuen, 1985), 102-121.

5. *Problems of Dostoevsky's Poetics*, translated by Caryl Emerson (Manchester: University Press, 1984), 122.

6. *Rabelais and His World*, translated by Hélène Iswolsky (Bloomington: Indiana University Press, 1984), 75.

7. *Desire in Language*, 65.

8. This definition of poetic logic can be found in *Desire in Language*, 70.

9. *Rabelais and His World*, 81.

10. I quote here from the interview mentioned in this paragraph, which is to be found in Magnarelli's *Reflections/Refractions Reading Luisa Valenzuela* (New York: Peter Lang, 1988), 204.

11. *Reflections/Refractions*, 206.

12. *Reflections/Refractions*, 208.

CLARICE LISPECTOR AND
THE HOUR OF THE STAR

Giovanni Pontiero

The central narrative of *The Hour of the Star* is deceptively straightforward. It relates the misfortunes of Macabéa, an orphaned, barely literate girl from the slums of Alagoas, whose future is determined by her inexperience, her ugliness and her total anonymity. Macabéa's speech and dress betray her humble origins. Swallowed up by the great metropolis, she merges with hundreds of other faceless creatures in Rio's red-light district. Gauche and rachitic, Macabéa has deprivation and ill-health written all over her. She is one of the world's born losers and is wholly superfluous in an overpopulated city where influence and know-how are essential for survival.

Her humdrum existence is summed up in a few terse sentences. Macabéa is an appallingly bad typist, she is a virgin and her favourite drink is Coca-Cola. Her one ambition in life is to look like Marilyn Monroe. Innocent to the point of eccentricity, she becomes the butt of her exasperated employer, her aggressive boy-friend and her experienced work-mate Glória who has all the self-confidence and sex-appeal Macabéa so sadly lacks.

Feeble attempts to come to terms with her body and soul come to nothing. And Macabéa's sudden demise under the front wheels of a yellow Mercedes driven by a handsome foreigner is as absurd and inevitable as all the other disasters that befall this hopeless misfit.

Lispector's asides in the book reveal just how difficult it became for her in this last phase of her career as a writer to transpose her dazzling insights into some coherent pattern endowed with substance and depth. Yet despite the naked struggle, strands do come together and apparent contradictions are finally resolved. Author, protagonist and reader are on the edge of a precipice for most of the time. Lispector confides that she was driven to narrate the misfortunes of Macabéa by an inner compulsion: 'I must write about this girl from the North-east otherwise I shall choke. She points an accusing finger and I can only defend myself by writing about her.' (17) The social and intellectual climate in which the author and character move are poles apart yet by the end of the novel they have been drawn into the same avid struggle with life and death. Their thoughts and responses oscillate in counterpoint; their thoughts and reactions frequently coincide despite obvious points of contrast.

Macabéa's tale operates at three inter-dependent levels. Symbolically, this anti-heroine embodies the Brazilian legacy of poverty and ignorance. She clings to the author's skin like some viscous glue or contaminating mud for as Lispector reminds us 'poverty is both ugly and promiscuous' (21).

At another level, Macabéa's harsh discoveries about existence confirm the author's wry perceptions about the universal human condition as she obsessively returns to the central question: 'Who has not asked himself at some time or other: am I a monster or is this what it means to be a person?' (15).

And at a third level, Lispector reveals her inner self, her life-long fears and anxieties, her private traumas as a woman and writer - fears that range from a horror of rats and rhinoceroses ('surely one of God's mistakes', 54) to her instinctive mistrust of human motivation; from her aversion to disorder both spiritual and material to her fear of the abyss and the 'Hell of human freedom' (36). Allied to these fears are the nagging doubts about her worth and integrity as a writer. Experience has taught her that the good writer prefers a denuded text to one submerged by superfluous detail, and that truth can be obscured by emotion. This makes Macabéa's story particularly difficult to relate for as Lispector courageously admits: 'What I can say is that melodrama was the summit of Macabéa's life. All lives are an art, and hers inclined towards an outburst of restless weeping with thunder and lightning.'(81)

As Lispector strives to establish truth - her own as well as that of Macabéa - the novel becomes increasingly rebellious and questioning. Lispector takes pauses to reassess where her narrative is heading at the risk of losing her reader. A dangerous manoeuvre for any writer, but not to be seen as wilful self-indulgence or mystification. By revealing the pitfalls in her craft, Lispector allows us to share the experience of forging Macabéa's future. The bleak portrait of Macabéa: 'so young and yet so tarnished' (25) is gradually enhanced with a spiritual substratum of faith and resilience. Macabéa's firm possession of 'that tiny essential flame: the breath of life' (38) helps her ultimately to transcend the puzzling mundane realities that threaten to suppress her. Macabéa's extreme poverty in material terms is unexpectedly mitigated by other values which the world at large chooses to ignore or despise. Without trying to gloss over the psychological scars of poverty and neglect, the author exposes Macabéa's intuitive awareness of some deeper justification for holding on to life, however grim: '[Macabéa] believed in everything that existed and in everything non-existent as well. But she didn't know how to embellish reality. For her, reality was too enormous to grasp.' (33)

The social evils underlying Macabéa's privations are treated mainly as asides, but the reader is left in no doubt where Lispector's sympathies lie. Educated, well-travelled and socially privileged, Lispector nevertheless understands the solitude of a marginal existence. She can state with all honesty: 'I belong to no social category, marginal as I am. The upper classes consider me a strange creature, the middle classes regard me with suspicion, afraid that I might unsettle them, while the lower classes avoid me.' She may never have experienced Macabéa's physical hunger, but she fully understands the sense of frustration which is set within the broader context of human vulnerability:

> ... One day, however, [Macabéa] saw something that, for one brief moment, she dearly wanted: it was a book that Senhor Raimundo, who was fond of literature, had left on the table. The book was entitled The Shamed and Oppressed. The girl remained pensive. Perhaps for the first time she had established her social class. She

> thought and thought and thought! She decided that no
> one had ever really oppressed her and that everything
> that happened to her was inevitable. It was futile trying
> to struggle. Why struggle? I ask myself: will she one day
> experience love and its farewell? Will she one day
> experience love and its deceptions? Will she experience
> love's rapture in her own modest way? Who can tell?
> How can one disguise the simple fact that the entire
> world is somewhat sad and lonely? (40)

Convinced that she is a 'lost cause', Macabéa picks up the pieces as one misfortune after another befalls her. When Olímpico callously abandons her for Glória, she substitutes laughter for tears. She shrugs off sadness upon reflecting that even 'sadness was the privilege of the rich, of those who could afford it, of those who had nothing better to do. Sadness was a luxury' (61).

In nearly all of her novels and stories Lispector has pondered the same 'impersonal limbo' in which Macabéa finds herself ... 'untouched by what is worst or best. She merely exists, inhaling and exhaling, inhaling and exhaling. Why should there be anything more? Her existence is sparse.' (23)

The Hour of the Star should also be read as a testament of faith. At the outset of the novel, Lispector defiantly informs the reader: 'So long as I have questions to which there are no answers, I shall go on writing' (11). Several critics have accused her of wilful incoherence. Any such view conveniently ignores the fact that Lispector is treading intangible territory, that her characters are guided by faith rather than logic. A personal faith and a personal God are frequently invoked in the narrative. The author's interventions are sometimes couched in language reminiscent of the mystics. Consider Lispector's thoughts on prayer. She explains:

> Prayer was a means of confronting myself in silence
> away from the gaze of others. As I prayed I emptied my
> soul - and this emptiness is everything that I can ever
> hope to possess. Apart from this, there is nothing. But
> emptiness, too, has its value and somehow resembles
> abundance. One way of obtaining is not to search, one
> way of possessing is not to ask; simply to believe that my
> inner silence is the solution to my - to my mystery. (14)

These are subtle concepts expressed with all the assurance and conviction of the trained theologian. Author and character merge in this pursuit of self-effacement. By different paths and means both author and character touch the essence of existence:

> Macabéa like some vagrant bitch was guided entirely by
> her own remote control. For she had reduced herself to
> herself. After successive failures, I have also reduced
> myself, but I still want to discover the world and its God.
> (18)

The one thing they share is self-abnegation, but without any hint of sentimentality:

> Meantime, I want to walk naked or in rags; I want to
> experience at least once the insipid flavour of the Host.
> To eat communion bread will be to taste the world's
> indifference, and to immerse myself in nothingness. (19)

The faith they sustain is not one of self-complacency or spiritual consolation.

Macabéa, like Lispector herself, is more familiar with the chill of indifference than with the world's understanding:

> One day Macabéa enjoyed a moment of ecstasy. It
> happened in front of a tree that was so enormous that
> she couldn't put her arms around its trunk. Yet despite
> her ecstasy, she did not abide with God. She prayed with
> total indifference. True. Yet that mysterious God of
> others sometimes bestowed on her a state of grace. (63)

With considerable skill, Lispector nurtures seeds of spiritual growth in Macabéa's primitive soul - a soul that is receptive because free of guile.

Alongside the reflections about God and grace, there are some thought-provoking reflections on death as Macabéa moves towards an irresistible destiny and the author, consciously or unconsciously, moves closer to her own sad demise. Macabéa's poverty of body and soul intensifies the author's own longing for life hereafter. Death is seen as transfiguration, an apotheosis capable of transforming Macabéa into the persona she craves:

> No one would teach her how to die one day: yet one day
> she would surely die as if she had already learned by
> heart how to play the starring role. For at the hour of
> death you become a celebrated film star, it is a moment
> of glory for everyone, when the choral music scales the
> top notes. (28)

But there is a further twist in the plot. Lispector deliberately prolongs Macabéa's final moments as she lies injured in the gutter. Dying is savoured to the point of revulsion:

> ... the enormous eyes went on blinking and her flat chest
> heaved and fell as she struggled for breath. But who can
> tell if she was not in need of dying? For there are
> moments when one needs a taste of death even without
> realizing it. (82)

Paradox and ambiguity permeate the entire book right up to the closing paragraphs when Macabéa finally expires. The technique is that of the camera lens set in slow motion which captures every detail of her ebbing strength: 'Macabéa adrift ... like a door swinging in a never ending breeze' (82). Death, purging and redeeming ... 'an encounter with self' (85) ... 'a painful and difficult reflowering' (84).

Whether by accident or design, the techniques employed by Lispector in *The Hour of the Star* are altogether idiosyncratic. Anyone looking for conventional form or neat experimentation will be disappointed. The novel progresses by fits and starts with a lengthy preamble, constant interruption as pages are mislaid or destroyed in the writing or as the author stops to catch her breath or to reassess where the plot is going and then that suspended finale.

> Macabéa lay helpless by the side of the road. She felt
> drained of all emotion as she looked at the stones
> around the sewer and sprouting blades of grass; their
> greenness conveyed the most tender hope. Today, she
> thought, today is the dawn of my existence: I am born...
> Was she suffering? I believe she was. Like a hen with its
> neck half-severed, running about in a panic and dripping
> blood. Except that the hen escapes - as one flees from
> pain - clucking in desperation. Macabéa struggled in
> silence.
> I shall do everything possible to see that she doesn't
> die. But I feel such an urge to put her to sleep and then
> go off to sleep myself. (80)

Why this cat and mouse game? Sheer perversity? A desperate need to cling to life? Whatever the explanation, the drama is clearly intensified by this pause for thought before death at last claims Macabéa.

> What do I see now, that is so terrifying? I see that she
> had vomited a little blood, a great spasm, essence finally
> touch essence: victory!
> And then - then suddenly the anguished cry of a
> seagull, suddenly the voracious eagle soaring on high
> with the tender lamb in its beak, the sleek cat mangling
> vermin, life devouring life. (85)

And there is one final unexpected twist as the deceased Macabéa inflicts death of another kind on the author:

> Macabéa has murdered me.
> She is finally free of herself and of me. ... Suddenly it's all over.
> Macabéa is dead. The bells were ringing without making any sound. I now understand this story. She is the imminence in those bells, pealing so softly.
> The greatness of every human being. (85)

As character and author simultaneously cross the frontier of death, intangible mysteries are clarified.

As she struggles with the facts and tries to give substance to her narrative, Lispector confides in her reader and exposes the raw process of moulding a text, the nervous energy it requires, the moments of uncertainty as the writer strives to transpose insights into words without falsifying them. Lispector's obsession with silence, with inner harmony and the mysterious undercurrents of life are much in evidence. She courageously shows her hand at every stage of the process.

Intent upon a narrative that will be 'open and explicit' (12), Lispector takes the reader into her confidence from the outset. 'This story,' she tells us, 'unfolds in a state of emergency and public calamity. It is an unfinished book because it offers no answer. An answer I hope someone somewhere in the world may be able to provide.' (8) She states that she is anxious to observe simplicity and impartiality. No easy task as she discovers for 'this is not simply a narrative but above all primary life that breathes, breathes, breathes' (13). Caught up in a web of perceptions, the author finds herself grappling with complex emotions and responses, 'something that is almost obliterated and can scarcely be deciphered' (18) ... 'a mute photograph', 'silence', 'an interrogation' (17). She compares the craft of writing to that of carpentry or sculpture - 'as hard as breaking rocks' ... 'Sparks and splinters fly like shattered steel.' (19) 'What I am writing is something more than mere invention: it is my duty, however unrewarding, to confront her with her own existence.' (13) Macabéa's discoveries about herself and the world around her erupt in a series of explosions. Her responses to pain, joy, desire and betrayal create their own syncopated melody, edgy and unpredictable - a stridency capable of touching the most alarming and unsuspected regions of the soul. And once Macabéa's tale has been told, the author finds herself as bewildered and abashed as in the opening preamble:

> And now - now it only remains for me to light a
> cigarette and go home. (86)

The relationship that emerges here between author and protagonist is intense and complex. Lispector hides behind a male narrator, Rodrigo S.M., allegedly in order to maintain a certain detachment and to avoid giving way to emotion. In my view, this otherwise valid strategy misfires. The relationship which develops in *The Hour of the Star* between the author and her character is unmistakably one of close identification. Despite her stated intentions, Lispector's impartiality and detachment remain suspect. Both author and character share the same probing attitude to life, society and a woman's role within that society. In moments of stress, Macabéa's fear of vomiting is much the same thing as Lispector's horror of Sartrean nausea. The avenues of escape also bear a striking resemblance. They are both mesmerised by words and their sonority.

Lispector confesses a maternal concern for the inept, unlovely Macabéa. But that concern is gradually compounded with feelings of guilt as she becomes increasingly involved. Lispector nervously asks herself:

> Is it possible that in penetrating the seeds of her
> existence that I am violating the secrets of the
> Pharaohs? Will I be condemned to death for discussing
> a life that contains, like the lives of all of us, an
> inviolable secret? (39)

At times, she even mistrusts this character who has become an obsessive, demanding presence, yet if she tries to ignore her even momentarily she finds that she misses her, irresistibly drawn by her ugliness and total anonymity.

In recent years, Lispector's narratives have inspired artists working in other media. Her texts have been set to music, or adapted for stage and screen. The most successful of these adaptations so far has been Suzana Amaral's prize-winning film *The Hour of the Star*. The cast is excellent and headed by an unknown actress from a provincial repertory company, Marcelia Cartaxo, whose touching performance as Macabéa won her the Silver Bear award at the Berlin Festival (1986). The central story is deftly handled by Amaral. Cartaxo is the embodiment of Lispector's heroine, a figure of almost unbearable pathos: ... 'she was inept. Inept for living' (24).

It was obviously much easier for Amaral to convey on the screen Macabéa's growing awareness of her body and the first intimations of sexual desire than to portray her spiritual growth. The unloved Macabéa whose 'sex made its demands like a sunflower germinating in a tomb' (70) is more in evidence than the 'biblical and subterranean Macabéa' (30) whose 'delicate soul didn't quite match her body' (31).

Inevitably some of the novel's most telling episodes are lost in the film: for example, the touching efforts of the ingenuous Macabéa to absorb the disconnected fragments of information transmitted during her favourite programme on Radio Clock. She tells Olímpico:

> - Do you know the best thing I've learned? They said on Radio Clock that we should be glad to be alive. And I am. I also heard some lovely music and I almost wept.
> - Was it a samba?
> - I believe it was. It was sung by a man called Caruso who they said died a long time ago. His voice was so gentle that it was almost painful to listen to. The music was called Una Furtiva Lacrima. I don't know why they couldn't say lágrima the way it's said in Brazil.
> Una Furtiva Lacrima had been the only really beautiful thing in Macabéa's life. Drying her tears, she tried to sing what she had heard. But Macabéa's voice was as rough and tuneless as the rest of her body. When she heard her own voice, she began to weep ... (50)

This is surely one of those moments of illumination and enlargement James Joyce referred to as epiphany.

On the whole, the film is stronger on pathos than humour, a fact borne out by most of the reviews. The other main characters also lose some of their complexity. Macabéa's emotionally unstable boyfriend Olímpico de Jesus Moreira Chaves is unmistakably a North-easterner in voice, appearance and outlook. But the crude macho image is inflated in the film at the expense of the more sensitive Olímpico who weeps at funerals (a secret passion) and carves delicate religious effigies which betray another side to his nature. In recompense, Amaral has faithfully projected the sharp contrast in the personalities of this ill-matched pair. Their social inadequacies drive them to quite different strategies for survival. Trapped by the stigma of illiteracy and poverty, Olímpico has been driven to deception and crime. For him, wealth and power are the supreme values. Macabéa, on the other hand, has settled for numb resignation and extravagant dreams within the orbit of her private world. Even the mundane spectacle of a butcher's shop elicits contrasting responses:

> For quite different reasons they had wandered into a butcher's shop. Macabéa only had to smell raw meat in order to convince herself she had eaten. What attracted Olímpico, on the other hand, was the sight of a butcher at work with his sharp knife. (53)

Other key roles, such as the sensuous Glória and Macabéa's exasperated boss, are carefully handled in the film, but the prostitute turned fortune-teller, as played by the veteran Fernanda Montenegro, is something of a disappointment. She comes over as a raddled eccentric, whereas in the novel she is much more formidable. Macabéa's nervous encounter with this droll, loquacious and crafty extortioner is one of the most memorable passages in the novel. Confronting experience with innocence, Lispector mingles tragedy with farce.

> Madame Carlota looked like a large china doll that had seen better days ...
> - Don't be frightened, my pet. Anyone at my side is also at the side of Jesus.
> Madame Carlota pointed at the coloured print on the wall which depicted the Sacred Heart of Jesus in red and gold.
> - I'm a fan of Jesus. I'm just mad about Him. He has always helped me. Mind you, in my heyday I had enough class to live the life of a lady. Things were easier then, thanks to Jesus. Later on, when I didn't rate quite so highly on the market, Jesus lost no time in helping me to set up a brothel with a friend ...
> - ... Do you know what the word brothel means? I always use that word because I've never been frightened of words. There are some people who get all worked up if you mention certain words. Are you frightened of words, my pet?
> - Yes, Madame, I am.
> - Don't worry, dear. I'll try not to shock you with swear words...
> Macabéa had never had the courage to cherish hopes. Yet she now listened to Madame Carlota as if she were listening to a fanfare of trumpets coming from heaven - her heart beating furiously. Madame was right: at long last, Jesus was taking some interest in her.

> Macabéa's eyes opened wide as she felt a sudden hunger
> for the future (bang) ...
> - ... You are about to come in for a great fortune that a
> foreign gentleman will bring to you in the night...
> Macabéa felt almost inebriated and could scarcely
> gather her thoughts. It was as if someone had delivered
> a sharp blow to that head of lank hair. Macabéa felt
> totally confused as if some great misfortune had
> befallen her. (72-77)

Regrettably, Amaral chose to leave out of her script an equally crucial episode in the novel when Macabéa borrows money from Glória to consult a doctor. This encounter, too, has its moments of high comedy but most important of all, it illustrates two opposed reactions to poverty within the same wretched community:

> This doctor had no ambition whatsoever. He saw
> medicine simply as a means of earning a living. It had
> nothing to do with dedication or concern for the sick.
> He was negligent and found the squalor of his patients
> utterly distasteful. He resented having to deal with the
> poor whom he saw as the rejects of that privileged
> society from which he himself had been excluded. It had
> not escaped him that he was out of touch with the latest
> trends in medicine and new clinical methods, but he had
> all the training he was likely to need for treating the
> lower orders. His dream was to earn enough money to
> do exactly what he pleased: nothing.
> He gave her an X-ray and said:
> - You're in the early stages of pulmonary tuberculosis.
> Macabéa didn't know if this was a good or a bad
> thing. But being ever so polite she simply said:
> - Many thanks. (67-68)

The novel's unorthodox ending clearly posed serious problems for Amaral. The screen version is rather like a standard television commercial for some new shampoo. But to be fair, the edgy, anxious statements in the closing paragraphs which border on panic scarcely lend themselves to purely visual techniques:

> Was the ending of my story as grand as you expected?
> Dying, Macabéa became air. Vigorous air? I cannot say.
> She died instantaneously. An instant is that particle of
> time in which the tyre of a car going at full speed
> touches the ground, touches it no longer, then touches it
> again. (85-86)

Yet this is a film to be seen more than once for the subtlety of its detail, just as the novel should be read several times in order to grasp the individuality and depth of Lispector's fictional world. Time was running out for Clarice when she laboriously worked at the fragments which constitute this book. It is uneven in execution and there is a disconcerting atmosphere of mental fatigue and despondency. Yet *The Hour of the Star* has all the ingredients of her best work - probing and imaginative, unconventional and incisive to the point of jolting one's sensibilities. And as for Macabéa - she will endure as one of the truly memorable portraits of twentieth-century Brazilian literature. Like the Marilyn Monroe she dreams of emulating, Macabéa is hungry for love. Like her idol, Macabéa is consumed by encroaching unreality and premature death. The irony and absurdity of her character's bid for stardom was not lost on Lispector as she herself began to long for apotheosis or, as she once wrote elsewhere, for 'the ultimate freedom'.

*All quotations in the text have been taken from my own translation of *The Hour of the Star* published by Paladin, London, 1987.

WOMEN CHARACTERS AND MALE WRITERS:
A CUBAN APPROACH

Nissa Torrents

Thirty years after the Revolution, looking back at the Cuban novel, the cultural historian may dare to draw some conclusions and remark on the paucity of women novelists, the scarcity of major narrative writers of any sex born after 1958-9, and the persistence of the revolutionary theme in a large percentage of the works published.

Revolutions are epic deeds that tend to dominate cultural production for many years. The Mexican Revolution was the centre of a vast literary output from Azuela's *Los de abajo* (1915), Martín Luís Guzmán's *El águila y la serpiente* (1926) and *La sombra del caudillo* (1929) through Yáñez's *Al filo del agua* (1947) to Rulfo's *El llano en llamas* (1953); Castellanos's *Balún Canán* (1957) and Fuentes's *La muerte de Artemio Cruz* (1962), but it could be argued that the novel of the Mexican Revolution went through different periods, and that no single major author approached the revolution with similar eyes. Distance, criticism and revisionism marked the different approaches, but the Cuban revolution has not undergone such a treatment in the fiction produced in the island. There is little criticism of any of its aspects and even less revisionism, whether favourable or unfavourable.

A manichean approach is favoured and revolutionaries and dissenters are treated like goodies and baddies in old-fashioned Westerns. There is no room for ambiguity or even for nuance. The apologetic presentation and the striving for an epic tone appear to be the accepted and generalised practices, and they often result in the production of simple propaganda which degrades both the product and its reader. Although it is true that Cuba did not have a strong tradition in fiction, it is also true that it lacked a film industry. Nevertheless, the Revolution was able to create a film industry which almost overnight became influential. Arguably because of its lack of tradition, it was neither conservative nor apologetic and its filmic discourse was innovative and truly revolutionary.

The Revolution immediately created institutions intended not only to advance and propagate culture, but also to control its practice and its practitioners. UNEAC, the Writers Union and ICAIC, the organisation that has overall control of all aspects of the film industry, were early creations, and bureaucrats mushroomed overnight eager to control and to censor. Indifferent writers - the role of Nicolás Guillén and Alejo Carpentier is waiting for reassessment - occupied central positions and were eager to exert control over the young and the non-conformist. Film makers were luckier as the very lack of an autoctonous tradition made ICAIC authorities much freer in their judgements.

Soviet social realism appeared to be an obvious choice for the less than mediocre writers who occupied positions of power in UNEAC, a discourse that, somehow, they managed to relate to a 'true' depiction of the Revolution. On the other hand, Eisenstein, Vertov and Pudovkin were creative referents for the new film industry.

All said, some writers escape the over-simplification of 'official' narrators. José Soler Puig only started writing after 1959. His novels and short stories are examples of a Spanish realist tradition scarcely practised in Cuba. Spiced with touches of magical realism, his work is highly readable and never servile. Unknown outside Cuba, his is a solid, honest writing that does not follow fashions and bureaucratic directions. Also, whatever their public behaviour, Lisandro Otero, Pablo Armando Fernández, Antón Arrufat, Cintio Vitier and Jesús Díaz, do not slavishly praise the Revolution and fall into manichean patterns of assessment. Their knowledge and experience of a wider world has allowed them to look beyond what others considered the 'unavoidable' tone of revolutionary literature.

It is early to say, especially as the young have become more and more interested in the genre, but Díaz and Otero may turn out to be the major novelists of revolutionary Cuba; however it is the more popular literature which I will attempt to tackle, as I believe that this literature yields great rewards for the cultural historian.

In 1971, Ambrosio Fornet, the Cuban writer and critic, in a review of Miguel Cossío's *Sacchario*, wrote that although Cuban novelists had avoided the danger of producing a schematic and paralysing epic, they had not escaped mimeticism and mediocrity. While it is easy to agree with the second premise, it is more difficult to do so with the first, especially when the reader is still confronted with works like Armando Cristóbal's *La batalla*, published as recently as 1988, a conventional, tedious 468-page novel, in which the same tired heroics, the same black and white characters parade in front of the reader's eyes.

Thus it would be easy to conclude that since 1971, when Fornet warned writers of the dangers, only cosmetic changes have taken place, a conclusion confirmed in the Fourth Congress of UNEAC (Union of Artists and Writers of Cuba) in 1988, a Congress held in the spirit of the 'rectification' process, which in its final resolution underlined that the poor quality of work produced was the direct result of '... the naively affirmative nature of the revolutionary process; the excessive lack of depth and the absence of critical inquiry'. This conclusion, an admission of the continuing hold of conservative forces on the creative life of the country, a conservatism that informs many aspects of Cuba's social and personal conduct, admirable as it may seem, has become ritualistic in all spheres of Cuban public life. The powers that be seem willing to accept and even describe their mistakes. "Rectification" is an "in" word but mistakes are seldom reversed.

An amazing degree of social equality has been achieved, and it has been accompanied by a cultural flowering which is the direct result of the government's policies, but the same government that nationalised the means of production and tackled illiteracy and disease in greatly successful 'battles' seems reluctant to accelerate changes at the level of consciousness, reluctant to tackle sexism beyond passing admirable laws, reluctant to tackle sexual and racial stereotypes, as a visit to the night club Tropicana will confirm. In the absence of affirmative action, the stereotypes persist and popular fiction mirrors the failure of the gradualist approach. Even in the otherwise 'progressive' sex education manuals, the pressures on the implementation of sexual control is put on the girls who are told that, because of their less active sexuality, moral responsibility falls on their shoulders. The manuals, originated in the German Democratic Republic, are not adapted to Cuban needs and customs. The images of boys and girls are those of tall, blonde Germans, and their words are merely translated, with obvious alienating results.

'Machismo' was strong in pre-revolutionary Cuba because of its recent slave past, where women were worth little, even as labour reproducers, and also because of the Spanish Catholic tradition which praised the female as mother, damning, belittling or just considering transient all other roles. When the revolution came, women were seen by Guevara and others as excellent back-up material but not as initiators or equals in the fight to overthrow the tyranny. After 1959, the 'revolution within the revolution', in Fidel's words, was declared. The massive exodus of professionals that followed made women's labour of prime importance. Labour was a necessity and so was their literacy. Prostitutes were re-educated and peasant girls taken into the luxury of the Hotel Nacional to learn to read, write, cut and make clothes, but seldom were they directed to other tasks.

Jobs were opened to women with the exception of those, as seen by male bureaucrats, that undermined their capacity as reproducers of the labour force. All women in the new Cuba were seen primarily as mothers, and the idea that a woman may voluntarily choose not to be one is as unthinkable in the new Cuba as it was in the old. The monogamic, nuclear family was the basis of society, and although the woman was no longer an exchange merchandise, her role within the household remained unchanged. What happened is that she acquired other roles and, certainly, other freedoms.

It was taken for granted that all women wanted to contribute their best to the building of the 'new man'. To this day, there has been no mention of a new woman, the owners of the word sheltering themselves under the excuse that in Castillian the collective is masculine. And how better could a female contribute to the new society than by giving birth, i.e., by fulfilling her biological condition? Next to the 26th of July and the New Year, Mother's Day is Cuba's biggest holiday and today it is not a pretext for a consumer frenzy but an exaltation of women's role in society, which remains the same as in the old, patriarchal, pre-revolutionary times. As in Soviet Russia, Cuba declared the nuclear family the mainstay of revolutionary society, dismissing Engelian fears of oppression and repression. The admirable Family Code of 1975 corrected many injustices and imbalances, but the fifty-fifty share of household and parental tasks that it codified remains to this day a noble expression of wishful thinking, and the double shift, effectively, prevents women's progress and promotion in all spheres of social life. Women's magazines and mass media in general still talk about 'helping' women in their household chores, thus reinforcing the notion that they are essentially 'feminine' in nature. And Castro's definition of women as 'the workshop of life' effectively created as many obstacles as it may have aimed to demolish by 'socializing' the act of motherhood.

Men may be deemed to share household chores, but both in everyday life and in the images presented by literature and the mass media, the outstanding difference between pre-revolutionary and post-revolutionary males is their politics. As the 'pater familias' of yesteryear, the 'new man' is represented enjoying leisure at home, i.e., reading the paper, while the equally working wife tries to cook whatever is available, educate the children in the new spirit, make their clothes and better her own education.

The *Plan Jaba* was aimed at 'easing' the load of working mothers by making everyday shopping easier, but this 'progressive' measure also implied the acceptance, at governmental level, that work sharing was merely desirable and would take a long time to implement. An illness in the family or simply lice in the *Círculo* (Kindergarten) sees the women staying at home and their careers suffering because of it, absenteeism being deemed almost a counterrevolutionary activity. All work is important, but, paraphrasing a well-known Western writer, some work is more important than others. Women are to be seen in most types of work, but there is still a marked tendency for them to occupy places in traditional female professions or their extensions, from teaching to medicine. The power posts in those professions nevertheless are not held by women, though they now constitute some 38% of the labour force in the island.

The Revolution is real enough but the cultural subconscious has not advanced in a comparable manner as those in power do not deem it necessary to force changes in everyday behaviour and thinking and reject as alien and capitalist such concepts as positive discrimination and women's liberation. 'El Hombre Nuevo' is still seen as encompassing both sexes. When Cuban women and men are addressed about this problem, the answer more often encountered is that the Revolution has freed all and, presumably, women have only themselves to blame if they do not attain the highest levels.

Cuban cinema has been one of the outstanding successes of the Revolution. Practically non-existent before 1959, the year ICAIC - the Cuban Film Board - was founded as one of the first cultural undertakings of the new Cuba, it soon had an impact worldwide, but since 1959, only one feature film, Sara Gómez's *De Cierta Manera*, has been made by a woman and that was in 1974! Even woman documentary film makers are few and far between. The double shift (work) and the double standard (social morality) have taken their toll, and film making which implies prolonged absences from home and ruling over largely male crews continues to be a male preserve.

While in the advanced capitalist countries the women's movement has led to an explosion of woman writers and film makers, in Cuba they are rare not only in film making but also as novelists. Before and after 1959, women appear more often as poets and even as short-story writers, activities that do not seem to require the same level of continuity and the famous room of one's own, once longed for by the very bourgeois writer from Bloomsbury, Virginia Woolf.

Virginia Woolf would have felt very strange in a society which rejected not only the specific needs of women but also any sexuality that did not have as its main aim reproduction, seemingly the ideal woman's creative activity. Men create, women procreate, and in Cuban fiction, this tenet seems still to hold.

If unmarried women are seen as an anomaly, homosexual women are not even imagined apart from in the traditional role of participants in an activity aimed at male titillation. It is assumed that lesbianism or the desire to live alone do not result from free choice but from circumstance. Lesbians are misguided or perverted women who want to be men, and when represented they behave like males or exaggerate their 'feminine' traits. Their conduct is simply a copy of men's behaviour. Bisexual men or women do not even get a mention either on film or in literature. The simple duality prevails in every realm of human and societal activity, with good and evil taking on different clothing without altering the manichean division.

Women thus appear in Cuban fiction largely through the eyes of male writers, and an alarming percentage of the popular writers seem unwilling and incapable of breaking voyeuristic and exploitative points of view. I would like to venture that this state of affairs promotes a very insidious (however 'soft') type of pornography, one which coyly withdraws from the explicit while skilfully maximising titillation. Soft pornography has been a highly successful form under capitalism, as the fortunes of Harold Robbins or Mickey Spillane prove, and my contention is that a similar pornography exists and is tolerated in revolutionary Cuba because the mentality of the hegemonic class has not changed.

A feminist critique of pornography is not primarily concerned with censorship but with the pervasive presence of sexism and pornographic structures throughout our culture. Political interests structure representation, and representations are made by the writers and read by readers. A text is never innocent and neither is any reading. A text is a real political form and its analysis requires the construction of a cultural theory of representation, an analysis of power relations. The problem is not whether sex is too explicit or obscene but what structures of sexuality, what sexual politics, what subject-object relationships are pre-represented.

In the texts I will examine, I believe that the sexual politics and the relationships between men and women are sexist in the extreme, even misogynist, with men playing the traditional domineering role and women, happily and masochistically, accepting their submission and their repression, and with other sexual relationships beyond the heterosexual being excluded, except for titillation. In these texts, the subjective author objectivizes his characters, and women characters are the object-victim *par excellence*. The voyeuristic author exacts the complicity of the readers by turning them into

180

voyeurs, a voyeurism legitimated by the 'artistic' credentials of the product - the book - that arouses it.

The Revolution itself is often used to cover authorial flaws. The poorer the craft, the more afraid the author is to stray away from the 'safe' haven of revolutionary themes, and the more he is forced to rely on familiar stereotypes both in character-formation and in the situations developed.

As in pre-revolutionary years, the novels offer the reader two clearly separate worlds. There is the private field in which women are wives, mothers and mistresses. They often try to stop men's efforts to advance with the new society, either through egotism or counter-revolutionary activities. Jealous, incapable of generosity, women are petty egoists who cannot see beyond the self, a self which is reduced to the physical. There is also a public field, that of labour and the construction of the new society, which is mainly inhabited by the male, happy to surrender his individuality, in order to become a part of a more meaningful collectivity.

Contrary to the reality of revolutionary Cuba, women workers occupy little space in the fictions I am to examine, where men represent the force open to change and progress and women the regressive tendencies. They are mere sexual objects, intent on using their sex to distract the male from 'higher' tasks, although they never succeed for long. The novels being dogmatically optimistic, the triumph of evil is short-lived. Men may die for a cause but they are spared corruption and/or illness, with sexual disease apparently having become a thing of the past or a malady of counter-revolutionaries. No syphilis or AIDS ever contaminates the body of the pure male revolutionary. Disease is the territory of the other, of women and counter-revolutionaries.

Notoriously sexist genres in capitalist narrative and film are the thriller and counter-espionage novel. Before the 1970's, such novels were as rare in Cuba as in most of the Spanish-speaking world. A genre largely identified with Britain and the United States, it was from this tradition that the models were to be taken. As Rodriguez Calderón explains, '...el novelista cubano carecía de una experiencia técnica en el tratamiento de esta temática; por este motivo, recurre a los modelos que le proporcionan las llamadas "escuela inglesa" y, sobre todo, la "escuela realista norteamericana". Pero como el objetivo cardinal es reflejar la transformación de la sociedad, la defensa de sus conquistas ante la agresión enemiga interna y externa..., el novelista no guarda una filiación definida: integra muy libremente elementos tomados tanto de la escuela inglesa como de la norteamericana'.[1]

The defense of the Revolution against internal and external enemies only became an important theme after the hardening of political attitudes that followed 1968, the failure of the Ten Million sugar harvest target and the Padilla affair. The thriller and the spy novel fused, maybe as a result of the determination to confine evil to the public sphere, and also because of the falling interest in the personal and psychological problems of the individual characters in line with the attempt to impose a new, collective morality. The central figure of the private and very individual detective and of the equally private and diverse personal motivation for crimes disappeared. The investigators belong to political or mass organizations and crimes are of a social or national nature: 'El delito, más que un atentado a la moral, es un reto a la nueva sociedad, de ahí que en gran parte de las novelas se vincule la delincuencia común a la contrarrevolución'.[2]

The inner and outer structures are binary, manichean. Neither the baddies nor the goodies can ever be individuals in the new narrative. The CIA or Cuban traitors are preferred as the evil partners and the police force or the counter-espionage arms of MININT or MINFAR as the good guys. Crimes of passion are excluded. There is no rape or sexual abuse, incest, child or wife battering - unless carried out by counter-revolutionary men. None of the heroes can possibly be homosexuals. Only economic or anti- revolutionary crimes are portrayed. Born in difficult times, the genre wanted 'to be of a didactic nature and to further awareness and prevent all anti-social and counter-revolutionary activities'.[3] Instantly popular, printings of 60,000 copies are average, and many more would be sold if it wasn't for paper rationing. Favoured by the authorities because of its attraction for a newly literate reading public, the thriller was seen by the political and cultural powers as an ideal means to educate and to raise the consciousness of these new groups, but it was also closely watched for dissent and deviation from the established norms.

It is interesting to remember that the principal institution that firmly backed the creation of the genre in Cuba was the MININT, the ministry responsible for internal order, anti-subversion and counter-espionage. Luis Rogelio Nogueras further stated that the genre was 'a tribute to the efforts of soldiers, classes and officials of MININT'.[4] Because of the use of the masculine in Spanish to cover both sexes, the sentence appears to refer only to men, an appearance confirmed by the secondary and subordinate role of women in the genre as practised in Cuba. If women ever took an active part in counter-espionage, the official narrative does not bear witness to their participation. Women are, at best, side kicks or patiently waiting mothers-wives-fiancées and, at worst, willing and perverse partners of male traitors who retain the initiative in spite of their evil nature.

Its purported didacticism, the attitude of the cultural authorities and the cultural and political fragility of the targeted public was understood by the writers, who did not wish to alienate the system, to mean that there was no room for moral ambiguity. The traitors were to be beyond change and redemption. Born bad, a familiar set of signs identified them to the defenders of the law within the fiction and to the new readership. Lechery, shifty eyes, greed, laziness at work, and love for the United States were common traits. The enemy wanted self-betterment while the good guy/s, almost always a member of MINFAR or MININT, could only see themselves as part of a team, and the team as a cog in the Revolution. The private field, normally in the shape of a woman, was incidental, a form of inconsequential entertainment, often dangerous as it distracted the hero/es from his/their main task.

El cuarto círculo (1976) by Nogueras and Rodriguez Rivera was a great success, but I would like to examine briefly a novel by Nogueras alone: *Y si muero mañana* (1978), which bridges the thin line between the thriller and counter-espionage novel. Significantly, this novel won the UNEAC 1977 novel prize and not just the MININT prize for genre novels, an honour that signified the 'coming of age' of the genre in Cuba's cultural establishment. Obviously familiar or well-informed with MININT procedure, Nogueras in his novel pays homage to those who fought in the Sierra. It is a common, though often unstated, trait of these novels that the main characters establish their persona and their revolutionary credentials by having fought in the Sierra with Fidel, a sure sign of heroic conduct. Noguera's hero goes from the Sierra to

Miami, a harbour for defectors and capitalist vices, where he will encounter the bad Cubans and fight the CIA plotters on their own terrain.

Our hero, in the house of defector León Ortiz, 'gordo y fofo', meets Arnaldo Rediles, a thinly veiled parody of Guillermo Cabrera Infante, but he also meets Ortiz's daughter: 'una rubia que se había sentado a la mesa con un pulover sin ajustadores, como para mostrar que tenía los pezones muy grandes'.[5] This anatomical treatment is never given to the male, even if they are defectors who own a chain of porn shops. The body, heavy with sexuality, always barely covered, is the terrain of the female. Men have no bodies. Even the worst have only perverted minds.

We are further informed that the blonde and the Cabrera Infante look alike 'la rubia de tetas de vaca...se habían ido a retozar como perros y/o gatos en alguna de las hamacas del jardin'.[6] Another feature that is common in the texts I will examine is that, although men always have names and surnames, women are identified as merchandise and possessions: 'la hija de Ortiz', 'la mujer de X', 'la amante de Z', thus confirming their secondary status. Another common trait is the unpleasant smell of women, a consequence of their sex and their tasks. Smells, i.e. bad smells, have traditionally been ascribed to women because of their occult sex, their menstruation and their secretions, which make their odours a symbol of their impurity. 'Legitimate' sources of odour, i.e., those created by sport or hard work, are only ascribed to the male.

In post-revolutionary Cuban literature, women, especially if they are 'gringas', have a tendency to nymphomania, the assumption being that the US male is not only an apalling colonialist but a poor sexual partner. Virility, potency and good revolutionary feelings are thus equated. This is the reason US women long for 'la macabia cubiche', not surprising in the case of Alice, 'una trigueña de grandes tetas, pero con las piernas bastante cobardes, como todas las gringas'.[7]

Cuban writers, like Freud, appear to be convinced that nymphomania is a female characteristic, as male sexual desire falls within the accepted and desirable norm. In Nogueras's novel, only Yolanda, the Cuban girlfriend from heroic times, gets a better treatment, but even she is naked under her robe, waiting eagerly for the hero's embrace and possibly being used to instruct the readers in the delights of orthodox sexuality.

Rodolfo Peréz Valero, well aware of the curtailment of rhetorical devices faced by revolutionary thriller writers, attempted a revisionistic approach. In *No es tiempo de ceremonias*, he tried to break stereotypes though he only managed to add homophobia to the existing list with the presence, as evil types, of a gay butler and an equally gay restorer of religious images.

One of the problems the genre faces is that criminals, in a society that has many eyes, are easily targeted, especially by their clearly anti-social behaviour. It is significant that nobody in these novels questions the information received and/or the possibility that such reporting may be the result of private revenge or may lead to abuse. In such a closely observed society, with many grass roots and state-operated systems of vigilance, the writer does not appear to be willing to question the role of such institutions or even less, their veracity. There is no place for shades of grey.

Guillermo Rodríguez Rivera, in a critical commentary on the Cuban thriller-counter-espionage novel, quotes Coronel Ramón Roa on the genre: 'There is no greater pleasure than to shoot one's enemy with their own gun',[8] a phrase which he sees as a seal of approval. Obviously in such terrain, women have little to do, as the lack of female practitioners of the genre proves.

Very popular although not thriller writers, the novels of David Buzzi and Manuel Cofiño are clear examples of the voyeuristic, subjective approach. I have chosen these authors because they are middle brow and very popular, and I believe that their success relies on the new conservatism engendered by a system that is slow in changing, and also by the persistence of pre-revolutionary attitudes in many walks of life. Although the novelists examined have paid lip service to formal experimentation by using some of the devices of post-Joycean narrative, their novels have a sense of 'déjà-vu' that brings them close to the 1920's and 1930's bourgeois novel which targeted women of the middle classes - Vicki Baum and Cecil Roberts among the well-known practitioners - offering them controlled titillation and acceptable levels of voyeurism in an ambiance sufficiently luxurious and protected as to be desirable.

David Buzzi (La Habana, 1932), has had a long career as a novelist and cultural civil servant. Very successful and the recipient of many national prizes, his work appears to be modern both in its technical awareness and in its treatment of sexuality. His first novel, *Los desnudos/The Nudes*, (1967) begins with the triumph of the Revolution and the return to the capital of Silvia, a woman from the bourgeoisie who joined the rebels in the mountains. Confronted with the new orientation of the Revolution towards communism, she has her doubts but manages to learn from her mistakes, becoming a full revolutionary. She is the only female who is given this opportunity, as the rest of the women characters are not allowed any change, being mainly represented as stereotypical women who are hysterical gossips and decadent bourgeois who drink, pick fights and toy boys. They only think about money and sex, often confusing them.

But even those foul-mouthed females in perpetual heat abhor lesbianism, offering an opportunity to the writer to describe and decry such activity. Another staple of male pornography - the all-women fight - also puts in an appearance, and even Silvia indulges: 'Joyita dile a la criada que me traiga otro trago. Estoy como Alina, que me acuesto hasta con un perro. Puff, mira. Estiró los labios Esther. Ahí tienes el negro ese que nos sirve, no está mal. ¿Verdad? Y me acuesto, pero le tapo los sobacos. ¿De verás? A Mirna va a haber que mandarle hacer un consolador. Mira Mirna este palito de jaibol. "Júrame, júrame que a ti te ha servido, degenerada". Muchachitas no peleen ... No hay negro bueno'.[9]

In Buzzi's *Caudillo de difuntos* (1975), the conventions that successfully allow soft porn to be acceptable are further refined and extended in their scope, but what is striking is that the hommage to Ernesto Sábato's *Sobre heroes y tumbas* (1961), seems to go beyond the accepted limits of intertextuality and even admiration. The very title evokes the earlier work. Characters, themes, and the to-ing and fro-ing between meaningful but widely separate historical times, all help to create in the reader a powerful sensation of 'déjà vu'.

Both novels have as protagonists a young couple. In Buzzi's novel, they are called Rosalía and David. In Sábato's: Alejandra and Martín, and it is especially in the women's characters that coincidences can be detected. The girls behave in a very similar manner. They frequent bohemian circles and their unorthodox sexual conduct becomes the source not of liberation but of guilt. Alejandra (rosafango) y Rosalía (rosa encharcada) share a guilty childhood. The reasons for this particular horror gradually unfold within the novel, and they constitute an important part of the plot. They share some witchlike powers and, although capable of entering people's deepest thoughts, unlike the male scientist, they are incapable of helping themselves. Their knowledge is not transmissible and the total unpredictability of their actions makes these unrewarding, at best. Quintessentially female, they are whimsical and unreasonable, definitely the dark continent with a very dark past.

In Sábato's novel, Martín meets Alejandra in Lezama park, under a statue of Ceres, the Latin goddess of agriculture. Buzzi's David meets Rosalía in another park under the statue of Martí, a god for all seasons within revolutionary iconography. Buzzi's Reemberto, the older man of the trio, is the counterpart of Sábato's Bruno, always understanding and willing to help the young with their erotic and existential problems.

Buzzi's Rosalía is described as a cross between 'God and the Devil' and Sábato's Alejandra's beautiful exterior also hides a double nature. She is the dragon and the princess, the devourer and the virgin. Both girls, as depicted by the different men (and that includes the authors), are never far from hysteria or even epileptic attacks, a sure sign in medieval times both of sin and witchery. Not too far from Freud's Dora, they suffer from insomnia and have a love-hate relationship with their own bodies, a situation that brings them to acts of suicidal daring. Coincidentally, both live in dread of blind men, the Oedipal curse, a dread that Sábato put into our literary map thanks to his masterful 'Informe de ciegos' in *Sobre heroes y tumbas*.

The offspring of conflicting ancestries who never manage to reconcile themselves, they could symbolise Latin America, but this possibility is not the main concern. Rosalía, a Mancebo and a Segura; Alejandra a Vidal Olmos and an Acevedo, the tension between the two strains is made worse by sexual abuse which in both cases is of an incestuous nature, though in Buzzi, more timid, the incest occurs between uncle and niece, while in Sábato, it is more classic. They have both been sexually abused as young children, but forever respectful and subservient to men and tradition, both Alejandra and Rosalía feel the abuse is a result of the essential impurity of their sex. The power of patriarchy is never taken into account as a primary source of abuse.

The two girls live in rambling old houses near collapse, and they tend to confuse the history of their families with that of their own country. Their houses are full of old relatives in several stages of madness or delusion, and the historical times covered in the novels comprise significant periods in the formation of the two nations. Alejandra's family is incapable of understanding the changes that the country has undergone during Peronism, and equally closed to the new reality is Rosalía's family which cannot understand or support the Revolution. Alejandra's grandfather Pancho becomes Rosalía's Uncle Pancho with an extra homophobic touch: he is a homosexual. The Argentinian's Niña Escolástica is the Cuban's Tía Tula (*pace* Unamuno), and Fernando Vidal Olmos, the ghost that haunts Sábato's novel, is Buzzi's Luciano Segura, a true ghost who never manages to come to life, though we are made aware of his 'dirty' activities. What in Sábato has a grandeur, in Buzzi becomes smut, dirty old jokes, made even dirtier by their derivative nature.

Bruno (Sábato) and Reemberto (Buzzi), fulfil similar roles. Friends of the young couple, they are sane and stable. Their function in the narrative is to give cohesion to its chaotic elements and explain the darker points, but again, what succeeds in the initiator, fails in its imitator. Bruno's relationship with Alejandra is one of support, as is Reemberto's with Rosalía, but neither can help the turbulent and unclean nature of woman, forever beyond reason and, as such, beyond change. The main difference between the two characters is that Bruno, basically in love with them all, is familiar with the three embodiments of woman: Ana María, Georgina and Alejandra, and does not become a judge of their actions, while Reemberto helps Rosalía because she may be recoverable for the Revolution. His purpose is didactic.

Both family histories are full of violence, sexual and national, which are the two levels at which Sábato's novel functions and Buzzi's aims to.

Curiously, the fascination for Sábato's novel and for the character of Alejandra will also be present in Manuel Cofiño's *Amor a sombra y sol* (1981), a very successful novel that has had many reprints.

Manuel Cofiño (La Habana, 1936-1989) became famous with *La última mujer y el próximo combate* (1971), a novel which depicted the struggle to convince the Cuban peasantry of the necessity to organize agriculture in the form of state farms. Well aware of the gap between the proposed system and the mentality and the praxis of Cuban peasants, Cofiño used in his novel two exemplary couples: Bruno and Mercedes as the hope for the future, and Siaco and Nati as the past that had to be overcome. Bruno is an executive in an agrarian venture run under the new system and Mercedes an active worker in the same organization, while Siaco is an idle person and Nati is a sensual animal who cannot fail to attract, and consequently lead to their downfall, the men who come near her womanhood. She is a 'femme fatale' whose early story of poverty and rape is but a proof of the unredeemability of her sex and never a factor in her 'wayward' ways. Long-haired and dark-skinned, traditional signs of the sinful female, she is 'toda una hembra' while Mercedes, the co-op worker, has small breasts, wears a demure handkerchief over her blond hair (thus covering an unmistakable sign of sexuality), and blushes when Bruno looks at her. It is not difficult to see behind these hardly changed images: the demure blonde girl and the sexy black-haired women, pre-revolutionary, class-ridden and racist stereotypes.

In *Cuando la sangre se parece al fuego* (1977), women act as a chorus for male endeavour and the only revolutionary, Laura, attracts the mistrust of the narrator, who dismisses her as somebody who believes that revolution is but a means to obtain a house in Altahabana. The protagonist comes from a humble background, but after the Revolution, he manages to marry a very white woman of impeccable bourgeois origins though revolutionary at present, a pattern all too familiar in Cofiño.

There is a clear increase in misogyny in Cofiño's output that reaches a height in *Amor a sombra y sol* (1981). Again, we have a rather familiar couple: an active revolutionary and hardworking man, Marcos, and a non-working, non-revolutionary woman, Magda, who appears to spend her days, naked on the bed, hair hanging down, musing on her lover and masturbating while waiting for his return. It is not difficult to recognize in Magda that well-worn stereotype, a clear product of male fantasy: the hot, beautiful young woman, all sex, always ready for the male, body free of clothes. Being a 'revolutionary' novel, however, Magda is given an actively counter-revolutionary father who loves her in a clearly incestuous manner and who, before the Revolution, was a criminal, mixed up in illegal gambling, and a lecher with a penchant for erotic mulattas and pubescent girls.

By now the Identikit of a traitor should be easy to draw. He - the father - keeps the daughter in a flat and gives her enough money for her not to work. The echoes of the 'casa chica', even if the other woman is his own daughter, are too loud to ignore, and although they may not be functioning at the explicit level, they are far more dangerous at the implicit one.

Another well-loved Western stereotype, the hot mulatta, is used by Cofiño, though he takes the 'revolutionary' care to ascribe such behaviour to the bad father who rapes a young Tomasa who does not resist because, being a mulatta, she is superstitious (another stereotype), and she knows that whatever is happening to her was foreseen by 'los caracoles'.

Women are masochists who, when they are, literally, broken into, assume their real nature: 'Nadie hubiera podido imaginar que estuviera hecha de aquel modo; era toda criatura de gozar. Y a la noche siguiente, cuando él entró en este cuarto, ya ella lo estaba esperando. Y había piñas y calabazas y el piso lleno de naranjas; y Tomasa estaba ahí, desnuda, acostada sobre las naranjas, embarrada de miel, olorosa a canela y salpicada de plumas de pavorreal, para que él se las fuera quitando con la lengua'.[10] Exemplary titillating language, soft porn mixed with cheap picture postcard exoticism. Poor Tomasa is Carmen Miranda as Hollywood moguls dreamt of but would not dare to film, and also Jorge Amado's mulatta without his sense of humour and his understanding.

Every trick in the book is used to titillate. The counter-revolutionary that allows evil men to talk evil:

> Tenías que comprarle la muñeca para acostarte con ella. Decía que ella no se vendía, que le paga por la muñeca. - Era una cabrona. - Un día me pasó lo más grande del mundo. Llegué y ví una muchachita nueva. Era muy joven. Se movía con timidez entre las mesas. La ataqué de lleno. La emborraché como una mula. La llevé a la

> posada de Agua Dulce, frente al Sierra, y... ¡sabes!...
> ¡agarrate!... Era señorita. Me dí un banquete como
> para chuparse los dedos...[11]

and the anti-clerical which tries to disguise the cheapest of voyeurisms as an
attack on the corrupting role of nuns, and all it does is follow the well-worn
tracks of nineteenth-century anti-clerical bourgeois pornography:

> Y después el colegio de monjas. Sor Ana, dura y seria
> por el día, y por la noche suave y dulce, con caricias
> borradoras de regaños, sofocada. La cara se le ponía
> como una manzana, y la caricia fría, como si un pez le
> estuviera subiendo por los muslos. Y al día siguiente
> santiguándose con los mismos dedos para la entrepierna
> que para la frente. Aquellas mujeres de blanco rostro y
> olor a sudor, a menstruo, a sexo, que manoseaban
> frenéticos rosarios con grandes crucifijos, los perfumes
> del altar, la frescura de las pilas de agua benditas y el
> resplandor tenebroso de los cirios.[12]

Bestiality is not excluded in Cofiño's project, a further point that
accentuates the degradation of the female: 'Y allá en la finca del padre, el
perro con que jugaba por la mañana, saltando por la noche sobre la muchacha
desnuda',[13] recalls Magda who, like Buzzi's Rosalía, is full of evil
remembrances, though she does not reach hysteria thanks to regular sex with
Marcos, the pure revolutionary, who states that he is going to liberate her
from 'questions and souvenirs', that is to say, from any dissent and from the
slightest questioning of the stated dogma.

Magda, a typical woman, wants Marcos all for herself and does not
wish to share him with the Revolution. In sharp contrast, Marcos often and
patiently reminds her that love helps to know the world and that it is not
necessarily an egotistical feeling.

Magda is all sex, a mass of 'carne tibia, turgente', with a body which is
either writhing or arching to further encourage penetration. She is just
another version, 'ampliada y aumentada' of Nati, the all-sex woman of *Ultima
mujer y el próximo combate*. But to Marcos, she is unstable and mysterious,
dark and, ultimately, fearful. Which is why, like so many 'revolutionary' men,
he feels better in the company of other 'revolutionary' men who are clean,
direct, without duplicity, keep their clothes on and do not smell. People like
Armando, a sound revolutionary who knows that men lose their heads for

women and that weakness makes them potentially anti-revolutionary. As in the priesthood, real revolutionaries are better consorting only with other men.

Cofiño shares with deodorant manufacturers in capitalism the conviction that smell is a peculiarly feminine trait. Even when recently washed, they expel 'un fuerte olor a hembra recién bañada'. Magda, who sweats profusely and is given to panting, has: 'el inmemorial husmo a hembra' and Julia sweats, 'como cuando hacemos eso' and, of course, there were the stinking nuns! Women are revealed by their secretions and even in death, the stench-producing secretions and juices which are the female response to the male presence are foremost: 'Por los muslos y las piernas chorrea despacio y gotea sobre la cama una, densa, insólita exudación de hembra terminada y reseca'.[14] Thus the death of faithful Tomasa, as hot as a she-cat and as faithful as a dog, the once honeyed mulatta who in old age became a procuress, is described.

Since the narrator and writer are men, the male characters talk and act, but unlike Marcos, who always keeps his clothes on, their physique is hardly sketched. Only the female physique is on display. Not unlike Victorian novelists, in spite of the apparent freedom of his sexual depictions, Cofiño, who has reduced woman's body to its sexual parts, has to make extensive use of synecdoche. Since no writer can ever name every single part of the body, he fragments Magda's, focussing on four centres: entrepiernas (a clear euphemism); hair, long in the head and 'frondoso'/thick in the pubis; breasts with large nipples that can be seen though blouses, and buttocks that move suggestively and invitingly because all women, or so the evidence would appear to suggest, have but one desire: to have sex with men.

Another female character, Julia, plays tricks with a glow worm in order that: 'Castaño introduce la mano y con los dedos toca el cocuyo y el pezón duro y parado. - No puedo más. Tengo mucho miedo - Vamos para adentro.- No, aquí. Me gusta aqui en el píso. Se levanta el vestido, desesperada'.[15] Julia, the insatiable, was forced into prostitution in childhood, but violence done unto women is lightly dismissed because women are all whores at heart. Even Castaño, a real counter-revolutionary, has more dignity than Julia, because he can control his 'urges'.

Male genitalia are depicted as clean, external, visible. They do not have secret insides like those of women: 'Sólo sabe que existe un lugar de tinieblas dentro de ella y que algo maligno habita esas tinieblas, y de vez en cuando despierta y late para lacerarla de dolor.'[16] Women die because of the evil that lies in their genitals, the same evil that may attack the male, suck him in (which is why women have large mouths), and kill him, like the snake with which they share duplicity and writhing.

Even women seen casually are described as drunk: 'Un hilo de baba brota de su boca y se le escurre por la barbilla y el cuello. Tiene los ajustadores desabrochados y la saya zafada en la cintura. La cremallera lateral abierta deja ver un pedazo de cadera y el pliegue de la ingle'.[17] Only Lidia, the factory worker and party cadre, escapes the abuse (though not the ritual castration), but only to become a revolutionary version of the Christian martyr as she loses a leg at work. Soon recovering from the shock, she gives all her fellow workers a great example by just longing to go back to the factory, her only regret being the impossibility of wearing a skirt...!

Cofiño's fears, his relentless voyeurism and exploitation of the female characters are transformed into 'acceptable' soft porn and commercialized as they would have been under capitalism. The difference may lie in the success of marketing strategies, not in the content or the voyeurism.

NOTES

1. Rogelio Rodríguez Calderón, 'Notas para el estudio de la novela policial de la Revolución Cubana' in *Novela de la Revolución y otros temas*, La Habana, 1983, 61.

2. Ibid., 65.

3. Francisco Garzón Céspedes. Prologue to Armando Cristóbal *La ronda de los rubies*, La Habana, 1973, 8.

4. Rogelio Nogueras, *Por La Novela Policial*, La Habana 1982, 39.

5. Rogelio Nogueras, *Y si muero mañana* (2nd ed.), La Habana, 1983, 35.

6. Ibid., 36.

7. Ibid., 111.

8. Guillermo Rodríguez Rivera, *El caimán barbudo*, n. 130, La Habana 1979.

9. David Buzzi, *Los Desnudos*, La Habana, 1966, 19.

10. Manuel Cofiño, *Amor a sol y sombra* (3rd. ed.), La Habana, 1987, 19.

11. Ibid., 22.

12. Ibid., 27.

13. Ibid., 27.

14. Ibid., 231.

15. Ibid., 156.

16. Ibid., 187.

17. Ibid., 272.

CONTRIBUTORS

Dr Jean Andrews is Lecturer at the School of European Studies and Japanese, University of Wales College of Cardiff. She is at present researching on comparative literary topics in early twentieth-century literature and is the author of *The Stone by the Elixir—Spanish Reactions to the Anglo-Irish Revival* (New York: Edwin Mellen Press, provisional title, forthcoming).

Dr Lisa Condé is Lecturer in Hispanic Studies at the University College of Swansea, Wales, and is the author of *Women in the Theatre of Galdós* (New York: Edwin Mellen Press, 1990) and *Stages in the Development of a Feminist Consciousness in Pérez Galdós* (New York: Edwin Mellen Press, 1990). Her most recent articles are 'The complexity of women's roles in Galdós's *Realidad*' and 'The adaptation of Galdós's *Realidad* for the stage: A preliminary manuscript study' (to appear in forthcoming editions of *Forum for Modern Language Studies* and *Anales Galdosianos*, respectively).

Linda Craig is Lecturer at the Polytechnic of East London and is currently researching on aspects of marginality and gender in the works of Onetti, Valenzuela and Puig.

Dr Catherine Davies is Lecturer at St Andrews University, St Andrews, Fife. Her publications include *Rosalia de Castro no seu tempo* (Vigo: Galaxia, 1987), an edition of *Follas Novas* (Vigo: Galaxia, 1990), and 'Feminist writers in Spain 1900-1988: from Political Strategy to Personal Inquiry', in *Textual Liberation: European Feminist Writing in the Twentieth Century*, edited by H. Forsas-Scott (London: Routledge, in press).

Judith Drinkwater is Lecturer in Spanish at the University of Leeds and is currently researching on the themes of *desengaño* and images of women in Golden Age literature.

196

Dr Evelyn Fishburn is Senior Lecturer at North London Polythechnic. Her publications include (with Dr Psiche Hughes) *A Dictionary of Borges* (London: Duckworth, 1990) and a forthcoming essay in *The Land that England Forgot: Argentina and Britain, a Special Relationship,* edited by John King.

Dr Stephen Hart is Lecturer in Hispanic Studies at Queen Mary and Westfield College (University of London) and is author of *Religión, política y ciencia en la obra de Cesar Vallejo* (London: Tamesis, 1987), *R. J. Sender: Réquiem por un campesino español* (London: Grant and Cutler, 1990) and *The Hispanic Connection: Spanish, Catalan and Spanish American Poetry from "Modernismo" to the Spanish Civil War* (New York: Edwin Mellen Press,1991), and editor of *¡No pasarán!: Art, Literature and the Spanish Civil War* (London: Tamesis, 1988).

Jo Labanyi is Senior Lecturer at Birkbeck College, University of London. Her publications include *Ironía e historia en "Tiempo de silencio"* (Madrid: Taurus, 1985), and *Myth and History in the Contemporary Spanish Novel* (Cambridge: Cambridge University Press, 1989). She has been commissioned by OUP to write a book on *Nature, Culture and Gender in the Spanish Realist Novel* and to prepare an edition of Galdós's *Nazarín* for OUP's World's Classics Series; she has also been commissioned by Longman to edit an anthology of criticism on Galdós for their Modern Literature in Perspective Series.

Dr Abigail Lee Six is Lecturer in Hispanic Studies at Queen Mary and Westfield College (University of London) and is the author of *Juan Goytisolo: The Case for Chaos* (New Haven and London: Yale University Press, 1990) and *Juan Goytisolo: Campos de Níjar* (forthcoming in the series *Critical Guides to Spanish Texts,* Grant and Cutler, London). Her most recent articles are 'Breaking Rules, Making History: A Postmodern Reading of Historiography in Juan Goytisolo's Fiction' and 'Juan Goytisolo's Portable *Patria*: Staying on Home Ground Abroad' (forthcoming in the *Yearbook of Postmodern Studies: History and Postmodern Writing* and *Renaissance and Modern Studies,* respectively).

Dr Melveena McKendrick is Lecturer in Spanish at the University of Cambridge and fellow of Girton College, Cambridge. Her publications include *Woman and Society in the Spanish Drama of the Golden Age* (Cambridge: Cambridge University Press, 1974), *Theatre in Spain 1490-1700* (Cambridge: Cambridge University Press, 1989), and *El Mágico Prodigioso: A Composite Edition of the Manuscript and Printed Versions* (Oxford: Oxford University Press, forthcoming).

Dr Giovanni Pontiero is Reader in Latin American Literature at the University of Manchester. His publications include the translation into English of Lispector's *Family Ties, The Foreign Legion, The Hour of the Star* and *Near to the Wild Heart* (all published by Manchester, Carcanet Press). He is currently preparing an English edition of Lispector's collected chronicles and essays published in the *Jornal do Brasil* (1967-73).

Dr Alison Sinclair is Lecturer in Spanish at the University of Cambridge. Her publications include *Valle-Inclán's "Ruedo ibérico": a Popular View of Revolution* (London: Tamesis, 1977), and 'The Consuming Passion: Appetite and Hunger in *La Regenta*' (*Bulletin of Hispanic Studies*, in press). She is currently researching on *Honour at Stake*, a comparative study of the portrayal of deceived husbands, and on a feminist re-reading of Unamuno's major novels.

Nissa Torrents is Senior Lecturer at University College, London. Her principal research interest is in women's cultural production in Latin America. Her publications include *The Garden of Forking Paths: Argentine Cinema* (London: British Film Institute, 1988) with John King and *La Habana* (Barcelona: Editorial Destino, 1989).

Dr Verity Smith is Senior Lecturer in Hispanic Studies at Queen Mary and Westfield College (University of London). Her current research is on aspects of twentieth-century Cuban literature and post-revolutionary cultural policy. Her recent publications include an article in *Cuban Studies* (1989) and a contribution to a collection of papers on *War and Revolution in Hispanic Literature* (Madrid-Melbourne: Voz Hispánica, 1990).